Gilbert Malcolm Sproat

Scenes and Studies of Savage Life

Gilbert Malcolm Sproat

Scenes and Studies of Savage Life

ISBN/EAN: 9783337314583

Printed in Europe, USA, Canada, Australia, Japan

Cover: Foto ©Lupo / pixelio.de

More available books at **www.hansebooks.com**

SCENES AND STUDIES

OF SAVAGE LIFE.

I DEDICATE THIS BOOK

TO

EDMUND HOPE VERNEY, R.N.,

WHOSE NAME, ASSOCIATED WITH GOOD WORKS,

WILL LONG BE

REMEMBERED IN VANCOUVER ISLAND.

CONTENTS.

CHAPTER IV.

Physical Appearance.

CHAPTER V.

Pursuit of a Fugitive.

CHAPTER VI.

Houses.

CHAPTER VII.

A Justice of the Peace on Circuit.

CHAPTER VIII.

Domestic Manners.

CHAPTER IX.

Feasts.

CHAPTER X.

An Attempt at an Inquest.

CHAPTER XI.

Acquisition and Use of Property.

CHAPTER XII.

Condition of Women.

CHAPTER XIII.

Escape from the Toquahts.

CHAPTER XIV.

Tribal Ranks.

CHAPTER XV.

Intellectual Capacity and Language.

CHAPTER XVI.

A Great Deer Hunt.

CHAPTER XVII.

Moral Dispositions.

CHAPTER XVIII.

Sorcerers.

CHAPTER XIX.

Traditions.

CHAPTER XX.

Usages in Warfare.

CHAPTER XXI.

Religious Practices.

CHAPTER XXII.

Usages in Fishing.

CHAPTER XXIII.

Usages in Hunting.

CHAPTER XXIV.

Diseases.

CHAPTER XXV.

Usages in Burial.

CHAPTER XXVI.

Miscellaneous.

CHAPTER XXVII.

Effects upon Savages of Intercourse with Civilized Men.

CHAPTER XXVIII.

Concluding Chapter.

PREFACE.

I did not intend, originally, to publish these observations, and have made no attempt, now, at literary ornament in producing them. Any value found in these pages will consist, I think, in their freshness and minuteness of detail, as well as in the more special consideration of social feelings, moral and intellectual characteristics and religious notions—matters which travellers among savages, ordinarily, have not full opportunity to do justice to. My private and official business on the west coast of Vancouver Island gave me an advantageous position for studying the natives themselves, and also the effect upon them of intercourse with civilized intruders. I lived among the people and had a long acquaintanceship with them; I did not merely pass through the country. The information which I give concerning their language, manners, customs, and ways of life, is not from memory, but from memoranda, written with a pencil on the spot—in the hut, in the canoe, or in the deep forest; and afterwards verified or amended by my own further researches, or from the observations of my friends. Among these, I am especially indebted to the late George Reid, of Alberni, and to the well-known traveller and naturalist, Mr. Robert Brown, F.R.G.S., whose knowledge of the North-West American Indians is extensive and accurate.

During this singular episode in my early career, I was for five years a colonial magistrate, and also a proprietor of the settlement at Alberni in Nitinaht (or Barclay) Sound, on the west coast of Vancouver Island—the only civilized settlement on the west coast. The condition of the native tribes on that coast has, hitherto, been quite unknown.

I have stated in the two concluding chapters the opinions which I have formed from my observation and experience of these savages. Some, perhaps, will read these chapters, who have not time to read the whole book.

Mr. F. Whymper has kindly given me the sketch for the frontispiece.

G. M. S.

London, January 1, 1868.

SCENES AND STUDIES

OF

SAVAGE LIFE.

CHAPTER I.

OCCUPATION OF DISTRICT.

Occupation of Alberni—Interview with the Natives—Threatened Hostilities—Progress of the Settlement—Cook, Meares, and Jewitt's Accounts of several of these Indian Tribes.

He took great content, exceeding delight, in that his voyage.—BURTON.
I pr'ythee now, lead the way without any more talking.—SHAKSPEARE.

IN August, 1860, I entered Nitinaht, or Barclay Sound, on the outside, or western, coast of Vancouver Island, with the two armed vessels, *Woodpecker* and *Meg Merrilies*, manned by about fifty men, who accompanied me for the purpose of taking possession of the district now called Alberni, a name taken from the Spanish navigator who first discovered the inlet at the head of the Sound. Reaching the entrance of this inlet, we sailed for twenty miles up to the end of it—as up a natural canal—

three-quarters of a mile wide and very deep, bordered by rocky mountains, which rose high on both sides almost perpendicularly from the water. The view, as we advanced up this inlet from the sea, was shut in behind and before us, making the prospect like that from a mountain lake. At the end of this singular canal, the rocky sides of which appear to have been smoothed by a continued action of moving ice upon their surface, and which itself gives an idea of having been the furrow of a mighty glacier moving downwards towards the sea, the high land on the right receded from the shore, and a large bay or basin, with a river flowing into it through level wooded land, met our view. The range of hills which opened on one side formed an elbow about ten miles distant from the canal, and crossing in a direction almost at right angles to the course of the inlet, met a continuation of the other range, and thus shut in the district known to all the Indians as the famous berry-land of Somass.

Near a pretty point at one side of the bay, where there was a beach shaded by young trees, the summer encampment of a tribe of natives was to be seen. Our arrival caused a stir, and we saw their flambeaux of gumsticks flickering among the trees during the night.

In the morning I sent a boat for the chief, and explained to him that his tribe must move their encampment, as we had bought all the surrounding land from the Queen of England, and wished to occupy the site of the village for a particular purpose. He replied that the land belonged to themselves, but that they were willing to sell it. The price not being excessive, I paid him what was asked—about twenty pounds' worth of goods—for the sake of peace, on condition that the whole people and buildings should be removed next day. But no movement was then made, and as an excuse it was stated that the children were sick. On the day following the encampment was in commotion; speeches were made, faces blackened, guns and pikes got out, and barricades formed. Outnumbered as we were, ten to one, by men armed with muskets, and our communications with the sea cut off by the impossibility of sailing steadily down the Alberni Canal (the prevalent breeze blowing up it), there was some cause for alarm had the natives been resolute. But being provided, fortunately, in both vessels with cannon—of which the natives at that time were much afraid—they, after a little show of force on our side, saw that resistance would be inexpedient, and began to move from the spot. The way in which these people move their encampments will be described further on. Two or three days afterwards, when the village had been moved to another place, not far distant, I visited the principal house at the new encampment, with a native interpreter.

"Chiefs of the Seshahts," said I on entering, "are you well; are your women in health; are your children hearty; do your people get plenty of fish and fruits?"

"Yes," answered an old man, "our families are well, our people have plenty of food; but how long this will last we know not. We see your ships, and hear things that make our hearts grow faint. They say that more King-George-men will soon be here, and will take our land, our firewood, our fishing grounds; that we shall be placed on a little spot, and shall have to do everything according to the fancies of the King-George-men."

"Do you believe all this?" I asked.

"We want your information," said the speaker.

"Then," answered I, "it is true that more King-George-men (as they call the English) are coming: they will soon be here; but your land will be bought at a fair price."

"We do not wish to sell our land nor our water; let your friends stay in their own country."

To which I rejoined: "My great chief, the high chief of the King-George-men, seeing that you do not work your land, orders that you shall sell it. It is of no use to you. The trees you do not need; you will fish and hunt as you do now, and collect firewood, planks for your houses, and cedar for your canoes. The white man will give you work, and buy your fish and oil."

"Ah, but we don't care to do as the white men wish."

"Whether or not," said I, "the white men will come. All your people know that they are your superiors; they make the things which you value. You cannot make muskets, blankets, or bread. The white men will teach your children to read printing, and to be like themselves."

"We do not want the white man. He steals what we have. We wish to live as we are."

These were the first savages that I had ever seen, and they were probably at that time less known than any aboriginal people under British dominion, not excepting even the Andamaners.

A civilized settlement was now formed almost immediately in their midst, and the natives stared at the buildings, wharves, steam-engines, ploughs, oxen, horses, sheep, and pigs, which they had never seen before.

Having myself remained amongst them for a considerable time—since the first occupation of Alberni—I am now able to give an account of their condition and customs, in addition to what has been written concerning several of the Aht tribes dwelling more to the north by Cook, Meares, and Jewitt. Cook's account is the best that has been published; that of Jewitt, though evidently authentic, has probably suffered in the hands of some professed bookmaker.

As evidence to some extent of the authenticity of Jewitt's book, I may here record that an old Indian told the late W. E. Banfield, a well-known trader on the coast, that he had been a youthful servitor in the family of the chief Klan-nin-ittle during the bondage of Jewitt and Thompson, and that he often assisted Jewitt in carrying the bows, arrows, and other weapons which Klan-nin-ittle used in hostile expeditions. He said further that the white slave generally accompanied his owner on visits of courtesy, which in quiet times he frequently paid to the tribes of Ayhuttisaht, Ahousaht, and Klah-oh-quaht. Jewitt, it seems, was a general favourite, owing to his good-humour and lightheartedness, and he often recited and sang in his own language for the amusement of the savages. He was described as a tall, well-made youth, with a mirthful countenance, whose dress, latterly, consisted of nothing but a mantle of cedar-bark. There was a long story also of Jewitt's courting, and, I think, finally abducting the charming daughter of the Ahousaht chief, Waugh-clagh; with which, however, I shall not trouble the reader.

CHAPTER II.

RIGHT OF SAVAGES TO THE SOIL.

The right of civilized Men to occupy savage Countries—Duty of Intruders —Plots of the Ahts to attack us—Arrival of H.M. gunboat *Grappler* —The Indian's notion of an English Bishop, and of the Crews of English Ships of War.

I say, by sorcery he got this isle,
From me he got it.—TEMPEST.

I SPENT some months very pleasantly directing the first work at the settlement. The vessels discharged their cargoes, and the carpenters worked on shore preparing timber for the houses and buildings. The first house that was built was made of logs, with split wood for the roof—rather a plain-looking hut, but nevertheless a comfortable house in all weathers. It was the kind of house that woodmen build with the axe alone. By-and-by, we had more ambitious houses of sawn wood. The place the Indians had moved to was about a mile distant, and our conversation naturally was very much about them. In the evenings we sat round the fire discussing their dispositions and probable intentions, and the Indians did the same about us in their new encampment. We often talked about our right as strangers to take possession of the district. The right of *boná fide* purchase we had, for I had bought the land from the Government, and had purchased it a second time from the natives. Nevertheless, as the Indians disclaimed all knowledge of the colonial authorities at Victoria, and had sold the country to us, perhaps, under the fear of loaded cannon pointed towards the village, it was evident that we had taken forcible possession of the district. The American woodmen, who chiefly formed my party, discussed the whole question with great clearness. Their opinion generally was that our occupation was justifiable, and could not be sternly disputed even by the most scrupulous moralist. They considered that any right in the soil which these natives had as occupiers was partial and imperfect, as, with the exception of hunting animals in the forests, plucking wild fruits, and cutting a few trees to make canoes and houses, the natives did not, in any civilized sense, occupy the land. It would be unreasonable to suppose, the Americans said, that a body of civilized men, under the sanction of their Government, could not rightfully settle in a country needing their labours, and peopled only by a fringe of savages on the coast. Unless such a right were presumed to exist, there would be little progress in the world by means of colonization,—that wonderful agent, which, directed by laws of its own, has changed and is changing the whole surface of the earth. I could not, however, see how this last-named fact strictly could form the groundwork of a right. My own notion is that the particular circumstances which make the deliberate intrusion of a superior people into another country lawful or expedient are connected to some extent with the use which the dispossessed or conquered people have made of the soil, and with their general behaviour as a nation. For instance, we might justify our occupation of Vancouver Island by the fact of all the land lying waste without prospect of improvement, and our conquest of a peopled and cultivated country like Oude by some such consideration as this—that the State was delinquent before the world, and by its corruption put the welfare of neighbouring and progressive English territories in danger. It would be necessary in all cases to remember that, though the right of the intruders might be justified by some of these considerations, the intruders would be bound to act always with such justice, humanity, and moderation as should vindicate fully those superior pretensions which were the ground of the right of occupying. Any extreme act, such as a general confiscation of cultivated land, or systematic personal ill-treatment of the dispossessed people, would be quite unjustifiable. Probably, no other circumstance than a continued wanton quarrelling with their fate, after the occupation of the country by a superior race, ought to be held as sufficient cause for depriving savage aboriginal inhabitants of their title to a limited and sufficient property, enjoyable under certain conditions. So much they could claim as our fellow-men, and they would also have other obvious claims on the consideration of a Christian nation. The whole question of the right of any people to intrude upon another, and to dispossess them of their country, is one of those questions to which the answer practically is always the same, though differently given by many as a matter of speculative opinion. The practical answer is given by the determination of intruders under any circumstances to keep what has been obtained; and this, without discussion, we, on the west coast of Vancouver Island, were all prepared to do. It can easily be supposed that we spent many anxious nights in our remote, isolated position at Alberni. It was discovered afterwards that various plans of attacking us were at this time entertained by the natives; and there, of course, were rumours of plots which never had existence. Happily, however, no disturbance took place, with the exception of a few individual brawls, and we gradually gained the confidence and goodwill of the people. On a rumour spreading that we had been attacked in our encampment, Governor Douglas sent the gunboat *Grappler*, Commander Helby, to our assistance, which remained at anchor for a short time near the settlement. During the stay of this vessel, several interesting and picturesque interviews took place between two neighbouring tribes and Commander Helby, accompanied by his guest the Bishop of Columbia.* The Aht notion of an English bishop is that he is a great medicine man or sorcerer; and they regard the sailors in her Majesty's ships as belonging to a separate, distinct tribe of whites. Being themselves all fighters, the Ahts cannot understand why the great King-George tribe should leave all their fighting to a few individuals.

* The latter, I believe, sent home an account of one of these interviews, and it was published in some of the missionary newspapers.

CHAPTER III.

LOCALITIES.

Localities of the Aht Nation—Topographical Features of the District—The large Sounds: the outside Coast: the Mountain Lakes: the Pine-Forests: the Climate—Native Population on the West Coast of Vancouver Island—Several Characteristics of Tribes—Tribal Names originally bestowed by Quawteaht—Subdivision of Tribes.

Fain would I here have made abode,
But I was quickened by my hour.—HERBERT.

I WILL now give the reader a short description of the wild country in which we were the first settlers. To many this subject may not be very interesting, but perhaps in a few years it may become desirable to possess a record of the state of this portion of the island in its now condition. Dr. Arnold said he always looked for descriptions of places in books of travel, though he seldom found one that gave him any clear notion of a place. I hope to have avoided this condemnation.

The localities inhabited by the Aht tribes are, chiefly, the three large Sounds on the west coast of Vancouver Island, called Nitinaht (or Barclay), Klah-oh-quaht, and Nootkah, the two former of which are native names borne by tribes at these places. In Nitinaht (or Barclay) Sound, is now the settlement and port of Alberni, the origin of which I have just described; Klah-oh-quaht was the scene of the destruction of the ship *Tonquin*, and massacre of her crew, as related in Irving's *Astoria*, an occurrence which to this day is spoken of among the tribes; Nootkah gave its name (whatever that may have come from, for there is now no native name resembling it) to a convention in 1790 between England and Spain. As will be seen in the map, these capacious inlets or sounds throw out arms in various directions inland; and into these arms, coming from mountain lakes known to a few Indians only, shallow rivers flow, which are diversified by falls and rapids, and deepen here and there when pent up between mountains approaching one another closely. The broad surface of the sounds is studded with rocky islets of various sizes—as in the Skär, on the North-west coast of Europe—covered with scrubby, hemlock, cedar, and pine trees. These trees—the pine predominating—also clothe the rugged sides of the hills that rise from the shore into peaks or serrated ridges, in some places almost perpendicularly, at other places with a gradual ascent.

The scenery visible from these great sheets of water, if not beautiful, is at all times interesting, though in broad daylight, the jagged, fissured, rocky islands, the bare-topped trees dwarfed by the sea-breeze, and the hard outline of the mountain-ranges, appear perhaps rather too distinctly defined to make any near view either pleasing or impressive. I found that perhaps the best time to linger in a canoe on these wide bays was just about the twilight, when the harsh sharp lines of the surrounding scenery were softened, and the shadows of islet and mountain lengthened over the singularly clear water. Among the islands, and on the shore of the Sounds, there is an endless number and variety of passages, creeks, bays, and harbours of all shapes and sizes, which can be discovered only on a near approach. Many of these marine nooks, these unexpected quiet retreats on this secluded shore, are deep enough to float the largest ship, and far down through the pellucid water, never moved by storms, gardens of zoophytes are visible at the bottom. Such places, on a summer day, strike the imagination of a loiterer like the creations in a happy dream; they are so small, calm, and remote—so margined by worn, strange-shaped rocks, and by diminutive trees, chiefly cedar and fir, under whose arched roots streamlets flow murmuring into the sea.

On the ocean coast outside, between the entrances to the great inlets, a different prospect is found: the line of the shore there is broken by low headlands which project from the seaboard, and appear with their shapeless, outlying rocks, not unlike the shattered angles of a fortified work; between these capes are narrow beaches, backed by a curtain of rock, over which hill upon hill appears, woody and rugged. As the coast lies exposed to the uninterrupted western swell of the North Pacific, the waves are generally large, and even in calm weather they break with a noise on the shore and roar among the caverns. During a storm in winter, those who care for terrible scenes are gratified by the sight of enormous billows rolling in from the ocean and dashing with fury upon the shore. The line of the raging surf on the beach extends before one's eyes for miles to some rocky cape, over which the waves foam, the spray being borne upwards and flung through the air. Wild black clouds approach the earth, and are hurried along by the blast. There is nowhere any sign of life now; the Indians crowd together in their houses, and the birds huddle behind the sheltering rocks. Speaking generally, however, navigators, since the publication of the Admiralty charts, do not consider the coast dangerous in average weather; they find anchorages in the Sounds, and the channels from the ocean are deep—too deep rather—and are free from rocks and rapid currents. The severest gales that I remember occurred in November, but during the whole winter there are heavy storms; in summer calms and fogs prevail—March and October being considered the foggiest months.*

Of the country along this coast, a short description will suffice. The whole surface, as far inland as I have penetrated, is rocky and mountainous, and is covered with thick pine-forests, without any of the oak-openings that enliven the scenery near Victoria in the southern part of the island. From some of the eminences near Alberni a great expanse of country can be seen on a clear day; but the view, looking inland, is not varied, consisting for the most part of narrow valleys and steep hills, weathered peaks with bare stony tops; here and there glimpses of shining lakes or rain-pools, and in the distance snow-covered mountains. "The back of the world, brother," with some truth the Gaelic-

* The kelp is one of the most extraordinary marine productions on the coast. It is found in masses which spread over the surface of the sea, and through these great weeds it is difficult for a small vessel to make way unless with a strong breeze. I do not know the greatest length of the stems of this plant, but I have seen it growing in twenty-five fathoms of water, and remember measuring a piece of kelp on the beach near the Ohyaht village, in Nitinaht Sound, that was fifty-five yards in length and an inch and a half in diameter at the thickest part.

woman said in her own expressive words on first seeing this district; "you are bringing me to the back of the world." Owing to the absence of any large tract of level land in the district, and the height of the land near the sea, the rivers are small, shallow, and rapid, and only navigable by canoes for a few miles.

Two days' rain, dissolving a portion of the snow on the hills, or gathering in the innumerable natural reservoirs and channels, will cause a rise of many feet in streams which before were extremely shallow. I know an instance of a fordable river—the Klistachnit at Alberni—which rose twelve feet in less than forty-eight hours. The mountains everywhere approach closely to one another, and form between them deep, thickly-wooded valleys or long narrow lakes. These lakes are a marked feature in Vancouver Island scenery. They have no main feeders, but generally receive their waters from the rain and melted snow, which come down the sides of the steep mountains. In fact they are extensive "tarns," and many of them are the finest and gloomiest of their class. They are most irregular in shape, seldom exceeding a mile or two in width, but extending between mountains for ten or fifteen miles in different directions like the legs on a Manx penny. The whole country—valley and mountain—is covered with pines, which, though rough-looking trees, yet by the deep verdure of their tops, preserve the scenery from the bareness and hardness which, for instance, characterize many of the West of Scotland Lochs. There are lakes, however, in the Aht district which are as deep, dark, and wild, as Loch Corruisken, and solitary beyond conception. I never knew what utter solitude meant till I went among these Vancouver lakes; all is silence but for the melancholy cry of the loon, the breaking of a decayed branch in the woods, or the rush of a torrent; and the feeling of loneliness is increased by the thought that you are in a savage country far from civilized men. As a journeyer in these wilds, I have often reclined on a decaying tree by the lake-side in the deepening twilight, looking at the black clouds and stormy rain, and have tried to imagine—as my last match sputtered out—that the lee of a cedar-tree would be a comfortable resting-place. In truth, not much imagining is required; for it is wonderful how easily a man becomes reconciled even to so poor a bed, if he is in good health and has a cheerful heart. One can sleep almost anywhere if one's clothes are dry and the cold not excessive. The conditions necessary to avoid positive physical discomfort depend greatly on habit: an old campaigner thinks that a sod turned up against the wind is a luxury. In the interior of the Aht country, it is hardly possible for the traveller to reach the edge of the forest, except at a lake; and then, through the darkness, whatever his bed promises to be, it is grand sometimes, as I remember, to see the lightning-flash lighting up the shaggy breast of the mountain opposite; and when the blazing glare comes again, to mark the long line through the trees made by the avalanche in rolling down for thousands of feet into the lake. He marks too the draperies of mist moving upwards from the gloomy fells, and that cataract just seen hanging like a silver thread to the cap of clouds on the far summit, which strikes the eye again, expanded into a torrent, a thousand feet lower at the exposed turn of some ravine, and then is heard rushing into the narrow lake just opposite to the spot on which the observer sits. I have seen many such nights in these wilds.

It is difficult to find in any part of the district more than a few patches of open land here and there, near the mouths of rivers and the borders of lakes. The soil is generally deep, and often rich from the accumulation of vegetable remains; but as rough wooded hills form a great part of the surface of the country, and rocks crop out everywhere, there is not room for many farms. Notwithstanding the deep shade in the forest, the undergrowth of shrubs is luxuriant at certain seasons, but it does not last long. In July and August—July being called *Kow-wishimilh* (from *Kow-wit*, salmon-berry, and *Hishimilh*, a crowd)—the graceful branches and wavy green leaves of the low berry-bushes in the woods are most pleasant to look upon, but are a great hindrance in travelling. Probably there is nothing in Vancouver Island more interesting to a stranger than the aged forests of pine—nearly all of one species, *Abies Douglassii*—which cover the country. Viewed commercially, though the wood is of first-rate quality, these forests are of little value, owing to the difficulty of getting the "logs" or "spars" over a rugged surface to a saw-mill or place of shipment. The traveller, accustomed elsewhere to trees of smaller growth, and to pleasing varieties of verdure and freshness, finds himself here amidst old, gigantic, thick-barked pines without branches to a considerable height from the ground, and with dark-green bristling foliage that hardly ever changes. The tops of these great trees are in many places so densely mingled as to scatter, if not to exclude, the rays of the sun. Here and there in the forest are open spaces where the trees burnt by a fire—caused perhaps by the careless Indians—lie blackened on the ground, or where they appear lying white and withered, as if destroyed by some blast or circle of wind that left the surrounding trees uninjured:

> "Blasted pines,
> Wrecks of a single winter, barkless, branchless."—MANFRED.

And many an old tree meets the eye, fit object of a contemplative and melancholy regard, which, after its long growth and towering position in the forest, has reached the period of its decline, and can no longer oppose the ravages of the insects that prey on its naked trunk. These aged trees are constantly falling one across another, and their great thickness and length make them, when prostrate, formidable obstructions in walking through the woods. On my leaping upon a fallen decayed tree, the bark has given way, and I have sunk to the thigh in a red mould. Judging from the fact that many clumps of young trees grow in the forest, it would appear that the seeds, on being shaken out of the cones by the wind, either are blown from the parent trees here and there in heaps, steered by their membranous sail, or that they cover the whole surface, and spring up numerously only where the conditions of growth are favourable. These young trees stand so closely together that they have a hard struggle to grow beyond a certain height; and I should think fifty trees die for every one that lives to throw out its green top under the heavens.

There is occasionally a good deal of snow in the Aht district—much more than falls in the neighbourhood of Victoria; but, as a rule, it does not lie long on the lower ground near the water, and it is seldom seen on the mountains in summer, except in clefts from which the sun is excluded. The third month or "moon" of the Indians, *Hy-yeskikamilh,* which means "the month of most snow," corresponds with our January. The climate on the west coast, as in all parts of Vancouver Island, particularly in the favoured locality of Victoria, is probably altogether the most healthful and delightful in the world. Most people fatten there, and feel strong and vigorous. I never was brisker than when exploring the unknown Aht district, carrying with me my food, and sleeping where I chanced to halt, generally beneath a spreading cedar.

I will now remark upon the population of the district, which has been thus roughly described to the reader. It is not easy to ascertain the exact native population at the present time; but so far as I know there are, between Pacheenah and Nespod, twenty distinct tribes of the Aht nation (see Appendix), numbering together about 1,700 men, capable of bearing arms. The largest tribe numbers 400 men; seven other tribes have between one and two hundred; the remaining fifteen tribes vary in numbers from sixty down to as few as five: the average number in each of the last-named tribes being about twenty-five grown men. Few of these natives have visited Victoria; and their condition, in fact, as already stated, is comparatively unknown to Americans as well as to Europeans. The Aht district lies quite out of the ordinary route of travellers, and can be reached conveniently only by engaging a vessel at Victoria. These tribes of the Ahts are not confederated; and I have no other warrant for calling them a nation than the fact of their occupying adjacent territories, and having the same superstitions and language. They evidently have had an ancient connection, if not a common origin. It may be noticed that, though living only a few miles apart, the tribes practise different arts, and have, apparently, distinct tribal characteristics. One tribe is skilful in shaping canoes; another in painting boards for ornamental work, or making ornaments for the person, or instruments for hunting and fishing. Individuals, as a rule, keep to the arts for which their tribe has some repute, and do not care to acquire those arts in which other tribes excel. There seems to be among all the tribes in the island a sort of recognized tribal monopoly in certain articles produced, or that have been long manufactured in their own district. For instance, a tribe that does not grow potatoes, or make a particular kind of mat, will go a long way, year after year, to barter for those articles, which, if they liked, they themselves could easily produce or manufacture. The different Aht tribes vary in physiognomy somewhat—faces of the Chinese and the Spanish types may be seen; they vary also in intelligence, in love of war, in fondness for many wives, in decorum of speech and manner, in several social usages, in taste for music and oratory, in habits of slave-dealing and gambling, and in their thievish propensities. No superior position in the political scale of the tribes is assigned by their traditions to any one tribe; but the Toquahts in Nitinaht, or Barclay Sound, are generally considered by their neighbours to have been the tribe from which the others sprung. Quawteaht, a great personage in the mythology of these barbarians, who, while on earth, lived at the Toquaht river, is said to have given the first part of the names to the tribes; for instance,

Toqu to the Toquahts, Ohy to the Ohyahts, Nitin to the Nitinahts, Klah-oh-Qu to the Klah-oh-Quahts, and so on. The natives added the termination Aht in honour of their instructor or progenitor, Quawteaht. Subdivisions of tribes occasionally take place by the secession of restless, influential individuals, who, with their families and friends, endeavour to start new tribes under their own chiefship. In this way—if a natural increase of numbers is possible in a savage state of life—we may suppose that the tribes now existing along the coast branched off formerly from a few parent stems; a supposition which accords with one of the legends of the people. These first families, leaving the parent tribes, and settling at good fishing-places, would forget their kindred in a few generations, and treat them in all respects as members of separate tribes. But against the supposition of such secession having occurred frequently in modern days, there is the improbability of the number of these natives having increased; and the fact (which will be proved farther on) that the Aht language has not changed materially within the last century, as would most likely have been the case if subdivisions and formations of new tribes had been common.

CHAPTER IV.

PHYSICAL APPEARANCE.

Physical Appearance of the Natives—Their Stature, Strength, Weight, Complexion—Their Teeth, Hair, Dress, Ornaments—Abbé Domenech's Book—Fish-eating Indians not weak in the Legs—Bathing common; Skill of the Ahts in Diving—Vapour-Bath unknown—Water colder than in England—Traces of old Spanish Settlement—Painting Faces—Custom of Moulding the Head—Appearance of the Natives in Infancy and Youth—Rapid Decay of Manly Strength—The Faces of the Ahts expressive of Settled Character.

. . . And yet more pleased have, from your lips,
Gathered this fair report of them who dwell
In that retirement.—Wordsworth.

The next part of my subject, which I hope will not be uninteresting to the reader, is the physical appearance and characteristics of these people. As their only article of dress is a blanket, and I was constantly among them, I can speak with some confidence as to their physique. The external features of all the natives along this coast are much alike, but one acquainted with them can generally distinguish the tribes to which individuals belong. I have noticed that the slaves have a meaner appearance than the free men, and that those few small tribes who dwell inland along lakes and rivers, and who live on a mixed diet of fish and flesh, have a finer stature and bearing than the fish-eaters on the coast. Of all the tribes in Vancouver Island the Klah-oh-quahts, who live in Klah-oh-quaht Sound, probably are, as a tribe, physically the finest.* Individuals may be found in all the tribes who reach a height of five feet eleven inches, and a weight of a hundred and eighty pounds, without much flesh on their bodies. The extreme average height of the men of the Aht nation ascertained by comparison of a number, is about five feet six inches, and of the women about five feet and a quarter of an inch—a stature which equals that of the New Zealanders.† Many of the men have well-shaped forms and limbs. None are corpulent, and very few are deformed from their birth. I have, however, seen several who had been born crippled; one, with withered crooked legs, stiff at the knees, was an excellent canoe-man. The men, as a rule, are better-looking than the women. The latter are not enticing, even when young, though one meets with some good-looking women, but these in a few years, after reaching womanhood, lose their comeliness. They are short-limbed, and have an awkward habit of turning their toes in

* "Klah-oh-quaht," in the native tongue, means "another people," but this tribe is now in every respect the same as the others.

† The following ridiculous account of the Ahts is contained in the latest book in which they are mentioned: Abbé Domenech's *Residence in the Great Deserts of North America*. "The men (the Nootkahs) are below the middle height, with thick-set limbs, broad faces, low foreheads, and rough, coppery, and tanned skins. Their moral deformities are as great as their physical ones. Their dialect is exceedingly difficult, and the harshness of their pronunciation incredible." The abbé evidently knows nothing about the people.

too much when walking. The men generally have well-set, strong frames, and, if they had pluck and skill, could probably hold their own in a grapple with Englishmen of the same stature. They want heart, however, for a close struggle, and seldom come up after the first knock-down. The best place to strike them with the fist is on the throat, or on the breast, so as to take away their wind; a blow on the head does them very little harm. The powers of endurance possessed by the natives are great in any work to which they are accustomed, such as paddling, or rowing, or walking in the woods. I have had men with me from sunrise to sunset whilst exploring new districts where the walking tried one's powers to the utmost, and they scarcely seemed to feel the exertion.* The natives can bear the want of food for a long time without becoming exhausted. Their complexion is a dull brown, just about, perhaps, what the English complexion would be if the people were in a savage instead of a civilized condition—the difference being explained by the habits of life of the Ahts, by their frequent exposure, and by the effect of their food of blubber, oil, and fish. The Queen Charlotte Islanders and other natives to the north are fairer in complexion than the Vancouverians, though living under the same conditions

* It is an error to suppose that these fish-eating Indians become weak in the legs from constantly sitting or stooping in canoes; mean-looking, thin-legged Ahts can travel for great distances in the woods without tiring. There is a fair proportion of well-limbed men among them. No finer men than the Queen Charlotte Islanders, a canoe-using people, can be found on the American continent; they will stand up and fight Englishmen with their fists, though the Aht fails on this point. The notion of the Coast Indians being deficient in muscular power in their legs, probably arose from their legs being always seen uncovered, which is a severe ordeal for any people. If the men wore blankets, how many presentable legs would there be in an ordinary crowd of Englishmen?

in a climate not much colder. Their young women's skins are as clear and white as those of Englishwomen. But it is different among the Ahts. Cook and Meares probably mentioned exceptional cases in stating that the natives of Nootkah had the fair complexions of the North of Europe. The prevailing colour of the people in Vancouver Island is unmistakeably, as here described, a sort of dull brown. During summer they are much in the open air, lightly clad, and in winter pass most of their time sitting round fires in a smoky atmosphere. All the natives swim well, but not so fast nor so lightly as Europeans; they labour more in the water. As divers they cannot be beaten; a friend of mine saw Maquilla, a noted warrior and fisherman of the Nitinahts, dive from the stern of a boat, in five fathoms of water, and bring up a pup seal in each hand from the bottom. On approaching the boat, one of the seals got away, but Maquilla, throwing the other into the boat, again dived and captured the seal before it could reach the bottom. Till beyond middle age many of the natives bathe every day in the sea, and in winter they rub their bodies with oil after coming out of the water.* The vapour-bath is not known on this coast. Mothers roll their young children in the snow to make them hardy. I should not call the Aht Indians a dirty people in their persons: they wash often, the fresh air circulates round their bodies, and they have not the disagreeable oniony smell about them which is common among the more closely attired poorer classes

* Throughout the year, though the climate on the whole is milder than the English climate, the water in the sea round Vancouver Island is colder than on any part of the shores of Great Britain.

in many countries. After their day's work, the women arrange their dress and hair, and wash themselves in fresh water.* The men's dress is a blanket; the women's a strip of cloth, or shift, and blanket. The old costume of the natives was the same as at present, but the material was different; for instance, a single robe of bearskin, or of four red catskins sewn together, was worn instead of a blanket. They use no covering for the head or feet except on canoe journeys, when hats and capes made of bark or grass are worn. There is no difference between summer and winter dresses, nor anything peculiar, on ordinary occasions, in the dress of the chiefs. The men's beards and whiskers are deficient, probably from the old alleged custom, now seldom practised, of extirpating the hairs with small shells. This custom, continued from one generation to another, would perhaps at last produce a race distinguishable as these natives are by a thin and straggling growth of beard and whiskers. Several of the Nootkah Sound natives (Moouchahts) have large moustaches and whiskers, and on that account are supposed to have Spanish or foreign blood in them. A few names and a cast of features reminding one of Spain, cross one here and there on this coast. I have heard an Indian from Nootkah count ten in Spanish. Few traces of the settlement at Nootkah remain, except an indistinct ridge showing the site of houses, and here and there a few bricks half hidden in the ground; but the older natives

* It is a characteristic of these natives, that men sometimes saunter along, holding each other's hand in a friendly way: a habit never to be observed in civilized life, except amongst boys, or sailors when intoxicated.

sometimes speak of the Spaniards. They say that the foreigners (who must have been Meares' men or the Spanish) had begun to cultivate the ground and to erect a stockade and fort, when one day a ship came with papers for the head man, who was observed to cry, and all the white men became sad. The next day they began moving their goods to the vessel.

The hair of the natives is never shaven from the head. It is black or dark brown, without gloss, coarse and lank, but not scanty, worn long, and either tied in a bunch or knot at the crown without an attempt at ornament, or allowed to hang loosely from under a handkerchief or wreath of grass, or of feathered birdskin, encircling the head. A favourite place of concealment for a knife carried as a weapon is among the hair behind the ear. The practice of tying the hair behind the head in the Chinese fashion is said to be peculiar to the natives on the outside coast of the Island. Slaves wear their hair short. Now and then, but rarely, a light-haired native is seen. There is one woman in the Opechisaht tribe at Alberni who had curly, or rather wavy, brown hair. Few grey-haired men can be noticed in any tribe. I once saw a middle-aged native with red hair, and he seemed a pure Indian, but it is difficult to say whether he was so or not. The women are careful of their hair, and have little boxes in which they keep combs and looking-glasses. There is a small white-flowered plant, of about three feet in height, the bruised roots of which are put on their hair by the Indians to make it grow. One frequently sees the women combing their hair and afterwards disposing it on each side into plaits, which taper to a point, and are there ornamented with beads; or it hangs loosely and is kept down by leaden weights affixed to the end. When at work the women tie up their hair so as not to be inconvenienced. Unlike the men, they are fond of toys and ornaments for themselves and children, and are seldom seen without rings, anklets, and bracelets of beads or brass. Their blankets are often tastefully ornamented with beads. To cut off the hair of an Indian is an effective punishment for minor offences, as he is thereby exposed to the derision of his own people. The face of the Ahts is rather broad and flat; the mouth and lips of both men and women are large, though to this there are exceptions, and the cheekbones are broad but not high. The skull is fairly shaped, the eyes small and long, deep set, in colour a lustreless inexpressive black or very dark hazel, none being blue, grey, nor brown. Some of the Chinese workmen brought to Nootkah eighty years ago by Meares, have no doubt left descendants among the Ahts. One occasionally sees an Indian with eyes distinctly Chinese. The nose, of all the features of the human face rarest for beauty, in some instances is remarkably well-shaped. A brilliant ring or piece of cockleshell, or a bit of brass, shaped like a horse-shoe, often adorns this feature. Similar ornaments are worn in the ear by both sexes. The teeth are regular, but stumpy, and are deficient in enamel at the points, as some think from the natives' eating so much dried salmon with which sand has intermixed in the process of drying.

No such practice as tatooing exists among these natives. At great feasts the faces of the women are painted red with vermilion or berry-juice, and the men's faces are blackened with burnt wood. About the age of twenty-five the women cease to use paint, and for the remainder of their lives wear feathers in their hair for full dress. Some of the young men streak their faces with red, but grown-up men seldom now use paint, unless on particular occasions. Hair cut short and a blackened face are signs of grief; at a time of rejoicing the face is also of that colour, except a space round the eyes; but in war every portion of the visage is blackened, and the eyes glare through. The leader of a war expedition is distinguished by a streaked visage from his black-faced followers.

The curious custom of moulding the heads of infants into a different shape from the natural form does not now extensively prevail among the Ahts, though almost every child's head receives a slight pressure, owing to the mode of resting in the cradle. The traveller leaves on this side of Cape Scott a people with fine, broad—though perhaps slightly flattened—foreheads, and heads well set on, and soon finds himself on the north side of the Cape, among the Quoquoulth nation, a people with disfigured heads, who speak a language different from that of the Ahts, though, of course, having many words in common, near the tribal boundaries. In other parts of the Island, also, as well as among the Quoquoulth natives, the practice of moulding the head is followed, but it is principally among the latter people that heads have been seen of the real sugar-loaf shape. I have never seen an Aht head so much distorted as the chief's head shown at page 317, vol. ii., in Wilson's *Pre-Historic Man.* In Barclay (Nitinaht) Sound, where the Aht tribes have intermarried with the Flatheads, on the American shore of the Strait of Juan de Fuca, many of the natives are proud of such children as have their foreheads flattened, but they do not regard this disfigurement as a sign of freedom, nor of high birth—as travellers have reported of the natives at the mouth of the Columbia river. The Ahts imagine that it improves the appearance, and also gives better health and greater strength to the infant. I could not satisfactorily discover whether the brain is injured by this change in the form of the skull. The natives say that no harm is done, but I have observed—from whatever cause the superiority arises —that several of the tribes of the Aht nation, the Klah-oh-quahts, for instance, who do not greatly flatten their heads, are superior to other tribes, not Ahts, known to me which flatten their heads excessively. This superiority, however, may be in the race: the Klah-oh-quahts, for instance—which, from their name, are probably a foreign tribe now assimilated to the other Aht tribes—may have originally possessed a superior organization to any others. It is extremely difficult to compare the intellectual faculties of any two tribes of suspicious, reserved, and weak-minded savages, without a particular acquaintance with both tribes, and a knowledge of their language and subjects of thought, their politics and management of individual and tribal affairs; but I may say that the general opinion which I have formed with respect to these natives is that the flattening of the skull in infancy cannot decisively be said to injure the intellect. The process by which the deformity is effected is similar to that described by Irving as usual with the Coast Indians near the Columbia river. The infant is laid, soon after birth, on a small wooden cradle higher at the head than the foot. A padding is placed on the forehead, and is pressed down with cords, which pass through holes on each side of the trough or cradle; these being tightened gradually the required pressure is obtained, and after a time the front of the skull is flattened. The covering or padding is filled with sand, or sometimes a maple mould is made to fit the forehead. It is said that the process is not painful, but some of the children, whom I saw undergoing the compression, seemed to breathe slowly, and their faces were pale. The origin of this singular custom cannot with certainty be ascertained. It may have been adopted to celebrate some particular event, or in honour of a great warrior whose head was naturally of that form. It is a fashion; that is all that can be said about it. During infancy the native children are big-headed and ugly, and are subject to eruptive diseases, but in a few years they become interesting and sprightly in appearance and manners. They are plump and fresh-looking, with smooth skins of a rich brown colour. About the age of puberty—which in both sexes is early—the visage of the men assumes the composure, and displays the cold serious traits of the savage. The eye, particularly, has a hard furtive expression that was not there in childhood.* After having reached a vigorous age, no other important stage takes place till their manhood fails, when the Aht natives become thin and wrinkled in a short time. They do not seem to have any intermediate stage in their existence corresponding with the attractive time in an Englishman's

* The face of the Indian, while it conceals present thoughts, seems to me to be a much more open book than the face of the white man in expressing settled character. It shows the very normal types of the vices plainly printed in the features, most especially those of anger, cunning, and pride.

life between full manhood and the first steps that lead downwards into age. They are either vigorous or weak, young-looking or old-looking. I have known many Indians who have become quite old in appearance within the five years since I first saw them.

CHAPTER V.

PURSUIT OF A FUGITIVE.

Strength of the Natives' Fingers—Speed in Running—Skill in Paddling—Escape of a Fugitive.

You have not seen such a thing as it is;
I can hardly forbear hurling things at him.
TWELFTH NIGHT.

THE Upper Canadians and the men of the Northern and Western States of the United States are the finest-looking men I have anywhere seen, with the exception, perhaps, of the Queen Charlotte Islanders, on the North-west of British Columbia. I thought so on seeing them in their homes in Canada and America, and my estimate was confirmed by the appearance of the British Columbian population and the inhabitants of my own settlement, who chiefly were of these nationalities. Finer men cannot be seen, in face and figure, than among the miners and woodmen, say, at a race-meeting in Beacon Hill Park, near Victoria, Vancouver Island, any summer afternoon. I had on an average about 270 men at Alberni—perhaps three-fourths of these Canadians and Americans—stalwart, handsome fellows, accustomed to work with their hands. One day, when the vessels were discharging cargo into the warehouse, we amused ourselves by trying who could carry round the room, on two fingers, the governor of a steam-engine—a mass of metal like a 10-inch shell—and not one of us could carry it half the distance. A middle-sized Indian, who was present, carried it round the warehouse apparently with ease. The constant use of the paddle may be supposed to make the fingers of the Indians strong; but would the use of the axe from childhood not also strengthen the fingers of the woodmen? Why should the fingers of a comparatively small Indian be stronger than the fingers of a powerful American woodman? The generally prevalent opinion, as regards the hand of the Indians, was that it exceeded the white man's hand in power. On a certain occasion, a disturbance having arisen, I armed my men, warning them earnestly not to strike or fire till the last extremity. Every one answered that if the Indians came to close quarters and grasped their clothes, they could not disengage the Indians' hold without drawing blood. The blanket worn by the Indians is a convenient garment in a close struggle. One of my men who had watched an Indian potato-stealer for weeks, gripped him at last one night by slipping round a tree upon him as he was filling his bag; but the savage got off by pulling out the bone skewer that fastened his blanket at the neck, and by running naked across the potato-beds into the thick wood. If an Indian is unarmed, one can hold him only by seizing his hair; if he has a weapon about his person, he should not be seized at all, but should be knocked down. The Indians, as already stated, often carry a knife concealed behind the ear in their long hair.

The Aht Indian runs well, but does not equal the Englishman in running. In pursuing a native in the open, he should always be turned from the forest, as, when once there, nothing but a hound can follow him. In November, 1864, on a day so dreary and snowy that we could not work, word reached the settlement that a notoriously bad Indian, who, we were well aware, had committed several murders, and was under sentence of imprisonment, but who had escaped from the constable in 1862, was visiting his married daughter at a temporary Indian hut on the bank of the Klistachnit River, about a mile from Alberni. Taking with me John Eyloc, a New Brunswick shipwright, a quick runner and a first-rate oarsman and paddler, with five other trusty men, all unarmed, and putting my six-barrelled Adams' revolver in my own belt, I went up the river in a boat, and landed on the bank a few hundred yards below the hut, towards which we walked. Before the inmates discovered our approach, we had surrounded the hut. Cautiously entering the doorway, I looked into the apartment, and saw no one but the son-in-law of the fugitive and two women sitting by the fire, who sprang to their feet on observing me. A noise outside attracted my attention, and, on going out, I found that the savage we wanted to capture had sprung unobserved from an opening at a corner of the hut, and was making for the wood at full speed over the snow. Eyloc was in pursuit, and having gained on him quickly, notwithstanding the disadvantage of shoes (which get clogged in the snow), the Indian abandoned his intention of reaching the wood, and turned towards a near point on the river. We ran to intercept him, but he reached the bank, and, throwing off his blanket, plunged into the stream. The excitement in our party was now so great that one of my men ran towards me, seized my arm, and almost ordered me to shoot, or he would escape. The fugitive had risen to the surface, and was swimming towards a canoe that was quite out of our reach, tied to a drift tree in the river. I covered him several times with my pistol, in the excitement of the moment; but had no intention of firing, especially as two of my own men had got into a small canoe some way down the stream, and were paddling up stream towards the coveted canoe. The Indian reached it, however, first. He looked to see if the canoe contained a paddle, then eagerly grasped the welcome instrument. His pursuers, by this time, were perhaps twenty yards from him, and were labouring with powerful, but unequal and unskilful strokes against the rapid current. We on the bank were not more than thirty yards distant. The river was about 250 yards wide. It was beautiful to see how boldly the Indian, now seated in a canoe, shot athwart his pursuers, and how skilfully he forced his light skiff both up and across the stream, while our men lost ground greatly in attempting to slant their canoe and follow him. There were more than fifty yards between the two canoes when the Indian reached the wooded bank opposite, and plunged into the forest. We, of course, then lost him. I believe he never again came near the settlement. As our party retraced their steps to the boat, cold, weary, and disappointed, I could see that my not having fired at this fellow was not approved by my companions. During the whole time of the pursuit, the two women,—one of them, as above named, the fugitive's daughter,—squatted near me and scolded bitterly. "*You* a chief!" repeated they. "*You* pretend to be a chief; and try to steal our papa! *You* a chief! You are a common man. So-and-so" (naming one of the foremen) "is a high chief. *You* are no chief at all." They are adepts in scolding; and it was done, in this case, so vigorously that I could not laugh at them. Next day the same women were quite friendly and chatty when they saw me at the settlement. Their papa, they said, was now far beyond my reach.

I remember many instances of Indians having escaped from us through their skill in swimming, and paddling, and travelling through the woods. The management by a single Indian of a canoe in crossing a rapid stream cannot be surpassed. At the same time, I may observe that I have seen a trained crew of white men beat a crew of Indians in a long canoe race on the sea. The civilized man seems to have more bottom in him, when the exertion is intense and prolonged.

CHAPTER VI.

HOUSES.

Houses of the Ahts—Custom of Changing Quarters—Mode of Shifting an Encampment—No Appreciation of Natural Scenery—Description of Dwellings and Furniture.

Carrying his own home still, still is at home.—DONNE.

A fish : he smells like a fish ; a very ancient and fishlike smell.
SHAKSPEARE.

THE framework or fixed portion of the houses in an Indian village here belongs to individuals, generally to subordinate chiefs, or to men of some station in the tribe. The name of the owner of the framework of any division of the house is given to the division formed by such framework for the use of a family, when the whole encampment is planked in for occupation. The planking is a joint contribution from the inmates. It is customary for the natives to shift their encampments several times during the year, so as to be near good fishing and root and fruit grounds. They cannot, however, be strictly considered as migratory tribes, as they always move to the same places, according to the season, and these different encampments are not far apart. The framework of the building is never removed, so that planking the sides and roofs is the only work on re-occupation. Planks required for repairing the houses are made during winter. Following the salmon as they swim up the rivers and inlets, the natives place their summer encampments at some distance from the seaboard, towards which they return for the winter season about the end of October, with a stock of dried salmon—their principal food at all times. By this arrangement, being near the seashore, they can get shell-fish, if their stock of salmon runs short, and can also catch the first fish that approach the shore in the early spring. Every tribe, however, does not thus regularly follow the salmon; some of the tribes devote a season to whale-fishing, or to the capture of the dog-fish, and supply themselves with salmon by barter with other tribes. If the natives did not thus often move their quarters, their health would suffer from the putrid fish and other nastinesses that surround their camps, which the elements and the birds clear away during the time of non-occupation. They remove in the following manner from an encampment:—Two large canoes are placed about six feet apart, and connected by planks—the sides and roofs of the houses—laid transversely upon each other, so as to form a wide deck the whole length of the canoe, space enough for one man being reserved at the bow and stern. On this deck are baskets full of preparations of salmon-roe, dried salmon, and other fish, together with wooden boxes containing blankets and household articles. The women and children sit in a small space purposely left for them. I have seen the goods piled on these rafts as high as fourteen feet from the water. Each canoe is managed by two men, who, with the women and children, often raise a cheery song as they float down the stream with all their goods and chattels. The principal men send slaves or others to prepare their quarters, and among the common people it is understood beforehand who shall live together at the new encampment. A willing, handy poor man sometimes is invited to live for the winter with a richer family, for whom he works for a small remuneration. The houses of the natives at their winter camping-grounds are large and strongly constructed. I have seen a row of houses stretching along the bank of a stream for the third of a mile, with a varying breadth, inside the buildings, of from twenty-five to forty feet, and a height of from ten to twelve. Cedar (*Thuja gigantea*) is the wood used in making the houses. Far from presenting a mean appearance, some of the permanent winter encampments on this coast suggest to us what the wooden halls of the old Northern nations in Europe may have been like. They are far superior, as human dwellings, to the hovels in Connaught, or the mud cabins in the west of Sutherland. The village sites are generally well chosen, and, though not selected for any other reason than nearness to firewood and water, and safety against a surprise, are often beautiful, occupying picturesquely the made* ground at the bend of a river, or a spot near some pleasant brook, where fantastic masses of rock, or the dense mixed forests, keep off the wind.† At such places, occupied for centuries year after

* This "made" ground consists of mud or earth, partly deposited from the river itself, and partly washed from the bank of the stream. This washing takes place especially at any bend or turn in the river.

† It is not my belief that these savages select pretty spots for their village sites, or that they have any appreciation of natural scenery. The notion that

year, shell-mounds have been formed, like the Danish "kitchen refuse heaps," and from some of these in Vancouver Island, on their being dug through, the materials for information respecting a past time may yet be got. A row of round posts, a foot thick, and from ten to twelve feet high, placed twenty feet apart and slightly hollowed out at the top, is driven firmly into the ground to form the framework of the lodge. These posts are connected by strong cross-pieces, over which, lengthwise, the roof-tree is placed—a stick sometimes of twenty inches diameter and eighty or ninety feet long, hewn neatly round by the mussel-adze, and often to be seen blackened by the smoke of several generations. Some of the inside main-posts often have great faces carved on them.* Heavy timbers cap the side-posts, and across from these to the roof-tree smaller cross-poles are laid, which support the roof. The

they find a charm in contemplating the beauties of nature while resting hour after hour on the grass near their houses, seems to me to have no foundation. It is easy to imagine, from an Indian's attitude, that he is watching tranquilly the floating clouds, or the light waves on the surface of the water, or that his ear enjoys the pleasant murmuring of the leaves; but the chances are, I imagine, that the savage either gazes with a dull eye on vacancy, or is half asleep. His rude. coarse organization cannot receive the impressions of which more civilized, elevated natures are susceptible. If his fancy roves, the images before the mind of the savage will be gross and common, and very different from the beautiful conceptions which a refined intelligence would form. The woods, to him, merely shelter beasts; an angry spirit makes a ripple on the water; and every shadow of a cloud causes alarm. The immediate necessities of his life, vague fears of the future, an unavenged wrong, or some torturing suspicions, fill the mind of the savage, and unfit him even for the sensuous enjoyment of fine scenery and climate.

* These are not idols, but rude artistic efforts undertaken without any view to symbolize the notions which the natives have of Quawteaht as a higher being. I could not find that the Ahts possessed any symbols or images that could be properly called idols, as objects of religious or superstitious veneration.

roof is formed of broad cedar boards, sometimes seen of five feet in width by two inches thick, overlaid so as to turn off water. The roof is not quite flat, but has a slight pitch from the back part. The sides of the house are made of the same material as the roof—the boards overlapping and being tied together with twigs between slender upright posts fixed into the ground. The building is now complete, except that the inmates have no place for the reception of goods. To get this, a sort of duplicate inside building is made by driving into the ground, close to the exterior upright posts, smaller posts shorter by about two feet. Small trees are tied to these shorter inside posts, one end of each tree being fastened to an inside post on one side of the house, about two feet below the top of this inside post, and the other end tied in a similar manner to the opposite short post on the other side of the house. At right angles to these small trees, slender poles are laid, on which the natives stow all sorts of things—onions, fern-roots, mats, packages of roe, dried fish, guns, and hunting and fishing instruments. There is no ceiling, and, with the exception of these poles, the interior is open to the roof. For about a foot deep inside of the building the earth is hollowed out, and on the outside a strong stockade of split cedar is sometimes erected, about six feet from the walls. At the Ohyaht village, in Nitinaht (or Barclay) Sound, I have seen a loopholed stockade of this kind, erected so as to face almost the only beach in the neighbourhood on which an enemy could land. The Nitinahts also have a fortified village. The houses of the Ahts are without windows, and the entrances are small, and usually at a corner of some division of the building. The chimney consists of a shifting board in the roof. There is access from division to division of the house. The inside is divided for family occupation into large squares, partitioned for four feet in height; in the middle of each square is the fire burning on a ring of stones; and round the sides of these squares are wooden couches, raised nine inches from the ground,* and covered with six or eight soft mats for bedding. A more comfortable bed to rest upon I do not know, and the wooden pillow, nicely fitting the head of the sleeper, and covered with mats, is a good contrivance. Boxes are piled between the couches, and also in the corners of these rooms or divisions. The floor is uncovered. There are no prescribed seats in these divisions for the different members of the family. All the houses are so much alike, and the habits of the natives differ so little, that in a night attack the stealthy enemy can enter, and in the dark know where to strike the sleepers. A strong fish-like smell, and rather more pungent smoke than is agreeable, salute the nose and eyes of the careless traveller who enters the Aht dwellings. The outside, however, is the worst, for the whole refuse of the camp is thrown there; and, not being offensive to the organs of the natives, is never removed. A pinch of snuff and a toothful of good brandy are very grateful to one who picks his way among the putrid fish and castaway mollusks that cover the ground. The principal occupant lives at the extreme end, on the left of the building as you walk

* It is worthy of remark that in several villages on the north-east of Vancouver Island, and in nearly all on the coast of British Columbia, the Indian houses are divided into small rooms. I have not seen a house so divided on the west coast of the island. It probably is an imitation of white men's houses.

up from the main door; the next in rank at the nearer end, on the left as one enters; the intermediate spaces being occupied by the common people. The half bulkheads between the different families are removed on great occasions, and the whole building kept clear.*

* The Indians saw our carpenters at work constantly, and were present at the building of perhaps a hundred wooden houses—both log-houses and frame-houses—yet, though furnished with sawn wood and the necessary tools and appliances, they built their new houses exactly like their old ones, never altering nor improving them.

CHAPTER VII.

A JUSTICE OF THE PEACE ON CIRCUIT.

A Mutinous Crew—My Canoe stolen—Left upon an Island—George the Pirate—Stormy Sea—Sensations from Freezing—Samaritan Woodmen.

Nature, whilst fears her bosom chill,
Suspends her pow'rs, and life stands still.—CHURCHILL.

THE comfort of even such a house as the Indians have is never so much felt, as when one has no house at all to sleep in. I remember one night when the poorest hut would have delighted me. During the afternoon a request had reached me that I would visit officially, as a magistrate, an English ship which had put into Nitinaht (or Barclay) Sound with a discontented crew. I went to the ship in a canoe manned by six Indians, and found her at an anchorage about forty-five miles from our settlement. After spending a night and the greater part of the next day on board, I succeeded in inducing the crew to lift the anchor and set the sails. They made some petty complaints, but the truth was they had a weak captain, and did not wish to proceed with the vessel. My canoe was alongside, the ship was beginning to move slowly through the water, and I was signing some papers for the captain, when a sudden hailstorm struck the vessel, and obscured the whole deck for several minutes. When the squall passed I prepared to depart, but on looking over the side found that my canoe was gone. The boatswain of the ship also was missing; he had sprung into the canoe during the squall, and had satisfied the Indians by some story of my going to sea in the vessel, that it would be according to my wishes if they proceeded with him alone—at all events the canoe was nowhere to be seen. Here was a pretty situation—several miles from the mainland, night approaching, the ship increasing her speed every minute, and the sea becoming rough. I need not relate at length how the ship managed to land me without again casting anchor. Suffice it to say, that after several hours I was landed, in the ship's gig, on a small wooded island near the entrance of Nitinaht (or Barclay) Sound; the boat returned to the ship, and she stood away and disappeared in the evening gloom. I had a pocketful of biscuits with me, but no blankets, as I expected to find an Indian encampment on the other side of the island. This chance failed me, however; for after scrambling across the island to the village, I found it empty—the Indians had moved to other fishing quarters. The night was falling, and there was nothing for it but to light a fire, and sit down beside it to chew a biscuit, and to wish the boatswain some well-deserved punishment. He was, no doubt, by this time far on his way, in my fine canoe, to some decent place of shelter. The want of a blanket I felt most; one does not like, on a January evening, to lie down at the foot even of a suitable tree without a covering of some sort. I sat by the fire till about midnight, and then made a bed of young fir-branches, and drawing several branches over me, fell asleep, with my feet towards the fire. The cold awoke me early in the morning, and I got up and moved about the island, and seated myself finally on an elevated rock, from which I could see numerous other small islands, and a considerable part of the open water of the Sound. I took a breakfast of biscuits here, and looked out anxiously for some Indian canoe. I at last saw one crossing the Sound, a long way off, and waved a handkerchief to attract attention. The Indians made no sign, but changed their course slightly in my direction. I kept on waving till I was certain they saw me, and then sat down to wait their pleasure. It was a wretched small canoe, with a man and woman in it. They did not come on steadily within hailing distance, but stopped now and then and talked, and then paddled a little way farther. Coming near at last, I shouted, "Are you Seshahts?" to which they replied by a great hoarse laugh, after the manner of the Indians. "Seshahts?" I again shouted interrogatively, and they answered, "No, Ohyahts." "Very well," said I, "come and take me to the Ohyaht village." The answer to this was another guffaw, and an objection that the canoe was too small. All this time they were endeavouring to find the real reason of one white man being there without a boat, and at the same time they were manœuvring for a hard bargain. I agreed to give them all they asked, and finally was taken by them to the village of the Ohyahts—three or four miles distant.

My first inquiry was for George the Pirate, a noted Ohyaht murderer and scoundrel, but a very good paddler.

On coming forward, he at once recognized me, and I began to be treated with distinction, which, in view of the inevitable bargain for a canoe, I was rather sorry for, as chiefs in this part are expected to pay like chiefs for everything they have. Kleeshin, the head chief of the Ohyahts, was sent for, and he invited me into his house, and spread a clean mat on a box for me to sit upon. After many questions and answers, we came to business. I wanted a large canoe, with six Indians, to take me quickly to Alberni. Such a canoe, I ascertained, could not be got—there were no large canoes at the village; so it was finally agreed that Kleeshin and scoundrel George should take me in George's small canoe, at the hire of three blue blankets. They insisted on this agreement being written on paper, to which, though unable to read it, they attached great importance.

We started about nine o'clock, and kept close to the shore, as the Indians generally do. About eleven the wind rose, and snow began to fall. We passed a point on which a dog was howling piteously. Kleeshin said this dog had been abandoned by the Indians. Entering the long canal described in the first chapter, the work became very stiff, as the sea was rough and the wind blew against the canoe; but the two paddlers worked hour after hour with regularity and vigour, and without speaking a word. I was told afterwards that we were in great danger during the whole of this time, and that nothing saved us but the extraordinary skill of Kleeshin and George with the paddles. The sea was rougher than they had expected, and there was no landing-place, and to go back was as bad as to go on. I was sitting with my back to the stern of the canoe where

Kleeshin was, but saw every movement of George the bow paddler; and not being aware of any danger, I watched his action with admiration. His manner showed no excitement; hour after hour his shoulder and arm worked like part of a steam-engine, and when an angry curling wave came close to the gunwale, he cut the top of it lengthwise with his paddle, and not a drop came on board. The snow all this time continued to fall; I was sitting on the bottom of the canoe, without any power of changing my position, and the flakes gathered round my feet and legs in spite of all my endeavours to free myself from their soft embrace. It was a long time before I felt any alarm; but when the line of foam on the steep rocks showed the impossibility of landing anywhere, and I remembered we were only half-way on our journey, a sort of dread crept over me. Using my hands as a scoop, I shovelled the snow out of the canoe: still, hour after hour passed, and the snow never ceased to fall. I spoke to the Indian in front, but he did not reply, nor make any sign that he heard me speaking. Mile after mile was thus slowly passed, and I recollect fancying that I felt the cold less, and that I should be warmer if the snow quite covered my legs. When, in changing his paddle for another lying in the canoe, George accidentally struck my leg, I remember it seemed odd to me that I should *see* and not *feel* something striking my leg. After that it was all like a dream; I seemed to be resting on a soft couch, in a great hall lighted by numerous lamps shedding a pleasant light, and beautiful people were tending me, and there were strains of music in the air. The fact was the cold was becoming too much for me. Then the scene changed to a rough hut, lighted imperfectly by a huge fire of logs under a large chimney in the middle of the hut, at some distance from which fire I was propped up by two strong woodmen, who were rubbing my legs. The pleasant words, "I guess, Jim, he's thawing," recalled me to earth from the land of dreams, and I began to estimate the whole position exactly, though I could as yet not utter a word, but only laugh in recognition of my attendants' kindness. Having had a warm dry shirt and drawers put on, I tumbled into a bunk, under a heap of blankets, and awoke next morning quite myself again. We were a long way from the settlement; but, fortunately for me, several of the men engaged in rafting timber happened to have occupied an old hut for the night; and the Indians, seeing the light and becoming aware of my condition, had steered for the place, and had succeeded in landing safely, though with damage to their canoe. I had no very kindly feelings towards the boatswain who was the cause of this mischance.

CHAPTER VIII.

DOMESTIC MANNERS.

Winter the time for Feasts—Domestic Manners; Fondness for Jokes and Gossip—Rarity of Serious Quarrels; Ignorance of Fisticuffs—Unwillingness to labour—Appetite, Meals, Food and Drinks, Cooking; Gathering Gammass Roots; Cutting down Crab-apple Trees in Despair—Hospitality to Friendly Unexpected Visitors—Observance of Formalities in Social Intercourse.

Come; our stomachs
Will make what 's homely, savoury; weariness
Can snore upon the flint.—Shakspeare.

In fine seasons, the Ahts, following the salmon up the inlets and streams, have been known not to return to their winter quarters till the end of November. A month sooner, however, is about the usual time. Mirth then prevails, as the whole tribe is gathered like a family round a fireside. There is a general holiday and time of feasting, called Klooh-quahn-nah, which ends about the middle of January, soon after which time the natives begin to look for fish that approach the inlets on the coast in the spring. The winter season is the time when, if one knew the Aht language thoroughly, and had the stomach and nose to live actually amongst them, their ways could be best learnt. The natives delight in gossip and scandal, and the strangest rumours circulate freely through every camp.

What talks there will be in the smoky houses about the past fishing season, the conduct of other tribes, the doings of the white men! These natives are not at all times so grave as out of doors they appear to us. When relieved from the presence of strangers, they have much easy and social conversation among themselves. Round their own fires they sing and chat, and the older men, lying and bragging after the manner of story-tellers, recount their feats in war or the chase to a listening group. Jokes pass freely, and the laugh is long, if not loud. According to our notions, the conversation is frequently coarse and indecent. A common fireside amusement is to tease the women till they become angry, which always produces great merriment. The men rarely quarrel except with their tongues, and a blow is seldom given. If struck in anger it must be paid for next day with a present, unless the striker chooses to leave the dispute between himself and his opponent open. The respect entertained for the head of the family is, however, generally speaking, sufficient to preserve order within the family circle. Quarrelling is also rare among the children. The use of the doubled fist as a means of offence is quite unknown among these people, and seemed at first very much to surprise them. I have never witnessed a fight between two sober natives; when drunk, they seek close quarters and pull each other's hair. When there is no dancing, their evenings are passed round the fire, and, as the stories slacken, they retire one by one to their couches. They sleep in the same blankets which they use during the day. To judge by their snoring, the natives seem to sleep rather heavily than otherwise. They rise from their beds at an early hour in the morning. The women go to bed first, and are up first in the morning to prepare breakfast. In their own work, among themselves, I should not call these Ahts a very lazy people, though they have no regular occupation, and though, from the toiling Englishman's point of view, they are the reverse of industrious.* They have a good deal to do in making house utensils, nets, canoes, paddles, weapons, and implements. The high chiefs, of course, are mere gentlemen at large. I have seen Indians hard at work on canoes in the woods at five o'clock on an autumn morning, a long way from their houses (*see* canoe-making, page 85). Their appetite is capricious and not easily appeased; but when necessary, they have great power of abstaining from food. When at work, only two small meals are taken—in the morning and evening; but, when not at work, cooking continues all day, and as many as six or eight meals are

* When I first employed Indians at Alberni, the price of their labour was two blankets and rations of biscuits and molasses for a month's work for each man, if he worked the whole time. The Indians became very tired after labouring for ten days or a fortnight, and many forfeited the wages already earned, rather than endure longer the misery of regular labour. It was instructive, yet almost painful to witness the struggle between the strong acquisitive instincts of the savage, and the real mental and physical difficulty and pain caused by the stated regularity of the hours for work and for meals. Some of the Indians became fair workmen, and their labour was worth half-a-dollar a day and rations, or about one-third the value of an ordinary white labourer's work; but, on the whole, I found that the Indians were unprofitable workmen. They make better sailors than labourers; a Tsclahllam slave from the opposite side of the straits of Fuca, whom we named Quartermaster Jack, often took the wheel of the screw-steamer *Thames* in inland waters, on the way to Alberni. He could see in the dark like a racoon.

eaten. The principal food of the natives, as before alluded to, is fish—salmon, whale, halibut, seal, herring, anchovy, and shell-fish of various kinds. Their commonest article of food at all times is dried salmon; whale-blubber, preparations of salmon roe, and the heads of smaller fish are esteemed delicacies. They are particularly fond of picking bones. Twenty years ago, when few trading vessels visited the coast, the Ahts probably were restricted to a diet of fish, wild berries, and roots; but they now use also for food, flour, potatoes, rice, and molasses. This change of food, from what I saw of its effect on two tribes with whom I lived, has proved to be very injurious to their health.

The dogfish is occasionally eaten, but is generally caught for the sake of its oil, to barter with the whites. Fur-seals and sea-otters are diligently pursued for their furs, but few good furs are got without going much farther north than any part of Vancouver Island. Only a few individuals in any tribe follow the chase; but there are always some hunters who pursue the bear, beaver, mink, marten and racoon for their skins. Geese, ducks, and deer are also used as food, but are not so well liked as fish, and are seldom kept in stock. The marrow of animals is esteemed a great delicacy by all the natives. They seem to be very improvident, or rather, perhaps, are unable to calculate their probable wants; and it happens sometimes that they are in straits for want of food, when the fish do not appear until late in the spring. Becoming weak and thin, they blacken their faces to hide their altered looks. What we call the refuse of birds and fish, particularly the head, is esteemed by the natives. When the canoes return to shore from fishing, the men fill the baskets with the fish, and place them on the women's shoulders. The latter, assisted by the slaves, immediately cut off the heads, open, and wash the fish, press out the water, and afterwards hang them up to dry in the smoke without salt. The roe is made into cakes or rolls, which are hung up and smoked. The commonest way of cooking fish or flesh is by spitting it on cedar sticks placed near the fire. Whale-blubber and pieces of seal are prepared for food by being boiled in a wooden dish, into which hot stones are thrown to heat the water. A kind of gravy soup is also made from pieces of fish. Another mode of cooking is to cover the fire with stones, on which water is sprinkled and the fish placed, mats saturated with fresh water being thrown over all. In this way as many as fifty salmon are cooked at once, and no better mode could be desired. When used immediately as food, the head, backbone, ribs, and tail are separated from the rest of the body, the heads and tails are strung together and dried, and the backbone, which has a large portion of the fish adhering to it, is generally eaten first.

As a corrective of the injurious effects of a continued fish and animal diet, various plants are used by the natives as food. The kammass,—a species of lily common in the north and north-west of America, so called originally, it is supposed, by the early French fur-trading voyageurs, but known to the Ahts as gammass,—comes into flower about the middle or end of April, and remains in flower till June, when it is in a condition to be gathered. Before that time its root is watery and unpalatable. The gathering of the gammass is the most picturesque of all Indian employments. One could hardly wish in his honeymoon, or in any like happy time, for a pleasanter dwelling than the little bush camps which the natives form in the gammass districts. It is pleasant to lie on the fern in these cosy abodes, and smoke, and read one of those old books of travel too wonderful by half to be produced in these days. This useful plant is found also in Oregon, and the root is there roasted until black, and is preserved in cakes. In Vancouver Island it is roasted and preserved whole in bags for winter use. The gammass has an agreeable sweetish taste, and, from the great quantity of starchy matter which it contains, is justly esteemed one of the most wholesome of the Indian edibles. It grows only in small quantities on the west coast, and is taken thither as an article of traffic from the south of the island, particularly from the neighbourhood of Victoria, where there are excellent gammass districts. One of the bitterest regrets of the natives is that the encroachment of the whites is rapidly depriving them of their crops of this useful and almost necessary plant. They have never attempted to increase the production of gammass by any kind of cultivation.

The roots of the common fern or bracken are much used as a regular meal. They are simply washed and boiled, or beaten with a stone, till they become soft, and are then roasted. All the different kinds of berries are a favourite food, either fresh plucked from the bush, or when pressed into cakes for use in winter. The gathering of berries in the woods by parties of natives, during the lovely summer and autumn days, is a pleasant and favourite occupation of the women and children. The tender shoots of several species of rubus are eaten as a delicacy or relish during the summer, as the shoots of the sweet-briar are eaten in Scotland. Canoes may be seen quite laden with these shoots. Hazel-nuts and sal-al berries are used in autumn. Many species of seaweed are collected for food, and one species is pressed into cakes for winter use. The dog-tooth violet, wild onions, and the roots or young shoots of several other plants that grow on the coast, form the food of the Indians at different times of the year. Crab-apples are wrapped in leaves and preserved in bags for the winter. The method of cooking them, when fresh plucked, is by simply boiling the apples; but, when they have lost their acidity, they are cooked by being placed in a hole dug in the ground, over which green leaves are placed, and a fire kindled above all. The natives are as careful of their crab-apples as we are of our orchards; and it is a sure sign of their losing heart before intruding whites when, in the neighbourhood of settlements, they sullenly cut down their crab-apple trees, in order to gather the fruit for the last time without trouble, as the tree lies upon the ground. The Indian,

> As fades his swarthy race, with anguish sees
> The white man's cottage rise beneath the trees.—LEYDEN.

Water is the only drink of the natives. They dislike salt; at least I have observed they will not boil potatoes in salt-water, even under the pressure of hunger. At meals a circle is formed; the natives sit like Turks, and eat slowly and without much conversation, until the pipe has been passed round, after which they begin to talk. Travellers are generally well received, but members of another tribe are not expected to take their guns or pikes inside the house with them—an act which, according to M. Huc, is contrary also to Tartar etiquette. A stranger, on entering a house, seats himself, and no word is spoken for several minutes. Food is then placed before him without his having to ask for it, and the host is displeased if the stranger does not partake of it. He also feels hurt if by any omission, the guest has to ask for refreshment. A small mat, specially kept for strangers, is spread as a seat, and at the end of the meal, a wooden box of water and some soft bark strips are offered for washing the mouth and hands. Next follows a pipe, if tobacco is plentiful, and then the host asks a string of questions at once: where the guest is from? where going to? on what business? and the news from his tribe? In reply to which, the guest makes a sort of speech, answering all the questions. Another family now expresses a wish to entertain him, and, though occasionally a traveller has to eat six or eight times in a night, such invitations cannot be declined without offence. In the morning, the guest receives another meal, and departs without any charge being made for his entertainment. On the arrival of a number of strange canoes on a friendly but unexpected visit, they are brought stern foremost to the shore, and the natives cease paddling and wait without speaking. Had they been expected, the canoes would have approached bow foremost, and the people on shore would have run down and helped to pull their bows on to the beach; but in the case of unexpected visitors, the inmates of the village simply come out of their houses and squat down, looking at the visitors. By-and-by, one, and then another, is asked to go up to the houses; but no person goes without a special invitation, and sometimes it is an hour or more before all the visitors find accommodation.

The Aht Indians have an etiquette by which the manner of receiving guests and visitors is laid down, and all their ceremonies on public occasions are regulated. Extreme formality prevails, and any failure in good manners is noticed. The natives of rank rival one another in politeness. Compared with the manners of English rustics or mechanics, their manners are simple and rather dignified. Since the whites went amongst them, it is amusing to observe the attempts that are made to imitate some of the forms of civilized intercourse. In meeting out of doors, they have no gesture of salutation; in their houses it consists of a polite motioning towards a couch.

CHAPTER IX.

FEASTS.

Feasts and Feasting—Description of a great Whale Feast—After-dinner Oratory: Skill in Public Speaking—Seta-Kanim "on his Legs"—Vocal Peculiarities—Indian's reply to Governor Kennedy—Singing: Blind Minstrel from Klah-oh-quaht; translation of one of his Songs—Amusements of Adults and Children—Dances and Plays; Description of five different Dances.

I could be pleased with any one
Who entertained my sight with such gay shows.—Dryden.

The great feasts, as before named, take place in winter, but feasting goes on at all times. There are always feasts and distributions when a new house is built. An Indian who thinks anything of himself, never gets a deer or a seal, or even a quantity of flour, without inviting his friends to a feast. The guests go early, and sit chatting while the food is being cooked. They eat in silence, and go away afterwards one by one, each taking the uneaten portion of his allowance with him in a corner of his blanket. After a whale is brought on shore, about a hundredweight of the best part is cut off and presented to the chief. The harpooner who first struck the whale, and the fish-priest—a sorcerer who prophesies as to the success of the fish seasons—next receive their shares; then the minor chiefs, in portions according to their rank; and, finally, the common people, until the whole fish is divided. A round of feasts is now expected from those who have received large portions. Messengers, with red and blue blankets tastefully put on, go to each house, and in a loud voice invite all the men of the tribe to attend a feast at a particular house. The women are not invited to a feast of this kind, and are seldom seen at any large entertainment, except at that called *Wawkoahs*, which is given by one tribe to another with which they are on very friendly terms. The common people—how odd to talk of common people where all seem so common—go early, and take their seats near the door by which they enter. It is the habit of men of rank to be late in going to a feast, and to have several messages sent to them to request their presence. Each person's place is duly reserved for him. For a feast of this kind, a large part of the whole building is cleared; all the dividing planks that separate the families are removed, and a clear space left, sometimes fifty feet wide by two hundred in length. Clean mats, or long twists of cedar fibre are laid round the inside of the lodge. On the entrance of a guest, he is announced by name and placed in his proper seat, where he finds a bunch of bark strips for wiping his feet. When a popular chief enters, he is loudly cheered after the Aht fashion, that is, by striking the walls with the back of the hand or with a piece of stick, in which way the natives also accompany their monotonous songs. The meal is never served till all the invited guests have arrived. Meanwhile the cooking goes on in a corner of the house in a manner new to Soyer. Hot stones are put, by means of wooden tongs, into large wooden boxes, containing a small quantity of water. When the water boils, the blubber of the whale, cut into pieces about an inch thick, is thrown into these boxes, and hot stones are added till the food is cooked. This imperfect boiling does not extract half the oil from the blubber, but whatever appears is skimmed off, and preserved in bladders as a delicacy to be eaten with dried salmon and with potatoes or other roots. Whale-oil is so much liked by the natives that they rarely sell it. The chief's wives at such an entertainment prepare the food, and afterwards wait upon the guests. On everything being ready, the host directs the feast to be served. Silence while eating is considered a mark of politeness. No knives are used; the blubber, which in tenacity resembles gutta-percha, is held in the hands while being eaten. Each guest receives a larger or a smaller piece according to his rank. During dinner, the host and one of his servants, who may be called a sort of master of the feast, walk round to see that all the visitors have been served with due attention. On finishing his meal, each person receives some soft cedar bark, that he may wipe his mouth and hands. The remains of each person's meal are carefully gathered by the servants of the host, and carried to the guest's dwelling. By-and-by, conversation begins; a few compliments are paid to the chief for his good cheer, and then, perhaps, some tribal topics are introduced, and animated speeches are delivered by various orators. Praises of their own and their forefathers' achievements in war, or skill in hunting and fishing, and boasts of the number of their powerful friends and the admirable qualities of each, form the burden of these after-dinner speeches. The principal chief always gives the signal to break up the party, and he leaves first. When the guests retire, it is usual, in fine weather, for small groups to meet and discuss the whole proceedings and criticize the speeches. I had no expectation of finding that oratory —the queen of human gifts—was so much prized among this rude people. It is almost the readiest means of gaining power and station. The Klah-oh-quahts excel in public speaking. Individuals sometimes speak at festive or political meetings for more than an hour, with great effect upon the hearers. My not being able always to follow the words enabled me perhaps more to notice the graces of action which the speakers exhibited. The blanket is a more becoming garment to an orator than a frock coat. The voices of one or two noted chiefs are very powerful, yet clear and musical, the lower tones remarkably so; their articulation is distinct, and their gestures and attitudes are singularly expressive. I have been tempted sometimes to cheer them.

There is a noticeable difference, I may mention, between the voices of the Ahts and those of Englishmen. I never more distinctly observed this than when a savage replied to Governor Sir Arthur Kennedy on his addressing an assembly of natives in front of the Government House at Victoria, soon after his arrival in the colony. The Governor is a soldier-like man, with a resolute, handsome face, and firm voice; but the contrast was striking between his measured voice and talk, and the deep, careless tones of the savage, as his utterance in reply burst on the relieved ears of the audience. There is a pith in an Indian's speech altogether, in voice, manner, and meaning, that startles one accustomed to the artificial declamation of English public meetings. It has occurred to me, while hearing savage oratory among the Ahts, that an actor or artist who wished to know what natural earnest manner in public speaking really is, should visit Klah-oh-qu, and hear Seta-Kanim on his legs. Viewing the matter artistically, it is quite a treat; but, from another point of view, the picture is saddening, even to one ignorant of the language, to see a savage in the open air, pleading, under a sense of injustice, for some object he has much at heart —perhaps his native land. There is nothing to be seen in England like it. We Englishmen converse well in-doors across green tables, but out of doors the savage beats us in public speaking beyond compare. In all the externals of oratory, the Bishop of Oxford at Bradford, or Lamartine at the Hôtel de Ville, would be tame, placed beside Seta-Kanim speaking for war.

Boys practise the recital of portions of celebrated speeches which they retain in memory; and occasionally, as the old men sit on the beach, watching the sunset on a summer evening, they point out future orators and envoys among the youngsters who play before them. Such winter feasts as I have described are often followed by singing and dancing. Singing is very common, but their musical attainments are not great.

They have, however, different airs or chants for times of grief or joy, for careless moments, and for the hour of triumph, all of which, rude and informal as they may be, have a distinct character about them. The most unmusical ear, of course, distinguishes at once the song of the mother fondling her child from the wail of the parent lamenting for her offspring; and not less marked is the difference between the terrible death chant and the song of mirth at a feast. And, I daresay, one might perceive, on comparison, a certain beauty of natural expression in many of the native strains, if it were possible to relieve them from the monotony which is their fault. The required expression is usually given by uttering the sounds in quick or slow time, more than by any attempt at musical cadence. It is remarkable how aptly the natives catch and imitate songs heard from settlers or travellers. They soon learn to sing the "Old Hundredth" as well as many a Scottish congregation; "Bobbing Around," and "Dixie's Land," were lately familiar tunes; and I have heard several natives join in "God Save the Queen," and sing it fairly well too, without the variations which destroy that grave, simple song. The musical faculty must be far from unimportant that enables the natives thus accurately to catch, after a few hearings, the right expression of songs, the meaning and tendency of which are quite unknown to them. The singer often acts while he sings, representing, for instance, the spearing of fish or the paddling of a canoe. In almost every tribe there is an old man who sings war-chants, and songs of praise at public feasts. One old man from Klah-oh-quaht Sound, blind from age, accompanied by his two sons who lead him about, visits the different tribes of his own—the Aht—nation every summer. He is one of the richest men in his tribe. On landing at a camp, this white-haired minstrel praises the tribe and the chief, and makes a song, to which they listen quite pleased, and some one, whose benevolence or vanity has been touched, gives him a present. The following is a free translation of one of his improvisations :—"The Ohyahts are a great people "with strong hearts, and all the tribes fear them; they "make good canoes and kill whales. I am an old man "who has seen many snows, but every snow I hear more "about the Ohyahts; they have a great chief who has "taken many heads, and has many slaves; his grand-"father was strong and took many heads. The Ohyahts "are lucky and will catch plenty of salmon; I have come "far and am old, and will need blankets in winter." The venerable beggar will sing thus for an hour, praising different people and their forefathers, if at every stoppage he receives a present; and should there be any backwardness in giving on the part of the audience, he will ask for a gift in a most unbard-like manner.

The men have few out-door amusements except swimming, or trying strength by hooking little fingers, which is always conducted with good humour.* Hunting and fishing may be called more occupations than amusements. The war-dance is now and then practised out of doors, but is little like the dance one's imagination would picture, consisting merely of a number of men with blackened faces running to and fro, now and then jumping on one leg, yelling and firing their guns. The native children are sprightly enough and amuse themselves in various ways; climbing poles, shooting with bows and arrows, and darting miniature spears at shapes of birds and fish made of grass;

* From some cause, perhaps the constant use of the paddle, their fingers are very strong; as already stated, I have seen middle-sized natives carry heavy weights with their fingers which stalwart woodmen could scarcely lift. For this reason an angry Indian should not be allowed to catch the clothes of an opponent; he should be knocked down.

or alone in a small canoe, upsetting by a quick movement the tiny vessel, soon to right it, and empty the canoe of water before the bold swimmer again gets in to paddle off and repeat the trick. Another boy's pastime, which their elders instruct them in, is cutting off with a knife the heads of clay models made to represent enemies.

After a great feast, as a signal for dancing to commence, the host claps his hands, and, in a loud tone, sings a few words of some well-known song. As a rule, the men and women do not dance together; when the men are dancing the women sing and beat time. Hardly an evening passes in winter without a dance in some part of the encampment, and if no one has a party, the chief invites some of the young men to dance at his own house. The seal-dance is a common one. The men strip naked, though it may be a cold frosty night, and go into the water, from which they soon appear, dragging their bodies along the sand like seals. They enter the houses, and crawl about round the fires, of which there may be fifteen or twenty kept bright with oil. After a time the dancers jump up, and dance about the house. In another dance, in which all the performers are naked, a man appears with his arms tied behind his back with long cords, the ends of which, like reins, are held by other natives who drive him about. The spectators sing and beat time on their wooden dishes and bearskin drums. Suddenly the chief appears, armed with a knife, which he plunges into the runner's back, who springs forward, moving wildly as if in search of shelter. Another blow is given; blood flows down his back, and great excitement prevails, amidst which, the civilized spectator shudders and remonstrates. The stroke is repeated and the victim staggers weakly, and falls prostrate and lifeless. Friends gather round, and remove the body, which, outside the house, washes itself and puts on its blanket.

I never saw acting more to the life; the performers would be the making of a minor theatre in London. Here, in fact, is theatrical performance in its earliest stage. The blood, which by some contrivance flows down the back at the moment the stroke is given, is a mixture of a red gum, resin, oil and water—the same that is used in colouring the inside of canoes. In these dances men only share, but there is a dance in which men and women join, and which they keep up for a long time. Both sexes are naked to the waist, and the best blanket is worn as a kilt. Such a scene brings Alloway Kirk to mind, and one peers through the smoky, dim-lighted Indian house for a vision of the shaggy fiddler in the corner. The hair is allowed to hang loose, and the women are ornamented with anklets and bracelets. The dancers sing, and the boys standing round keep time with sticks on bearskin drums. No notice is taken of the women except, occasionally, when a gallant youth throws a string of beads round an active maiden's neck. The dancing is not with partners, and each seems to quit the dance alone, and without ceremony. The dancers move slowly through a kind of figure—the nature of which I could not understand — and pass strips of blanket under the arm so quickly to one another, that one cannot see them till some performer, tired out, stops and walks away with a strip in his hand.

I may mention here a few more of the Aht dances, which, accompanied with singing, are called by the natives "Nook," as I witnessed them at Alberni, during a large intertribal feast.

Nook 1.—The great aim in this dance was, that it was to be carried on with energy and without cessation ; when some one was tired out others joined in ; and those who had stopped returned to it again, when they had recovered their strength. The words of the song were equivalent to "keep it up." Many of the dancers kept it up till the perspiration appeared freely on their half-naked bodies : some went out and plunged into the river, and returned to renew their exertions.

Nook 2.—There was a peculiar song here, as in all the other dances ; but I do not know the words. Probably in this, as certainly in some other instances, there were no words, and tradition had only retained the notes of the tune, and the peculiar feature of the dance. The aim of the performers was to bend the knee excessively, while at the same time they kept time with the quick drum-beating and singing to which they danced. Only a few of the Indians excel in this dance.

Nook 3.—This might be called the doctor's (Ooshtukyu) nook. During the song and dance, which at first seemed to present nothing peculiar, a well-known slave (one, however, who was in a comparatively independent position, being employed as a sailor on board the steamer *Thames*,) suddenly ceased dancing, and fell down on the ground apparently in a dying state, and having his face covered with blood. He did not move or speak, his head fell on one side, his limbs were drawn up, and he certainly presented a ghastly spectacle. While the dance raged furiously around the fallen man, the doctor, with some others, seized and dragged him to the other side of the fire round which they were dancing, placing his naked feet very near the flames.

After this, a pail of water was brought in, and the doctor, who supported the dying man on his arm, washed the blood from his face; the people beat drums, danced, and sang, and suddenly the patient sprang to his feet and joined in the dance, none the worse for the apparently hopeless condition of the moment before. While all this was going on, I asked the giver of the feast whether it was real blood upon the man's face, and if he were really wounded. He told me so seriously that it was, that I was at first inclined to believe him, until he began to explain that the blood which came from the nose and mouth was owing to the incantations of the medicine-man, and that all the people would be very angry if he did not afterwards restore him. I then recalled to mind that in the early part of the day, before the feast, I had seen the doctor and the slave holding very friendly conferences; and the former had used his influence to get a pass for the latter to be present at the entertainment, to which, probably, he had no right to come. I feel sure that many of the Indians really believed in this exhibition of the doctor's power. When the affair was over, many of the natives asked me what I thought of it, and referred to it as if it must set at rest for ever any possible doubts with regard to the abilities of their native doctors. The Indian, who explained this and other performances to me, said, that the cure was not entirely owing to the doctor, but to the large body of dancers and singers who all "exerted their hearts" to desire the recovery of the sick man, and so procured the desired effect.

Nook 4.—This is the roof dance, a performance peculiar to the Seshaht people. Suddenly, during an apparently ordinary course of singing and dancing, the majority of those engaged climb up the posts of the house, thrust the boards aside, and the next moment are heard leaping on the roof and making a noise like thunder. This goes on for a time, some descending from above and joining those below, and others climbing up to take their places on the roof. It may be mentioned, in connection with this roof-dance, that after all the dances were over, on the occasion I speak of, an old man came forward and made, apparently, a very eloquent speech. He said that the roof-dance was one belonging to the Seshahts, and could not be omitted; but, at the same time, noticed that it was an injurious thing for the roof, as it was apt to split the boards and let in the rain. This was intended as an apology to the owner of the house. Afterwards, several Indians came forward, and each gave a small stick, which was received as a present by the owner of the house. These sticks intimated a gift of roof-boards, and the person presenting one of them undertook, at some future time, to redeem it with a roof-board.

Nook 5.—This dance was characterized by having a greater number of dancers, and a movement and song which, though cheerful, was not so quick nor loud as those which had preceded it. It seemed to be intended to have a sort of confidential and conversational tone. The dancers moved softly but actively about, and seemed to address each other in praises of the building; they looked cheerful, and turned the head quickly, as if speaking first to one and then to another, and sang, "It is a very great house; a very great house; a very great house." Upon a movement of the leader, who with voice and arm never failed to direct all the performances of the company, they changed their words (while they kept the same tune, certainly the most pleasant one of the entertainment,) to "It is a very warm fire; a very warm fire; a very warm fire;" and finally ended by praising the household furniture: "These are very nice things; very nice things; very nice things." On the whole, this dance-song was much the most pleasing of those which we witnessed. There was something dramatic in the way in which these rudely-painted and half-naked creatures attempted to represent, in dance and song, the idea of an animated conversation.

CHAPTER XI.

AN ATTEMPT AT AN INQUEST.

Depredations of the Indians—An Indian shot with Peas—English Staff Surgeon—Soft-hearted Yorkshireman—Absurd Verdicts of the Jury.

(After they'd almost por'd out their eyes)
Did very learnedly decide
The bus'ness on the horse's side.—HUDIBRAS.

I WAS roused from my bed one dark rainy night at Alberni, by a messenger from our farm up the Klistachnit River, bringing word that the man in charge of the farm had shot an Indian. The farm was about two miles distant, and being on the opposite side of the river, could only be reached by water. Not knowing very well what it might be necessary to do, I asked Mr. Johnston, a gentleman in our service, to take a few men and go to the farm and see what had happened. This party had some difficulty, owing to the darkness, in getting their boat past the drift-trees at the entrance of the rapid stream, but in an hour or two they reached the farm. Two men were employed there—an American and a Yorkshireman—who both were sitting in the kitchen, looking at the fire, when

Mr. Johnston entered the house. It appeared that the foreman, the American, had for several nights past been watching a field of potatoes which the Indians were plundering. They came in numbers up a long creek, and half filled their canoes in a few hours, and before morning were many miles distant. The foreman, two nights previously, had caught one of these Indians, a fellow who seemed a ringleader, but he had escaped by slipping off his blanket and running naked into the forest. The same Indian had again returned with his plundering gang. On the evening in question the foreman went out to watch the field, and took with him his gun, loaded with five hard peas, thinking that, if he could not catch an Indian, he would frighten them by shooting the peas amongst them. As usual, the depredators were in the field filling their bags, and as soon as they became aware of the foreman's presence, they ran with them to their canoes. He could not overtake them, but having fired his gun with as good an aim as he could take in the dark at the supposed ringleader, he was horror-struck to see the Indian fall flat upon the ground. Rushing back to the house with his discharged gun, the foreman cried to his companion, the Yorkshireman, on entering, "Jack, I've shot an Indian." These particulars being learnt, Mr. Johnston and two others took a lantern and visited the field, where, after looking about for some time, they found the Indian lying dead. He had fallen over his potato-bag, and his hands were clutching the soil. The body was dragged to the river; but the men forming Mr. Johnston's party objected to take it on board the boat, and proposed tying a string round the ankle, and towing the body astern. Finally, however, a small abandoned canoe was found, and the body was placed in this and towed behind the boat to the settlement, where it was put into a room full of old casks until the morning.

After breakfast next day I proceeded to examine into this affair. The peculiarity of the case was that everybody in the district was in my own employment. I took the word of the American that he would appear when wanted, knowing this to be a better security for his appearance, than locking him up in a room from which he might have escaped. The feeling among the settlers as to the death of this Indian was that nothing was required to be done. Several men came to me and said, "You are not going to trouble Henry about this—are you, sir?" I could only answer that we must do what the law required us to do. It was easy to summon a jury, but where could we get a doctor to make a post-mortem examination of the Indian's body? The difficulty was solved by a workman advancing from a gang employed in carrying wood, and asking to speak with me. He was a careworn, middle-aged man, dressed in common clothes. We went into the room that served as an office or court-room, and on entering into conversation, this man told me that he had been a staff surgeon in the British army, and that he had his diploma and certificates of service in his chest. He brought me these, and they proved the truth of his statement—so, of course, I gladly accepted his services. The next step was to get a jury. I selected twelve of the most respectable and intelligent workmen, and opened the court: this jury consisted of Canadians, Americans, and Englishmen. We inspected the body, and did everything in proper form. The doctor proved that death was caused by wounds in the chest, and he produced a pea, which he had found in the left lung. The Yorkshireman, who lived in the farm-house with the American, a fine young fellow above six feet in height, was next examined. He stood in the middle of the room with his cap in his hand; the jurymen standing half-a-dozen on each side of the room. I asked the Yorkshireman to tell the jury what happened that night. He said his "chum" had gone out of the farm-house, and had come back in about an hour. He took his gun out, and had brought it back. The witness had heard a gun-shot. He knew no more. I asked this witness what his companion said when he returned to the house? At this question he blushed, and then grew pale, and twirled his cap round, and said nothing. I repeated the question, and told the Yorkshireman to take time, and not to shrink from telling the truth. He seemed embarrassed, and did not reply. Noticing he was ill at ease, I left him alone for a little, and then again asked him the question in a mild tone. His agitation increased, the cap fell from his hands, he staggered, and finally fainted where he stood. Some of the jurymen caught him in their arms, and carried him outside. I have never seen a strong man faint from mental agitation before or since this occasion; it is probably a very unusual occurrence. The witness must have had a large heart, and he believed that his evidence as to the words of his companion, "Jack, I've shot an Indian," might be fatal words. The examination continued, and, after several other witnesses had given testimony, I stated the case to the jury, and sent them into another room for their finding. There was, it appeared, a long debate: for nearly half an hour passed before they returned to my room. One after another entered, and when they had ranged themselves again on the side of the room, I inquired what their finding was. The answer was, "We find the Siwash was worried by a dog." "A what?" I exclaimed. "Worried by a dog, sir," said another jury-man, fearing that the foreman had not spoken clearly.

Assuming, with great difficulty, an expression of proper magisterial gravity, I pointed out to the jury the incompatibility of this finding with the evidence, and went again over the points of the case, calling particular attention to the medical testimony, and the production by the doctor of the pea found in the body of the Indian; after which I, a second time, dismissed the jury to their room, and begged them to come back with something, at all events, reasonably connected with the facts of the case. A longer time than before elapsed. The jury, on this occasion, left their room, and walked about the settlement, and I saw knots of men conversing eagerly. There was some hope now, I thought, of a creditable verdict. When the jurymen at length sidled into my room for the second time, I drew a paper towards me to record a finding which I expected would suitably end this unpleasant inquest. "Now, men, what do you say?" Their decisive answer was, "We say he was killed by falling over a cliff." I shuffled my papers together, and told them they might go to their work; I would return a verdict for the jury myself. The farm, I may mention, for a mile every way from where the dead body was found, was as level as a table. I could not but think it strange the jury did not decide upon an open or evasive finding, instead of those extraordinarily absurd ones. The fact was the men were determined to shut their eyes, and they shut them so close that they became quite blind. Not a bit of a joke was in their minds; they acted with perfect seriousness throughout, and this made the comic parts of this tragi-comedy still more ludicrous.

I arrested the American, and sent him in our own steamboat to Victoria in charge of a constable, but he escaped from custody. He was an excellent fellow, and I am sure had no intention of killing the Indian. The victim belonged to a distant tribe, but they were too much ashamed of the circumstances of his death to send for the body. We accordingly buried it in the forest. The Indians who lived beside the settlement were rather pleased than otherwise with the death of this Indian, and many of them pointed to the body and said, "Now you see who steals your potatoes; our tribe does not."

I beg the reader to observe that the foregoing statement is not in the slightest degree exaggerated or distorted; it is a mere simple statement of the facts of the case as they actually occurred.

CHAPTER XI.

ACQUISITION AND USE OF PROPERTY.

Acquisition of Property—Sharpness in Bargaining—Restrictions upon Trade—Land considered as Tribal Property—Description of various kinds of Personal Property; Muskets, Bows and Arrows, Canoes, Hand-adze, Bone Gimlet, Elkhorn Chisel, Stone Hammer, Household Utensils, Mats, Clothing—Method of Making and Managing Canoes—Prevalence of Slavery and Slave-Dealing—Condition and Treatment of Slaves.

Takes what she liberal gives, nor thinks of more.—THOMSON.

COMMODITIES are obtained among the Ahts from one another by bartering slaves, canoes, and articles of food, clothing, or ornament; and from the colonists by exchanging oil, fish, skins, and furs. All the natives are acute, and rather too sharp at bargaining. The Ahts are fond of a long conversation in selling, but seldom reduce their price; living at no expense, they can afford to keep their stock of goods a long time on hand. I have known an Indian keep a sea-otter's skin more than three years, though offered repeatedly a fair price for it. News about prices, and indeed about anything in which the natives take an interest, travels quickly to distant places from one tribe to another. If a trading schooner appeared at one point on the shore, and offered higher prices than are usually given, the Indians would know the fact immediately along the whole coast. An active trade existed formerly among the tribes of this nation, as also between them and the tribes at the south of the island and on the American shore. The root called gammass, for instance, and swamp rushes for making mats, neither of which could be plentifully produced on the west coast, were sent from the south of the island in exchange for cedar-bark baskets, dried halibut, and herrings. The coasting intertribal trade is not free, but is arbitrarily controlled by the stronger tribes, who will not allow weaker tribes to go past them in search of customers; just as if the people of Hull should intercept all the vessels laden with cargo from the north of England for London, and make the people of London pay for them an increased price, fixed by the interceptors.

There is no very strict notion of individual property in land among the Ahts. The land belongs to the whole tribe. In dealing with other tribes the hereditary chief represents the proprietory body. I have, however, known several instances in which claims to portions of land were put forward by individuals. On one occasion a minor chief, who with his family and friends had for some years occupied a small island near the main encampment of the tribe, claimed to be regarded individually as the possessor of the island. I knew, also, an instance of a man of rank in one tribe who controlled ingress to a lake, and would allow no one to pass without his permission; but this may not have been so much for his own benefit as that someone should have authority, in the interest of the whole tribe, to prevent the salmon from being disturbed in their ascent up the river. The occupier of a detached house

—of which there are very few—built by his family on the same spot for several generations, will probably be found to have so far an idea of his right to the land, that he will prevent other persons from cutting down any valuable tree near his dwelling, or from occupying ground immediately adjoining. Trees, when they are cut down, belong to the feller. A noted hunter, in a small tribe where there are few to question his right, will sometimes regard the country along one side of a stream as his own hunting-ground; or the land will be claimed by the head of a powerful family who will allow none but his own friends to hunt over it. But these are exceptions to the general rule, among all the Aht tribes, that the whole extent of the tribal land is the common property of all the free men in the tribe. This rule is the more easily preserved as the land really is of little use to individuals, except for the berries which the women collect, or unless it is a good hunting-ground for the beaver, mink, marten, or deer. Agriculture is not here practised, and probably separate ownership of the soil nowhere exists generally until cultivation begins. While, however, private property in land is not fully recognized among these people, each tribe maintains the exclusive right of its members to the tribal territory—including all lands periodically or occasionally occupied or used, sites for summer and winter encampments, fishing and hunting grounds and spots for burial—and would strongly resist encroachment upon these places. They believe (see chapter on religion) that their villages existed and were occupied by birds and beasts even before the Indians themselves took the human form. What Captain Cook said of this people, that "nowhere in his several voyages did he meet with any uncivilized nation or tribe who had such strict notions of their having a right to the exclusive property of everything that their country produces," is quite true of these tribes, as tribes. In the numerous bays and rivers, the limits of the fishing-grounds, and the ownership of the islands, are strictly defined. But on the sea-shore, at any distance from a village, the exact boundaries of the land owned by the different tribes frequently remain open until settled in the discussions following some dispute about a stranded whale or some other waif. None of the natives have any clear views as to the mode in which the tribes acquired the land which they now claim as their own, beyond the general impression which some of them have, that it was bestowed by Quawteaht. The property owned by individuals consists chiefly of slaves, blankets, canoes, muskets, pikes, lances, tools, mats, wooden dishes, fishing spears and nets, inflated seal-skins, trinkets, skins, oil, and furs. Every free man keeps what his own labour earns; and it was an old custom of the tribes that younger men in a family, until they had wives and children, should give their earnings to the eldest brother. I speak of the customs of the tribes before these were influenced and weakened by closer intercourse with the colonists.

Perhaps about three-fourths of the grown men on this coast possess muskets, common smooth-bore flint-lock weapons, which are sold in Victoria at about forty shillings each. They prefer flintlock guns, being apt to lose or wet percussion-caps, or to run out of the supply. The muskets are kept in flannel cases, and great care is taken of them. The stocks are generally ornamented with brass-headed tacks. Neat powder-horns and seal-skin shot-pouches are made by the young hunters. The natives seldom shoot at game flying or running. As in other parts of the world, the bow was the weapon formerly used before the musket was known, or could be got. The native bow, like the canoe and paddle, is beautifully formed. It is generally made of yew or crab-apple wood, and is three and a half feet long, with about two inches at each end turned sharply backwards from the string. The string is a piece of dried seal-gut, deer-sinew, or twisted bark. The arrows are about thirty inches long, and are made of pine or cedar, tipped with six inches of serrated bone, or with two unbarbed bone or iron prongs. I have never seen an Aht arrow with a barbed head. Two such arrows weigh as much as the bow. The bow is held horizontally, and the string is pulled to the right side. It is said that a good native bowman can kill a small animal at fifty yards, but I have not seen any good archery among these tribes. Since muskets were introduced, the bowmen probably have been out of practice. I can understand that the native bow was formerly a formidable weapon.

Canoes are made on this coast principally of cedar, and are well shaped, and managed with great skill by men, women, and children. They are moved by a single sail or by paddles, or in ascending shallow rapid streams, by long poles. I have seen an Indian boy with a single pole make good way with a small laden canoe against a stream that ran at the rate of six miles an hour. Canoes are of all sizes, but of a uniform general shape, from the war-canoe of forty feet long to the small dug-out in which children of four years old amuse themselves. Outriggers are not used, but the natives sometimes tie bladders or seal-skin buoys to the sides of a canoe to prevent it from upsetting in heavy weather. The sail—of which it is supposed, but rather vaguely, that they got the idea from Meares some eighty years ago—* is a square mat tied at the top to a small stick or yard crossing a mast placed close to the bow. It is only useful in running before the wind in smooth water. The management of a canoe by natives in a heavy sea is dexterous; they seem to accommodate themselves readily to every motion of their conveyance, and if an angry breaker threatens to roll over the canoe, they weaken its effect quickly by a horizontal cut with their paddles through the upper part of the breaker when it is within a foot of the gunwale (*see* page 48). Their mode of landing on a beach through a surf shows skill and coolness. Approaching warily, the steersman of the canoe decides when to dash for the shore; sometimes quickly countermanding the movement, by strenuous exertion the canoe is paddled back. Twenty minutes may thus pass while another chance is awaited. At length the time comes; the men give a strong stroke and rise to their feet as the canoe darts over the first roller; now there is no returning: the second roller is just passed when the bow-paddler leaps out and pulls the canoe through the broken water; but it is a question of moments: yet few accidents happen. The paddles used by the Ahts are from four to five feet long, and are made of crab-apple or yew. Two kinds are used; the blade of one is shaped like a leaf, and the other tapers to a sharp point. The sharp-pointed

* Would it be fanciful to connect their first notion of a canoe sail with their observation of the membranous fan of the pine-seed, which they often see floating through the air, in the forest, after falling from the cones?

paddle is suitable for steering, as it is easily turned under water. It was formerly used as a weapon in canoe-fighting for putting out the eye—a disfigurement which many of the old Aht natives show. In taking a seat in a canoe, the paddler drops on his knees at the bottom, then turns his toes in, and sits down as it were on his heels. The paddle is grasped both in the middle and at the handle. To give a stroke and propel the canoe forward, the hand grasping the middle of the paddle draws the blade of the paddle backwards through the water, and the hand grasping the handle pushes the handle-end forward, and thus aids the other hand in making each stroke of the paddle: a sort of double-action movement. As a relief, the paddler occasionally shifts to the handle the hand grasping the middle of the paddle, and *vice versâ*. Such a position looks awkward, but two natives can easily paddle a middle-sized canoe forty miles on a summer day. The Strait of Juan de Fuca is about fifteen miles wide, and trading canoes often cross during the summer season to the American shore.* The Indians paddle best with a little wind ahead; when it is quite calm, they often stop to talk or look at objects in the water. It is useless to hurry them: they do quite as they please, and will sulk if you are too hard upon them. In a small canoe, when manned by two paddlers,

* I read with surprise the doubtful opinions of ethnological writers as to whether savages could cross in canoes from the Asiatic to the American shore. The Aht natives, and particularly the bolder Northern Indians, could do so in such canoes as they now have without any difficulty. It is not easy to determine what motive could induce savages to undertake such a voyage, or to migrate at all over the sea. The hope of reaching a better country would not be likely to enter the mind of a savage. He would not move unless forced to move. (*See* Paper by G. M. Sproat in the *Transactions of the Ethnological Society*, 1866.)

one sits in the stern and the other in the bow. The middle is the seat of honour for persons of distinction. An Indian sitting in the stern can propel and steer a canoe with a single paddle. In crowded war-canoes the natives sit two abreast. No regular time is kept in the stroke of the paddles unless on grand occasions, when the canoes are formed in order, and all the paddles enter the water at once and are worked with regularity. The most skilful canoe-makers among the tribes are the Nitinahts and the Klah-oh-quahts. They make canoes for sale to other tribes. Many of these canoes are of the most accurate workmanship and perfect design—so much so that I have heard persons fond of such speculations say that the Indians must have acquired the art of making these beautiful vessels in some earlier civilized existence. But it is easy to see now, among the canoes owned by any tribe, nearly all the degrees of progress in skilful workmanship, from the rough tree to the well-formed canoe. Vancouver Island and the immediately opposite coast of the mainland of British Columbia have always supplied the numerous tribes to the northward with canoes. The native artificers in these localities have in the cedar (*Thuja gigantea*) a wood which does not flourish so extensively to the north, and which is very suitable for their purpose, as it is of large growth, durable, and easily worked. Savages progress so slowly in the arts, that the absence of such a wood as cedar, and the necessity of fashioning canoes with imperfect implements from a hard wood like oak, as the ancient people of Scotland did, might make a difference of many centuries in reaching a stated degree of skill in their construction.

The time for making canoes in the rough is during the cold weather in winter, and they are finished when the days lengthen and become warmer. Few natives are without canoes of some sort, which have been made by themselves, or been worked for, or obtained by barter. The condition of the canoe, like an Englishman's equipage, generally shows the circumstances of the possessor. Selecting a good tree not far from the water, the Indian cuts it down laboriously with an axe, makes it of the required length, then splitting the trunk with wedges into two pieces, he chooses the best piece for his intended canoe. If it is winter, the bark is stripped and the block of wood is dragged to the encampment; but in summer it is hollowed out, though not finished, in the forest. English or American tools can now be easily procured by the natives. The axe used formerly in felling the largest tree,—which they did without the use of fire—was made of elkhorn, and was shaped like a chisel. The natives held it as we use a chisel, and struck the handle with a stone, not unlike a dumb-bell, and weighing about two pounds. This chisel-shaped axe, as well as large wooden wedges, was also used in hollowing the canoe. The other instruments used in canoe-making were the gimlet and hand-adze, both of which indeed are still generally used. The hand-adze is a large mussel-shell strapped firmly to a wooden handle. The natural shape of the shell quite fits it for use as a tool. In working with the hand-adze, the back of the workman's hand is turned downward, and the blow struck lightly towards the holder, whose thumb is pressed into a space cut to receive it. The surface of the canoe, marked by the regular chipping of the hand-adze, is prettier than if it were smooth. The gimlet, made of bird's bone, and having a wooden handle, is not used like ours; the shaft is placed between the workman's open hands brought close together, and moved briskly backwards and forwards as on hearing good news; in which manner, by the revolution of the gimlet, a hole is quickly bored. Thus, also, did the natives formerly produce fire, by rubbing two dry cedar sticks in the same way. A few slits, opening on one side, were made in a dry flat stick, and on the end of the rubbing stick being inserted into one of these, and twirled round quickly between the palms, a round hole was made, at the bottom of which ignition took place among the wood dust. When the wood was in bad order for lighting, two or three natives were sometimes employed successively in the work, before fire was obtained. The making of a canoe takes less time than has been supposed. With the assistance of another native in felling and splitting the tree, a good workman can roughly finish a canoe of fifteen or twenty feet long in about three weeks. Fire is not much used here in the hollowing of canoes, but the outside is always scorched to prevent sun-rents and damage from insects. After the sides are of the required thinness, the rough trunk is filled with fresh water, which is heated by hot stones being thrown into it, and the canoe, thus softened by the heat, is, by means of cross-pieces of wood, made into a shape which, on cooling, it retains. The fashioning is done entirely by the eye, and is surprisingly exact. In nine cases out of ten, a line drawn from the middle of the extremities will leave, as nearly as possible, the same width all along on each side of the line. To keep the canoe in shape, light cross-pieces fastened to the inside of the gunwales are placed about four feet apart, and there remain. The gunwale is turned outwards a little to throw off the water. The bow and stern pieces are made separately, and are always of one form, though the body of the canoe varies a little in shape according to the capabilities of the tree and the fancy or skill of the maker. Red is the favourite colour for the inside of a canoe, and is made by a mixture of resin, oil, and urine; the outside is as black as oil and burnt wood will make it; the bow and stern generally bear some device in red. The natural colour of the wood is, however, often allowed to remain. The baling-dish of the canoes is always of one shape—the shape of the gable-roof of a cottage—and is well suited to its purpose.

Of all the household articles, the prettiest is the common basket, which is of different sizes, and is used by the women in carrying salmon or berries—being supported on their backs by a thong passing across their foreheads. The dishes used are wooden, either hollowed from a block, or having the sides fastened together with wooden pegs; cedar and alder are commonly used in making them. Some of these dishes are very neatly formed. Water is brought from the stream in square wooden boxes, by the younger women and children. Similarly shaped are their wooden pots, which, of course, are not placed on the fire; the practice is, to throw hot stones into them till the water boils. For keeping fish-hooks, gun-flints, and other small necessaries, a cedar-bark case is used, which fits into another similar case, like the common cigar-cases sold in England. Three kinds of mats are used, one made of rushes for bedding, one of white-pine bark for bed-clothing and such purposes, and one of cedar-bark for use in canoes. To get the black colour considered ornamental in a portion of the mat, the strips of bark are steeped in a mixture of charcoal, oil, and water. The inside of the curious hats worn by the natives in canoe voyages is made of white-pine bark and the outside is made of cedar-bark, the hat being shaped so as to shade the head and throw the rain off the shoulders. The upper part of the body is, on these occasions, protected by a cape made of white-pine bark, which is soft, but not close in texture, and which looks pretty when clean, and edged with marten fur. A strong fine thread is made of this bark, of which the Aht natives, who all are expert with the needle, make constant use. Their needle is a slender twig sharpened at one end. It is unnecessary to give any further account of their property in personal chattels, which, as may be supposed, are all of the simplest description. I may mention that the stock of salmon collected for consumption in winter is not quite regarded as common property, but is an article which a native, in case of need, will give freely to another. If a quantity, the product of one man's fishing, is stored in his particular division of a house, he will not object to another industrious Indian using it for food, should he be destitute. The Indians give food ungrudgingly to one another; they have generally plenty and can be free with it. In connection with the descriptions of property owned by the Ahts, I must not omit to refer to the slaves.

No institution is more specifically defined among the Ahts than that of slavery. It has probably existed in these tribes for a long time, as many of the slaves have a characteristic mean appearance, and the word "slave" is used commonly as a term of reproach. If a man acts meanly or is niggardly in his distributions of property (see chapter on Tribal Ranks), it is said that he has a "slave's heart." Next to a "heart of water," which means a coward, the "heart of a slave" is the most opprobrious epithet. It is the fashion for slaves to wear short hair. Formerly almost every well-born native owned a slave, and some of the chiefs had five or six. A slave was considered a useful and honourable possession, and if sold or lost, was replaced immediately by another. Women and children, as well as men, were enslaved. Slave-women are at the present day bought and sold on this coast like sheep. A slave never sat at meat with his owner; he waited upon the family and their guests, and took his own meals afterwards. His duty was to split salmon, pluck berries, carry wood and water, and to do all that he was told to do, without remonstrance or remuneration. There were means, though what they were I do not know, by which a person recently enslaved might regain his freedom; but this was a rare occurrence, and I could not discover any instance of a person becoming free who had been born in slavery and was basely descended. Stories, however, are told of great chiefs in former times, such as *Tsosiatin* of the Kowitchans, who occasionally freed a number of slaves in order to show their magnanimity. I believe that a well-born native, captured in war and reduced to slavery, could be bought back by his friends for a large price; and if he remained a captive until death, and left an orphan born of his own wife, the child, in some cases, on growing up, would, on account of his better descent and unfortunate condition, so far become free that he could not be sold out of the tribe. On this subject, however, I found it difficult to get accurate information. Like other native institutions, slavery has been shaken by the approach of civilization, and sometimes what the traveller now might mistake for old customs are, in reality, but the mere portions or remnants of them.

The natives take great pride in honourable birth, as distinguished from the base mixed extraction from slaves.* One instance, however, is known to me of a chief having promoted a slave to be one of his inferior wives.† The slave is at the absolute disposal of his master in all things; he is a bond-servant who may be transferred without his own consent from one proprietor to another. A master sometimes directs a slave, on pain of death, to kill an enemy, and the slave dares not again appear in the presence of his master without the head of the person. The behest of the Sheikh Al Jebel is not more faithfully obeyed. The case, in this instance, is one in which—native evidence being excluded by the working of the British criminal law as administered in Vancouver Island—the slave would be put to death, while the chief, who cares nothing for a slave's life, would probably go free, and boast of his successful crime. So complete is the power over slaves, and the indifference to human life among the Ahts, that an owner might bring half a dozen slaves out of his house and kill them publicly in a row without any notice being taken of the atrocity. But the slave, as a rule, is not harshly treated; he is clothed and has plenty to eat, and is seldom beaten except for desertion, when a severe flogging is administered. A runaway slave, if belonging to a chief, is occasionally

* The Vancouver Indians dislike and have a contempt for Chinamen and negroes. They regard them as inferior people to themselves.

† The fathers of the offspring of female slaves are not known, as the slaveholders hire out the women to infamy.

returned, through courtesy, by the chief of another friendly tribe; but more frequently he is seized and immediately conveyed along the coast for sale, the captors being unwilling to risk the hostility of his owner by detaining him. As it is the practice of powerful tribes to prevent the canoes of smaller tribes from passing their villages in search of customers, the price of a slave increases at each stage, as he is conveyed along the coast to the best market. Men formerly were preferred to women, but since the island has been colonized women have brought higher prices, owing to the encouragement given to prostitution among a young unmarried colonial population. A young woman worth, say, thirty blankets on the west coast towards the north end of the island, will, at Victoria, be worth fifty or sixty blankets, or about thirty pounds. I know of several instances of slave-dealing between the west coast and Victoria within the last two years. The coast of British Columbia, and the islands towards the north are, however, the chief sources of this odious and shameful traffic with Victoria. On the west coast of Vancouver Island there is not much slave-trade with Victoria; it is directed chiefly from that quarter to the American side of the Strait of Juan de Fuca, where the Cape Flattery Indians are great promoters and supporters of this hateful commerce. Being comparatively rich and numerous, they induce the larger Vancouverian tribes to attack the small neighbouring tribes on their own shores, and capture persons fit for the slave-market. Some of the smaller tribes at the north of the Island are practically regarded as slave-breeding tribes, and are attacked periodically by stronger tribes, who make prisoners, and sell them as slaves.

CHAPTER XII.

CONDITION OF WOMEN.

Condition of the Aht Women—Unmarried and Married—their Betrothal—Marriage—Divorce—Widowhood—Polygamy—Polyandry.

Allegiance and fast fealty
Which I do owe unto all womankind.—SPENCER.

THE condition of the Aht women is not one of unseemly inferiority; the men have their due share of the labours necessary for subsistence. The women do all the work of the camps, prepare fur-skins, collect roots and berries, take charge of the fish on the canoes reaching the shore, manage the cooking, and prepare food for winter. They also make mats, straw-hats and capes, wreaths and ornamental niceties of grass or cedar-fibre. I have met women in the woods in autumn, at four o'clock in the morning, staggering under a great burden of cedar-bark. They are seldom invited to feasts, and do not share in public ceremonies, except as assistants. On reaching puberty, young women, on a given occasion, are placed in the sort of gallery already described as in every house, and are there surrounded completely with mats, so that neither the sun nor any fire can be seen. In this cage they remain for several days. Water is given to them, but no food. The longer a girl remains in this retirement the greater honour is it to the parents; but she is disgraced for life if it is known that she has seen fire or the sun during this initiatory ordeal. Feasts are given at this time as part of the ceremony, by her parents or by other near friends.* The average age at which native women marry is about sixteen. They suffer little during pregnancy or at childbirth, but seldom bear children after the age of about twenty-five. As a rule they have few children, and, I think, more boys than girls. Their female relations act as midwives. There is no separate place for lying-in. The child, on being born, is rolled up in a mat among feathers. Instances are known of women having been at work twelve hours after their confinement. They suckle one child till another comes. I have seen a boy of four following his mother for her milk. The women are good and kind mothers, and the crime of infanticide after birth is unknown; but, in order to spite their husbands after a quarrel, they frequently take means to procure abortion. I could find no evidence among the Ahts for the past prevalence or present existence of the custom of the *couvade*, by which, among some savages, when a child is born, the father, not the mother, goes to bed and is treated as a patient. Before meeting with white men, it is supposed that the Aht women were

* This reminds one of the Mexican superstition at the rekindling of the sacred fire, according to which women were confined to their houses with covered faces, lest, if they saw the fire, they should be changed into beasts.

generally faithful to their husbands, who, according to the accounts of former travellers, valued them so much as sometimes to show jealousy on their account—a feeling not found often in savage bosoms, but which implies a certain degree of affection. The Ahts, indeed, within recent times, were distinguished by the respect which they showed towards their women, and especially towards their wives. A girl who was known to have lost her virtue, lost with it one of her chances of a favourable marriage; and a chief, or man of high rank in an Aht tribe, would have put his daughter to death for such a lapse. He would not, for any consideration, have prostituted his wife, but his female slaves were readily devoted to such infamy. The reverse, as far as the wife is concerned, is the case farther north among the tribes on the coast of British Columbia: the temporary present of a wife is one of the greatest honours that can be shown there to a guest. Generally speaking, wives are not harshly treated among the Ahts. They have the important privilege, with the consent of their own friends, of at any time leaving their husbands, who thus have to treat them well if they wish them to remain. An active female slave, however, is more valued than any wife who does not bring riches or powerful connections, for the slave cannot leave the master's service. Wives may be divorced at the will of their husbands, and a discarded wife is not viewed with disfavour. A singular mode of punishing an unfaithful wife came under my notice. The frail fair one was taken to the beach, and her husband, kneeling upon her, surrounded by wailing friends, fired a succession of blank musket charges close to her head. The woman was much frightened, and afterwards sat by herself weeping for several days. On separating from his wife, a husband has to give up the fishing or hunting grounds acquired with her at marriage. The property reverts to the woman's sole use, and is a dowry for her next matrimonial experiment. In the case of a marriage between persons of different tribes, and their separation while the children are young, the children go always with the mother to her own tribe. Separations and new connections are ordinary occurrences. The baskets and mats made by a wife for sale belong to herself, and she has also a certain small share of all the property acquired by her husband. He cannot interfere with her portion, which is a sort of pin-money used by the wife in the purchase of personal requirements. Additionally, as the traders well know, a wife has an important say in the disposal of articles. She and her husband talk together, and argue as to what shall be asked for oil or furs. The one may want blankets, and the other cotton. Privileges such as these prevent the women from being treated otherwise than with consideration. Early betrothals are common, and in the betrothal of chiefs' children the parents on both sides deposit a number of blankets to ensure good faith. Betrothals are so much respected that the wounded pride of a disappointed suitor or his tribe will not be satisfied by the mere return of the pledge. It is pretty well known at the betrothal what the price at marriage will be; but a chief can raise the price up to ten blankets above the original agreed number, if his daughter is pronounced by a majority of her own tribe to have greatly improved. Strange to say, this happens less frequently than might be expected. Prices for marriage, when the price has not been fixed at the time of betrothal, are sometimes offered formally, year after year, by the betrothed man; and the reception of the third offer is considered to show truly whether the betrothal is likely to be respected. It is an understood custom that if the third offer is rejected, the original betrothal is cancelled, and the pledge forfeited by the woman's friends. This leads always to bitterness of feeling, and is only done when some more distinguished native chief, or rich white man, seeks the woman in marriage. There is, however, a way of cancelling a betrothal by mutual agreement; and as a symbol of such termination, if the parties are well-born, each tribe sends a canoe laden with blankets, and manned with a full crew, who paddle to a distance from land, and, singing all the while a song, throw the blankets one by one upon the waves. For several days before a young girl's marriage the old women are busily engaged with her in a variety of ceremonies. The young men, under the like circumstances, to show their pluck, scratch their faces till blood comes.*

Wives, as has been before stated, are obtained by purchase, and the price is regulated by the rank and wealth of both parties. There is no particular mode of courtship; the matter has generally to be arranged with the parents. No English father, in his library, raising his spectacles to survey a diffident youth who longs to be his son-in-law, is sterner in the matter of "settlements" than a family man among the Ahts. I was offered a young,

* A fond practice in courtship among the common people (not among the chiefs) is for the woman to search the man's head, and give him to eat the fattest and least nimble of the population which she is able to secure.

pretty, well-born woman for one hundred blankets; but a wife can be bought sometimes for an old axe or half-a-dozen mink-skins. Though a wife is always purchased, it is a point of honour that the purchase-money given for a woman of rank—not for a common woman—shall, sometime or other, be returned by her friends or her tribe in a present of equal value. A man occasionally steals a wife from the women of his own tribe; but it is much like eloping in England, for both parties understand each other: and, after all, it is a purchase, as the friends of the woman must be pacified with presents. Though the different tribes of the Aht nation are frequently at war with one another, women are not captured from other tribes for marriage, but only to be kept as slaves. The idea of slavery connected with capture is so common, that a free-born Aht would hesitate to marry a woman taken in war, whatever her rank had been in her own tribe.

Polygamy is permitted in all classes, but, owing to its inconveniences, is not generally practised. There is no rule by which any wife obtains precedence over the others; the oldest wife, if she has children, seems to have most authority in the house. It is not uncommon, on the death of a poor native, for a friend to take the widow for one of his own wives, and to adopt the children. These children are kept much in the position of slaves, and, in the course of time, the younger ones are regarded as slaves, but they cannot be sold out of their tribe. Unless widows have property of their own, their position is hard. The eldest son takes all that property of his father not given away to the deceased's friends, during his last illness, nor buried with him.

I could find no traces of the existence of polyandry among the Ahts. The people have a strong idea of blood-relationship; so strong that it may be described as the principal constituent in the structure of their simple society. The groups of relatives round the different heads of families are very noticeable in a tribe, and any injury to a member of such a group is resented by the family and all the family's friends. The feeling of relationship is not confined merely to their offspring, nor is it of temporary duration, as in the case of animals, but it extends to all kinsmen—to the son and grandson, and, also, collaterally to marriage connections. Whether kinship is now, or ever was, considered by the Ahts to be stronger when derived through males than females, I do not know; the fact of its great influence at present among these primitive tribes on this coast is undoubted.

Intermarriage with other tribes is sought by the higher classes to strengthen the foreign connections of their own tribe, and, I think also, with some idea of preventing degeneracy of race. Before the house of the head chief of the Khah-oh-quahts there is a large stone which a man must lift and carry, in the presence of the people, before he may woo the chief's daughter. The poorer orders are unable to do otherwise than marry among their own people. By the old custom of the Aht tribes, no marriage was permitted within the degree of second-cousin. The marriage of a patrician is an important affair. He loses caste unless he marries a woman of corresponding rank, in his own or another tribe. Affection or attachment has little to do with the marriage; the idea is to preserve the family from a mixture of common blood. The marriage of a head chief must be with the descendant in the first line of another chief of similar rank, and no head chief is permitted to take a first wife for himself, or to agree to a marriage for his children by such first wife, without the consent of his tribe. Few of the head chiefs have more than one wife. Should a head chief wish for more wives than one, it is not necessary that he take other than his first wife from women of his own rank; but the children of his extra wives have not the father's rank. The purchase of wives is made in public, and great ceremony is observed when a chief's wife is purchased. Grave tribal discussions as to the purchase-money, the suitableness of rank, and all the benefits likely to follow, accompany any such proposal of marriage. Most of the tribes have heralds or criers, who announce important events, and their office, like the harpooner's, is obtained by inheritance.* On this official giving public notice that distinguished visitors are at hand, every person in a native encampment comes out, and squats down, covered with a blanket to the chin. Further proceedings are awaited in silence. If it is a marriage visit, thirty or forty canoes sometimes escort the suitor to the shore. No word is spoken on either side for ten minutes. At last, on the question being asked, where the visitors are from, and what is wanted—a form that is gone through, though the object of the visit is perfectly well known—a speaker rises in one of the canoes, and addresses the natives on shore in a loud voice. Talk of a voice, it would fill St. Paul's! He gives the

* The Bishop of Columbia and Commander Helby of the *Grappler* will remember the Seshaht herald who interpreted their speeches to the tribes assembled at Alberni in 1860.

name, titles, and history of the expectant husband, and states the number and influence of his friends and connections in his own and among other tribes; the object being to show that the honour of marrying so great a person should suffice without much purchase-money. At the end of the speech a canoe is paddled to the beach, and a bundle of blankets is thrown on land. Contemptuous laughter follows from the friends of the woman, and the suitor is told to go away, as he places too small a value upon the intended bride. Then some orator on shore in turn gets up, and praises the woman; and thus, with speeches and additional gifts, many hours are occupied, until finally the woman is brought down to the shore, stripped to her shift, and delivered to her lover. His first wedding present is the necessary covering of a blanket. After the marriage, a feast is spread which lasts for several days. Instead of throwing the proffered blankets on shore in a bundle, the natives sometimes land from their canoes, and, standing a few paces apart, hold up the red, white, blue, and green blankets in a long pretty line before the eyes of the woman's tribe. But this is not the ordinary practice of the Ahts: in the few cases in which it has been done among them, the custom of some other tribes has been imitated. When the man's rank is much higher than the woman's, the latter is sometimes brought to the man's tribe to be married; and Raleigh's courtesy is then outdone, for blankets are laid, not only over the puddles, but all the way, for her to walk upon, from the canoe to the house. There are several minor ceremonies in marriage, which, however, are hardly worth mentioning, as they vary greatly, and no one can explain their meaning.

A wooden head-piece, fringed with human hair, and having a long snout, is worn by the bridegroom on his head. At great marriages, such as I have just alluded to, this ugly covering is simply thrown upon the beach; but on common occasions, when merely the friends of the "young people" and not the whole tribe are present, the bridegroom, decorated with feathers and accompanied by a friend, walks into the woman's house, and throws the head-piece upon the floor, returning afterwards to his canoe. When the feasting, the speeches, and marriage mummeries are over, I have been told that the women's friends light two torches in her late house, and after a time extinguish them in water that is spilt for this purpose on the ground.

CHAPTER XIII.

ESCAPE FROM THE TOQUAHTS.

Respect for Rank—Visit to the Toquahts—Dangerous Encampment—Indians circumvented.

In vain thy Kate awaits thy comin',
Kate soon will be a woefu' woman.—BURNS.

THE high consideration in which rank or actual authority is held by these savages is extraordinary. After deciding whether a stranger is a friend or enemy, the first question, in the mind of a native, is as to his rank,—whether he is a chief or a common man. If several travellers are together, the natives are not satisfied till they know who is the leader, and who is next in command. At Alberni, where more than two hundred men were engaged in various employments, the Indians in the neighbourhood knew particularly the position of every person in the settlement. In their own villages, the common men point out the chiefs to a visitor, and show the differences of rank by holding up one forefinger for the highest chief, and placing the other forefinger against it, at points gradually lower and lower, for the inferior chiefs. I once visited, with a companion,—leaving three of my party in a boat at the entrance of the Toquaht river—the ancient and somewhat rascally tribe of Toquahts, now reduced by war to comparatively a small number,* whose village is in a dreary, remote part of Nitinaht (or Barclay) Sound. As our canoe rounded a corner of the shallow river, and came suddenly upon their village, a loud yell was raised by a group of natives, who sat on a bank making cedar-traps for salmon; and the shout was repeated by the inmates of the houses, who rushed out of doors. There is a strange wildness in the half-human, half-beast cry which these savages raise on being thus surprised, and it made the blood go back to our hearts; however, as we much wanted a fish for our supper, we hauled up the canoe, and walked towards the group. There was no fish to be got; so we lighted our cigars and entered into conversation. The natives ceased work, and formed a half circle round a middle-aged, important-looking savage, who was pointed out to us as the chief, and who sat looking unconcernedly before him, while all the others surveyed us with curious eyes. We did not speak much, and I daresay ten minutes passed before any of the natives opened their mouths. The evening was approaching; it was a wild remote place: the dense, motionless pines were everywhere around, and no sound broke the stillness but the murmuring of the shallow stream, as it flowed past the village. I began to have a feeling of apprehension as to these crouching Toquahts, wrapped all round in bearskins to

* In the list of the tribes, given in the Appendix, the real Toquahts appear as few; but many fugitives from other tribes join them.

the chin, above which their savage, furtive eyes looked out upon us.* At last, a grey-haired man commenced a song in praise of the chief, to whom he pointed often while singing, and who, with his hands crossed before him, carried himself, all the while, as a man of rank. Our visit seemed to have been turned into an occasion of glorifying this chief of twelve men—the remnant of a large tribe distinguished formerly in war and for savage arts. The time for speeches, and explanations, and presents was arriving; but being hungry, and having to trust to our guns or hooks for providing our supper, and having to select our camping ground for the night, we lost patience and retired to our canoe. The Toquahts, no doubt, thought us unmannerly visitors, and, in fact, aroused us next morning, on discovering our encampment, in a way which made us glad to get out of their neighbourhood.

I will relate how this occurred. After leaving the village, on our way down the river, we met several fierce-looking savages in canoes, one of whom, as he passed, grinned at us and presented a large horse-pistol. This was meant probably as a joke on his part, and, as a joke in return, I showed him the muzzles of our two six-barrel revolvers. He grinned still more, and asked where we were going. "Very far," I answered, and we pushed away from him, and by-and-by joined the remainder of

* The Indians rarely kill a well-known white man, as they know that he would be inquired for; but they think no more of cutting off a common man's head than of killing a salmon. You may, perhaps, travel safely alone, from one tribe to another, all round the island; but it is a matter of chance: your head may be cut off at any time. The Indians are the creatures of impulse; you never know what they will do; they are like grown children subject to ferocious demoniacal possession.

our party, whom we had left in the boat. We were now five in number; we had the prospect only of biscuit and coffee for our supper, as no fish had been got. It was with great difficulty we found a camping place along the shore. Not trusting the Toquahts, we wanted to go a long way from them. There were few streams of water in this part of Nitinaht (or Barclay) Sound; one place was too stony, another too wet; so it was almost dark before we found a place for our tent. One very suitable place was reached as we coasted along, where there was a nice stream and the remains of an Indian camp, but the smell of the decayed fish was so offensive we could not stay there. Taking with us a slender hewn pole from the standing framework of the temporarily abandoned huts, we proceeded farther, and at last encamped—just beyond a point—on a narrow stony beach, fifteen yards wide from the forest to the water, and perhaps two hundred yards long. Having pitched the tent with the pole above mentioned, we boiled some coffee, drew up the boat, and lay down to sleep. In using the pole for this purpose, we cut off about a foot of its length. The night was dark, and we let the fire burn, without fearing that the smoke would be seen. I remember we all looked uneasy; though, as often happens on such occasions, we laughed and talked a good deal about the very objects of our suspicions, namely the Indians we had just left. At length we fell asleep, I waking occasionally during the night when startled by the scream of the owl (known to ornithologists as the "great owl") from some neighbouring high tree.

Having awoke about five o'clock, I lay still, and occasionally lifted up a corner of the tent to observe the morning. On doing so once, I thought I saw the form of an Indian through the mist moving about between the wood and the water. I do not know whether it was an Indian or not, but the appearance rather startled me, for there were no Indians but Toquahts in the neighbourhood, and, as already stated, we rather wished to avoid them. Waking my companions, we thought it prudent quietly to pack everything within the tent, without appearing outside; then first one and next another went out of the tent; and, with apparent unconcern, made the usual arrangements for breaking up the camp. Breakfast we thought we would take later in the day; our present object was to remove quickly from the spot. Our supposition that Indians were near was soon confirmed, for, in a short time, about a dozen Toquaht Indians appeared coming towards us along the beach, sauntering with their usual undecided step, and their blankets tightly folded round them. A large canoe with a crew of twenty Indians was also seen through the mist coming round the point, near which, as above stated, we had placed our camp. The canoe stopped near the shore, and we saw that the crew wore their war-paint. The Indians on shore had no war-paint; they saluted us, and came near and began talking. One commenced a song, and accompanied it by imitating the action of paddling. We continued our preparations for embarking, when all at once, for the first time, we remembered that our heavy boat was fast aground. I shall not forget my sensations at that moment; I was certain that the savages meant mischief, and we seemed to be fairly trapped. Badly as all this looked, I was glad it was daylight. The shore party of the Indians had now mixed with us, and laughed and chatted; we working quietly, but on our guard. I asked why the Indians in the canoe wore war-paint, while those on shore did not, and was answered that the canoe was going to surprise a party of You-clul-ahts who had a fishing station somewhere near. As we moved about packing our things and collecting sticks for a make-believe fire, one of our party, a quick-witted woodman from the State of Maine, whispered, "Manœuvre to make them launch the boat for us." I was about replying, when a wild angry shout from one of the Indians on shore arrested the conversation; it was followed by a louder howl from the canoe. The song of the paddler ceased; angry exclamations and shouts filled the air, and the savages literally danced with passion. It appeared that, in search of a cause of quarrel, one of them had stumbled on the tent-pole we had cut, which they said belonged to the Toquaht tribe. "Toquaht house," "Toquaht stick," "steal stick," "steal stick," "you come here to steal stick," were among the cries the maddened Indians uttered. We were now familiar with the danger, and had reckoned our chances; we were getting into that dogged state of feeling very noticeable in the English race during a time of danger; and which would be expressed by saying, "Come now, if you mean business, set to work; we have had enough of this." The excitement of the Indians drew them all together, so that we had them before us, and they seemed at a loss how to proceed. The canoe came near the shore, and landed half its crew, who joined the shore party. Still we stood ready, but without drawing our pistols. When a party of the Indians tried to slip along the shore with the evident intention of getting behind us, we moved back one by one, till their movement was neutralized. Their excitement continued, but they hesitated to attack. At length I shouted to them, "Where is your chief, I want to talk to him: we did not know the stick was yours; we will pay for it." A score of voices answered "The chief is up the river." "Well, go and bring him," said I. "No," they replied, "you go to the chief." A thought having struck me, I said, we would go to the chief; our hearts were good to the Toquahts: they must get into their canoe, however, and show us the way, as the channel of the river when reached was intricate. The Indians talked this over among themselves for a short time, and seemed pleased with the proposition. Finally, they got into their canoe, and remained close to the shore, leaving half a dozen common men to help us to launch our boat, which still was aground. Stowing everything in it, we placed the oars handy, shipped the rudder; and went to work to shove the boat off, not with a "Yo-heave-oh!" but with the Indian "Tchoo, Tchoo, Tchoo." It was odd to see how the frantic excitement of the Indians had now subsided, and how willingly they seemed to comply with our wishes. They, no doubt, thought they had us nicely in a trap of our own contriving, forgetting quite that once up the Toquaht river was enough for any one. No sooner, with a great "Tchoo, Tchoo," did the keel of our boat cease to grate on the bottom, than each man sprang on board to his place, shipped his oar, and pulled vigorously in an *opposite direction* from the Toquaht river and from the expectant Indian canoe. The Indians in the canoe said nothing, but rose to their feet and sat down again; those who had helped to launch our boat stood in the water stupefied. I watched them for a long time through a field glass, and they were still about the same place. A stern chase after a boat with five men in it, each armed with a six-barrelled rifled revolver, was not to their mind. These Indians had expected to find our encampment during the night, but coming unexpectedly upon our party in the morning, and finding us moving, they were disconcerted. This trip was the last trip I made to the Toquaht river; their tribe was the most mischievous I saw on the west coast of Vancouver Island.

CHAPTER XIV.

TRIBAL RANKS.

Use made of an Accumulation of Personal Chattels—Custom of Distributing Property—Object of such Distribution—Degrees of Tribal Ranks—Position of Hereditary Chiefs; of Minor Chiefs; War Chiefs, and Military Officers—Rank bestowed on Women.

Let it not then seem strange to you,
That here one strange thing more you see.—MACE.

THE principal use made by the Ahts of an accumulation of personal chattels is to distribute them periodically among invited guests, each of whom is expected to return the compliment by equivalent presents on like occasions. The following particulars refer to the distribution of property by individuals to others of their own tribe: Blankets are usually given to men; beads, trinkets, and paint for the face, to women. Not more than two blankets are usually given to any person at one time. Sometimes a new musket is divided, and the stock, lock, and barrel given to three different persons. The destruction of certain kinds of property serves the same purpose as its distribution. Canoes, for instance, are rarely given away. The practice is to make a hole in them, and allow them to sink. The distributor shows by this act his total indifference to his property; he gives it away, he destroys it; his heart is very strong. Yet the same man, who has rid himself of almost his whole property, will haggle the next minute about the price of a trinket. Slaves are rarely given away at a distribution. This singular custom of distribution, which prevails among the coast tribes here, is thought by some to have been necessary, owing to the thievish habits of the people which prevented any individual from retaining what he had collected; but, whatever may have been its origin, the continuance of the custom probably is secured by the gratification which the practice affords to two strong propensities in human nature—pride of rank, and love of display. A lavish distribution of property among the Ahts shows what the natives call the "strong heart" of the distributor.* The practice is not so highly appreciated now as it was a generation since; still, the gaining of property with a view to its distribution is a ruling motive for the actions of the Ahts, and without bearing this in mind no one can understand their character, nor appreciate the difficulties in the way of reclaiming them. The collection of property for the purpose of distribution is the constant aim of many of the natives who, to the common observer, seem listless and idle. The Indian who stands by your side in a tattered blanket, may have twenty new blankets and yards of calico in his box at home. Whatever he acquires beyond immediate necessaries goes to increase this stock, until his high

* This term expresses what is frequently meant by our word "manliness."

day comes in the winter season, when he spreads his feast and distributes gifts among the guests, according to their rank. To include all present at such a feast, a single blanket is sometimes torn into twenty pieces; and it is said, but this I can hardly believe, that the exact quantity or value given to each guest is accurately remembered. It is customary to throw the article briskly into the face of the receiver, to show that it goes from a willing heart. The giver does not now consider that he has parted with his property: he regards it as well invested, for the present recipients of his largess will strive to return to him at their own feasts more than he has bestowed. The person who gives away the most property receives the greatest praise, and in time acquires, almost as a matter of course, but by the voice of the tribe, the highest rank obtainable by such means. This rank is not of the highest class. It is only for life, and is different from the ancient hereditary tribal rank. With each step in rank there is usually a change of name; and thus, bearing different names, the industrious or acquisitive native may rise from one honour to another, till finally he reaches a high position.

The head chief in an Aht tribe occupies apparently a position of which the type is patriarchal. His authority is rather nominal than positive. He generally calls the old men together to consider weighty matters, but neither he nor they can do anything without the consent of the people. At these public councils, where the tribal interests are debated with much shrewdness, the principal persons are seated according to their rank, and much respect is shown throughout to the ancient ceremonies. There is no formal way of taking a vote; the will of the tribe is expressed by acclamation. The chief has no officers, except his slaves, who could enforce obedience in his own tribe; but there are proper tribal officers through whom he communicates all resolutions of his own people to other tribes. He cannot give in marriage, nor betroth his children, contrary to the tribal custom or will. He never joins an embassy, nor leads an expedition in war. Though frequently receiving presents from his tribesmen, the chief is not often wealthy, as he has to entertain visitors and make large distributions to his own people. There is at this day one instance, which possibly is the remnant of an old general custom among the Ahts, of all the members of a tribe paying tribute to their chiefs. The instance to which I allude is that of the Klah-oh-quahts, some of whom pay annually to their chief certain contributions, consisting of blankets, skins, oil, and other articles. On public occasions, or in intertribal communications, the hereditary chief is an important person, whose official dignity is maintained by strict etiquette. But his actual influence in the tribe is frequently exceeded by that of some vigorous underchief. It is not uncommon for the principal chief, under his people's displeasure, to abandon his property, and abdicate his position in favour of the next heir. On retiring into private life he is little noticed. When a chief is childless, his next of kin, male, commonly succeeds to the chiefship, but occasionally a more distant kinsman is preferred by the tribe, if his property is large and his character approved of. As with the

Irish septs in old times, and with most Eastern people, much reverence is shown by the Ahts to the true reigning family, though individuals belonging to it are occasionally set aside in the line of succession. Minor tribal rank, of what may be called the first degree, is hereditary, but children only can inherit it, and in default of children, the dignity ceases. Unless accompanied with wealth, inherited rank in a tribe is a poor possession. The native grandee without blankets is like an English peer without land. The value of his distributions of property among the people is expected to befit his rank, and he gets no commendation for what would bring praise and honour to a plebeian. Whatever may have been the origin or purpose of these dignities, it is evident that the particular rank and position of every person in an Aht tribe are well understood. Some are called high chiefs, others half chiefs or small chiefs; and any insult, wrong, or injury offered to a chief by another tribe, is resented by his own tribe according to the rank of the sufferer. But his "blue blood" avails not in a dispute with one of his own people; he must fight his battle like a common man.

In marriage, however, or at burials, feasts and public ceremonies, and in a council of the tribe, the privileges of a man of rank are strictly regarded. The sons of high chiefs often have a following of eight or ten free-born youngsters, who, unremunerated, follow them about, and receive their commands. In the actual conduct of war, civil rank fails to secure for the possessor an important position. The war chiefs and the under officers in war are, as a general rule, chosen for their special fitness for military command, and not at all on account of their rank. Success in war, is a broad stepping-stone in an ambitious career. So far as I can learn, there are among the Ahts the following degrees or classes of rank. It must be understood that I speak of what is already almost of the past. So great has been the disturbing force of contact with the colonists, that rank has lost much of its value, and as regards some of their ancient customs, they are now but little regarded by the natives. First, then, as to ranks; there is the head chief's rank, which is hereditary in the male line, and to which, owing to the respect generally entertained for the true lineage (if not in all cases for the immediate heir), it is almost useless for any low-born native directly to aspire. Next are the various degrees of rank which probably have been held by inheritance from generation to generation. Degrees of rank are sometimes acquired, by the consent of the tribe, for great services or special acts of valour, but these are not altogether of so high a character as the former. The way the natives have of fixing the intended degree of rank is by saying that it is the will of the tribe, that so-and-so shall be equal to so-and-so, or next under him. The harpooner, in the tribes that live on the seaboard, possesses high hereditary rank. Inferior to these are the various degrees of rank, obtained by the consent of the tribe, consequent upon large distributions of property. This practice of distribution, it may be observed, is not confined to any particular class; all ranks find it useful in supporting their influence. All the ranks above mentioned appear to be hereditary. There are two additional descriptions of rank, both ending with the possessor's life; one, which, in our own country, we should call a courtesy title or rank, is enjoyed, as a matter of course, by well-born youths; the other it is the privilege of the hereditary chief and the principal chiefs to confer. This last-named rank is generally conferred during the festive period following the return of a tribe to winter quarters. I did not know that the chiefs had this power, or that rank could be possessed except with the expressed consent of the people, till I learnt that the right was exercised by the chief or chiefs independently, at this season, in a tribe near which I lived. This rank can be bestowed on men or women, adults or children; and its bestowal is preceded, if not actually obtained, generally by presents to the chiefs. Those seeking such rank signify their wish to the chief, who, on ascertaining the number of aspirants, directs them, at stated times, to assemble at his house, where they dance, sing, and go through various exercises, day after day—sometimes for weeks—before they receive the honour. The women, on these occasions, dress in their best; they are ornamented with beads and brass rings, and pretty shells are attached to their noses and plaited among their hair. This is the only description of rank which the women can acquire, by any tribal usage, but they partially inherit their parent's rank, to the extent, at least, of a regard being paid to it at their marriage. In an Aht tribe of two hundred men, perhaps fifty possess various degrees of acquired or inherited rank; there may be about as many slaves; the remainder are independent members, less rich as a body than the men of rank, but who live much in the same way, the difference of position being noticeable only on public occasions.* It is among the idle, poor, and low-born youth of the last-named class that the worst Indians are found; as a rule well-born natives, and especially the heads of families in a tribe are quiet and well-behaved.

* Was Darwin long enough among the Fuegians to be enabled authoritatively to affirm that perfect equality exists among the individuals composing the Fuegian tribes?

CHAPTER XV.

INTELLECTUAL CAPACITY AND LANGUAGE.

Intellectual Capacities—Mode of Numeration—Division of Time—Language; its Imperfect Structure; Formation of New Words—Remarks on some Peculiarities of the Language—Nitinaht Variations—Cook's List of Words—Little Change in the Language since Cook's Time—The Aht Language probably Allied to the Real Chinook—Tribal Names.

He in the lowest depth of Being framed
The imperishable mind.—SOUTHEY.

Speak what terrible language you will, though you understand it not
Yourselves, no matter! Chough's language, gabble enough, and good enough.
SHAKESPEARE.

UNTIL the effect of a judicious education of the Aht natives has been fairly tested through several generations, it will be difficult for any one to express a confident opinion as to their capability for improvement. Mr. Duncan, the missionary, has succeeded beyond his expectation in his educational efforts among the Tshimpseans on the coast of British Columbia; and there is no such great difference, apparently, between the Tshimpseans and the Ahts as to lead us to suppose that the one nation would be incapable of what is evidently within the capacity of the other. I could not be easily persuaded that any barrier exists to prevent savage races from attaining a fair degree of mental cultivation, whatever might be their capacity for advancing ultimately in civilization beyond a certain point. The cleverness shown in modes of hunting, fishing, and warfare, and in the adaptation of their manufactures to intended uses, might be exhibited, no doubt, by savages in other studies and pursuits. I had abundant proof, in conversing with the Ahts about matters in which they took an interest, that their mental capabilities are by no means small. It is true that the native mind, to an educated man, seems generally to be asleep; and if you suddenly ask a novel question, you have to repeat it while the mind of the savage is awaking, and to speak with emphasis until he has quite got your meaning. This may partly arise from the questioner's imperfect knowledge of the language; still, I think, not entirely, as the savage may be observed occasionally to become forgetful, when voluntarily communicating information. On his attention being fully aroused, he often shows much quickness in reply and ingenuity in argument. But a short conversation wearies him, particularly if questions are asked that require efforts of thought or memory on his part. The mind of the savage then appears to rock to and fro out of mere weakness, and he tells lies and talks nonsense. I do not doubt, however, that in course of time the mental powers of the Indian could be greatly improved by education. The chief difficulty is that the people would vanish from before the white man during the polishing process, as so many tribes of savages have done in other parts of the world.

I will mention the system of numeration of the Ahts,

in connection with the question of their intellectual capacity.

It will be seen from the list of Aht numerals in the Appendix, that there is no impediment to prevent the Indian from counting up to any number. As a matter of fact, he has seldom any necessity to use the higher numbers. The young men are, many of them, not well acquainted with their own numeration, and not unfrequently make *kochtseyk* "thirty," *sootcheyk* "fifty," and so on; but this is certainly repudiated by the elders and those who still place a value upon the national mode of enumeration (*see* "Numerals," in the Appendix).

It may be noticed that their word for one occurs again in that for six and nine, and the word for two in that for seven and eight. The Aht Indians count upon their fingers. They always count, except where they have learnt differently from their contact with civilisation, by raising the hands with the palms upwards, and extending all the fingers, and bending down each finger as it is used for enumeration. They begin with the little finger. This little finger, then, is one. Now six is five (that is, one whole hand) and one more. We can easily see then why their word for six comprehends the word for one. Again, seven is five (one whole hand) and two more—thus their word for seven comprehends the word for two. Again, when they have bent down the eighth finger, the most noticeable feature of the hand is that two fingers, that is, a finger and a thumb, remain extended. Now the Aht word for eight comprehends *atlah*, the word for two. The reason for this I imagine to be as follows:—Eight is ten (or two whole hands) wanting two. Again, when the ninth finger is down, only one finger is left extended. Their word for nine comprehends *tsow-wauk*, the word for one. Nine is ten (or two whole hands) wanting one.

The classical reader will recollect that the Greeks expressed such a number as, for instance, "thirty-nine" by saying "forty, wanting one," or such a number as "thirty-eight" by saying "forty, wanting two."

On this point, then, I think a similarity of view must have existed in the mind of the polished Greek, and the rude, but shrewd savage. There seems no cause to doubt the above reasonable explanation, which I had from an intelligent Indian.*

A curious feature in connection with the numerals is that, in agreement with a certain class of words, they are used simply as they are set down in the list (*see* Appendix); but, with another class of words, the numerals have the affix of *kamilh* or *kumilolah;* and again with other words, the affix of *sok* or *sokko.* Thus the Ahts say, *tsow-wauk* or *atlah,* that is, "one" or "two," *ko-us* (man); or *klootsmah* (woman); or *tsoowit* (salmon); or *waw-it* (frog); but with other words, for instance, with the words for dollar, paddle, house, stone, bird and beast of any sort, articles of clothing, and, in fact, with the majority of common names, the numerals *noop-(kamilh)*, *atlah-*

* It may be interesting to notice some of the modes in which certain of the British Columbian Indian tribes express their numbers. For 6 the Carrier says twice 3. In 7, the Tshimpsean, like the Aht, has a 2. Into 8, the Indians who live near the English towns of Douglas and Yale introduce a 1; while the Carrier, strong in his arithmetic says twice 4. For 9, the Douglas and the Carrier have 10 save 1, and the Yale and Lytton Indians have 9 and 1 for 10, borrowing their *Temilk* from *Teemilh*, their Shewshwap neighbours' term for 9.

(*kamilh*), *kochtsa*-(*kamilh*), &c., are made use of. The affix *sok* or *sokko* is used of trees or masts, as *sootcha-sokko klakkahs,* "five trees;" *kochtsa-sokko-kloksem chaputs,* "a vessel with three masts." Of compound words in which numerals appear, I may mention *tsow-wauchinnik,* "unaccompanied;" *atlahchinnik,* "with one other" (*i.e.* "himself the second"); and so on with the other numbers: *tsow-wauklus,* "sole occupant" of a house; *tsow-wista, atlista, kochtsista,* &c., "a canoe manned by one, two, three," &c.; *tsow-wautshamma, atlistshamma,* "with one wife," "with two wives."

The method in which the natives divide the year may also be stated.

The natives divide the year into thirteen months, or rather moons, and begin with the one that pretty well answers to our November. At the same time, as their names are applied to each actual new moon as it appears, they are not, by half a month and more (sometimes), identical with our calendar months.

1. *Mah-mayksoh* is the first moon, to which, meaning "elder brother" (*see* Vocabulary), the word is appropriately applied. "In this month the seals pair."
2. *Kathlahtik* means "brother." Of this moon, and of another occurring seventh from it, they say, "It does not travel, but stays for two days."
3. *Hy-yeskikamilh,* "the month of most snow." (So described and probably so derived, *ei-yeh quees, i.e. hy-yes*).
4. *Kahs-sit-imilh.*
5. *Ay-yak-kamilh,* "when the herrings spawn."

(*Ayyak*, perhaps, is *Ei-yeh-yahk*, *i.e.* "very long").

6. *Outlohkamilh*, "the month in which the geese leave for the lakes to breed."
7. *Oh-oh-kamilh.* "In this month the strange geese from a distance fly at a great height on their way to the inland lakes."
8. *Tahklahdkamilh.* "Before the end of this month the salmon-berry has just begun to ripen, and a small bird, with a single human sort of whistle, has arrived."
9. *Kow-wishimilh.* So named from *kow-wit*, "salmon-berry," and *hishimilh*, a "crowd" or "quantity," this being emphatically the salmon-berry month. Like *kathlahtik*, "this moon stays for two days."
10. *Aho-sit sis.*
11. *Satsope-us.* Evidently from the salmon so called.
12. *Enakonsimilh.* Evidently from the salmon so called.
13. *Cheeyahk-amilh.*

I notice that this last moon (about October) and the fifth moon (about March), have each *yak* or *yahk* in them, which, by itself, as well as in composition, has the meaning of "long."

I will now make a few remarks about the language of these people.

Language of the Ahts.

If the language has any grammatical construction at all—of which there certainly seem to be some traces—still it is in a most imperfect and partially developed state.

Case, gender, and tense are not found, number is only recognised in the personal pronouns, and the inflection of the verbs, which is very irregular and imperfect, marks, so far as I know, little difference between singular and plural. The special characteristic of the language is that it is evdently made up of roots expressive of natural sounds and generic ideas. In many instances, in the case of newly formed or derivative compound words, in which, perhaps, one root retains its full form and significance, and the other or others retain their significance, but have partially lost their form, the Indian immediately recognises the unaltered root, and quickly also the roots of altered form when they are pointed out to him and his attention is given to them. Connected with this extensive use of roots in composition, is the readiness with which the natives invent names for any new objects. A compound word is suggested by some individual in the tribe who is considered skilful in forming appropriate names, and who, for the sake of sound, subjects the roots to great change and, often, abbreviation in the process of compounding. Yet all the Indians who hear the new word at once recognise its meaning, and it is added to their vocabulary. It is surprising to find how quickly universal among the tribes any such new name becomes. As a rule, in the formation of Aht compounds, one root remains unchanged, or nearly so, in the compound word, but the other roots in it are freely altered. A marked feature of the language is the numerous terminations to words which, evidently, have been formed from the same root. Mr. Anderson (*see Cook's Voyages*) mentions this as a defect of the language, as if the variety were useless and unreasonable;

but there is no doubt that these various terminations have their proper significance, though this may often be difficult to discover.

The extensive use of roots and great variety of terminations may be mere barbarisms in a language; but these peculiarities, on the other hand, may be usages and even proofs of qualities that are beautiful and valuable in the highest degree,—all depends on the language itself, its genius and capabilities. In the Greek, which in Homer's time, was used in a very primitive state of society, these peculiarities are at once observed; and the scholar is well aware how adapted that most perfect language is for the conveyance of spiritual and moral truths, and how much this power of conveyance depends on its abundant use of root terms. I do not offer an opinion on the capabilities of the Aht language—these may, perhaps, be comparatively small—but, without for a moment comparing it with any more civilized language, I name the beauty and value of a great variety of terminations and an extensive use of roots, both alone and in compound derivative words,—usages which, in themselves, in the Aht language, cannot be considered as defects. The language of the savage came from the same source as the most perfect and philosophically constructed language, that is, from God Himself; and it is a wonderful proof of wisdom, as regards language, that it should be simple enough for the use of even a savage, and yet contain elements, in common with the most refined and beautiful of languages, by which it is fitted for a development equal to the requirements of the most advanced stages of divine knowledge, of civilization and taste.

A few instances of the Aht manner of compounding

words may be given. We find the root *yats* or *yets*, which expresses the idea of movement of the feet or legs: *yetsook*, is "to walk;" *yetspannich*, "to walk and see;" *yetshitl*, is "to kick;" and *yetseh-yetsah* (their only way of expressing either a frequentative or plural being by reduplication), is "to kick frequently." *Yetseh-yet-sokleh*, undoubtedly from the same root, is a "screw steamer." When the natives first saw one of these vessels, noticing the disturbance of the water astern, they attributed the propulsion to some action analogous to the stroke of the legs of a swimmer, and so the name of "continual kicker" was at once invented and universally received. This is an Indian's explanation, without suggestion or assistance. I may add that, in compound words, several consonants or syllables of the component parts are often run into one. This being the case, it is not unlikely that the *tsok* in the above word gives (as in many other instances) the idea of water (*chu-uk*). Another example of a new name, adopted within my own knowledge, may be mentioned, which shows that parts of different Aht words, expressing different ideas, are sometimes brought together and combined into one word. *Yahk* means "long," and is probably connected with the yet more radical *yeh*, *yah*, which I have noticed seems in some words to give the idea of distance. *Apuxim* is "hair upon the face," *hynmuxhel* is "the mouth;" and there are other words of a similar sound showing the *uxim* and *uxhel* to have a particular reference to the face. These roots are formed into *yahkpekuksel*, "a beard." From this word, and *ko-us*, "a man," a combination of six syllables, the two-syllabled word *yakpus* is derived.

Yakpus is a proper name, meaning "beard-man," and was applied by its Indian inventor or suggestor to my dear friend, the late George Reid, of Alberni.

Klahchoochin, "a stranger," or literally, "the newly-come," is derived from *klah*, a root signifying "present time," and *chookwah*, "come." This last word is connected with the Chinook word *chako*. The radical *klah* is found also in the word *klahooye*, "now;" *klah-huksik*, "the present generation;" and probably in *klah-oh*, "another," with its derivatives, *klah-oh-quill*, "the day after to-morrow," and *klah-oh-quill-ooye*, "the day before yesterday." The *quill* in the two latter words is found also in *atlah-quill*, "eight," and *tsow-wauk-quill*, "nine," and probably means "beyond," or "in addition;" and the *ooye* of the last word is a word of time, used by itself to express "soon" or "presently," and found in words implying both the present and the past, as *klah-ooye*, *ahm-ooye*, *klah-oh-quill-ooye*. Even to one possessing only an imperfect knowledge of the language, the continual presence of significant roots in compound words is evident. The peculiarity may be noticed in instances where the meaning of the root is entirely unknown (that is, unknown to any Indians I conversed with); thus, while *chaputs* is the word now used for canoe, the syllable *kleet* is found to occur in many words connected with a canoe. The similarity of the following words—*kleetcha*, "the steersman;" *kleetchaik*, "a rudder;" *kleetshitl*, "to steer;" *kleetsuppem*, "a sail;" *kleetsmah*, "stuff to sit on in a canoe;" and even *klootsinnim*, "the board which the paddler kneels upon," can hardly be accidental.

Next to these prominent features of the Aht language, which may be further verified by consulting the vocabulary,—to which I must generally refer the reader, as it is not my intention to comment on the language at length,—some of the most usual terminations of words deserve notice. *Ah* or *mah* is, in verbs, the termination of the first person both in the singular and plural; *huk* or *ayts*, of the second; and *mah*, *win*, or sometimes *utlma*, of the third person. These terminations, however, are not so bound to the verb but that sometimes they are transferred to an accompanying adverb, the exact manner of expression being apparently a good deal determined by phonetic considerations, subject to rule. From *wik*, "not," and *kumotop*, "to understand," we get either *wikah-kumotop*, or *wimmutomah*, both equally meaning, "I do not understand;" but the latter word has lost two prominent consonants in the process of composition. In contradistinction to the terminations *mah* and *utlma*, which are applicable to the third person, the ultimate *win*, also applicable to the third person, has specially the curious meaning, in some instances, that the speaker has not seen that which he speaks of, and in other instances, that the object is not in sight at the time of his speaking. This reference to a past and a present may indicate a growth of the language towards the formation of tenses, but the form has reference at present to space and locality, rather than to time, though the idea of time is often necessarily included in the expression. What I mean to observe is that perhaps ultimately the savage may use this termination "win" to express one of the two times (past or present), and adopt some other termination to express the other time. The "w" and the "n" sounds frequently are found in compound words, the one implying a negative, and the other the idea of sight. It might, however, be considered fanciful to look for the derivation of the syllable *win* in these, even although *waw-win,* "to hunt by shouts from unseen hunters" (the game hearing only, and not seeing, their pursuers); and *tupwin,* to gird or girdle the waist (and so to conceal the nakedness), might seem to point in the same direction. The first syllable in *waw-win* is obviously the same as in *waw-wah* or *waw-waw,* "to speak" or "shout."

The expression of number is more definite in the Aht language than that of time. Reduplication of a significant syllable is used to describe number in objects and frequency in action. The words *waw-waw* and *tseka tseka* are both used of sustained speech; *waw* means simply "to utter a shout," or "to say." I find the single word *tsechkah* in a vocabulary of eighty years ago, though I have not myself heard it without the reduplication. Of three words in the Aht language, meaning "to work," two, *oo-ooshtuk* and *pe-pe-sati,* have the doubled syllable, implying, no doubt, repeated action. *Yetseh-yetsah* and *yetseh-yetsoklch* have been already mentioned. *Maht-mahs* means "all the houses" or "the entire population," *mahte* or *mahs* being the word for a single "house" or "settlement." The significance of the following terminals must be considered as only implying a general rule, more or less liable to exception. Instruments end in *ik*—as *hukkaik,* "a knife;" *hissik,* "a saw;" *kleetchaik,* "a rudder." Colours end in *uk* or *ook,* as *ey-yoh-quk,* "green; *kistokkuk,* "blue;" *klay-hook,* "purple;" *kleesook,* "white;" *toop-kook,* "black" (*hissit,* "red," is an exception).

Trees and grasses end in *pt*, as *kow-whipt*, *see-whipt*, *ootsmupt*, *klakkupt*, *klakkamupt*, and many others.

Genera end in *oop* and *toop*, as *eesh-toop*, "household things;" *sush-toop*, "beasts of the forest;" *tel-hoop*, "fishes of the sea." The word *kleetstoop* means "blankets," in contradistinction to the special name given to each blanket according to its colour.

Verbs often end in *shitl*, *shetl*, and *chitl*. This termination is, on the whole, well-marked, though exceptions are very numerous. It would, in fact, be more correct to say that these endings, when occurring, are generally found in verbs, than to call them verbal terminations. They probably imply action or movement. Thus, apart from verbs, we meet with these ultimates in *kleeshitl*, (from *kleesook*, "white,") "the growing light of morning which comes before sunrise;" in *toopshitl*, (*toop-kook*, "black,") "the increasing darkness of sunset and immediately after;" and in *moolshitl*, "the flood, or flowing tide."

The most common termination in the language is *lh*. It is difficult to assign any uniform meaning to this termination. I have sometimes thought that it expresses the application of the meaning of a general word to a word of a more particular import. Thus *ey-yoh-quilh*, the usual term of the Ahts for a green blanket, means "a green one." The general term for blanket, as named above, is *kleetstoop*; as this word has no apparent connection with *ey-yoh-quilh*, and as the Ahts use now almost exclusively blankets for dress, we must suppose that in saying "a green one," they are referring to their usual and almost only covering. The word for a black blanket is *toopkulh*; for white, *kleeselh*; for red, *klayhulh*; (*klayhoòk* is purple, *hissoolh* is bloody.) *Attalh* or *uttalh* is an Aht word for black, evidently formed from *attyh* or *uttyh*, night.

Terminations in *up* seem to convey the meaning of loss, curtailment, injury, as *châ-tay-up*, "to cut off with a knife;" *kââsup*, "to hurt, to wound;" *hy-yusatyup*, "to lessen or diminish;" *kawkushup*, "sickness of the eyes;" *ash-sup* "to break a cord or string;" *quoy-up* "to break a stick."

The Nitinaht Dialect.

Among the various tribes living round Nitinaht (or Barclay) Sound, that called the Nitinahts is the largest tribe of all those both round the Sound and on the coast. The Nitinahts live on the seaboard close to the Sound, and it is worthy of remark that they have more words and changes of verbal form peculiar to themselves than any other of the Aht tribes. Their speech differs more from that of the other tribes in Nitinaht (or Barclay) Sound than from the speech of the tribes immediately north of the Sound, though the latter are farther removed from them. This probably arises from the circumstance of the seaboard tribes of the Ahts having more intercourse with the tribes of other nations of Indians speaking different languages than the Aht tribes have who live inside the large Sounds. The Nitinaht tribe, known specially by that name, is nearer to the Indians on the other side of the Strait of Juan de Fuca; and, additionally, as being a powerful tribe, represses, to a certain degree, the foreign intercourse of other seaboard tribes, and, therefore, naturally has most mixture of language, as the Nitinahts most visit and are visited by foreigners. Also, both Nitinahts and all other seaboard tribes have more foreign intercourse than the tribes living inside the Sounds, their position hindering these latter from visiting other nations, and strangers, on their part, being afraid to venture into the Sounds or inland.

In common with several of the seaboard Aht tribes to the north, the Nitinahts have *boouch* (*moouch*) for "deer;" and I have also heard Nitinahts use *atlah-sib*, *tsow-wau-sib*, (*Atlah-sim* and *tsow-wau-sim*) for "eight" and "nine." On the other hand, the tribes inside Nitinaht (or Barclay) Sound use *ahtoosh* and *atlahquill* and *tsow-wauk-quill* respectively for the same, that is, for "deer," "eight" and "nine." The Nitinaht dialect, however, is understood by all the tribes, though now and then one notices that, in conversation with Indians of other tribes of their own nation, the Nitinahts have to repeat their words with some alteration of expression in order to make themselves understood. Much of the difference of their dialect from that of others of the Aht tribes consists in the fact that, in almost every instance, the *m* and *n* of the other tribes are changed by the Nitinahts into *b* and *d*; this, with the frequent abbreviation or expansion of words in composition, often leads to singular alterations. Thus, for the common Aht words *noowayksoh*, "father," and *oomayksoh*, "mother," the Nitinahts have respectively *dooux* and *abahx*; for *quequenixo*, "a hand," they have *kookadooxyeh*; for *nismah*, "country" or "territory," *dissibach*; for *mamook* "to work," *baboik*. Two of the Nitinaht numerals I may remark, *chayukpalh*, "six," and *klah-whа*, "ten," are entirely different from those of the other tribes; the rest are substantially the same.

Cook's List of Nootkah Words.

Any one duly appreciating the difficulty of collecting the words of an unknown language without an interpreter will admire the industry of Mr. Anderson, surgeon of Cook's ship, the *Resolution*, who, in the short space of less than a month, obtained in the neighbourhood of Nootkah some 280 native words. The tribes who live in that neighbourhood, I may state, are the Moouchaht, Ayhuttisaht, Noochahlaht, and these form part of the Aht nation—a fact hitherto unknown. On examining Mr. Anderson's list, I recognize, inclusive of the first ten numerals, 133 words which are substantially the same as words now spoken by the tribes in Nitinaht (or Barclay) Sound. The distance along the coast between Nootkah and Nitinaht is about 90 miles. When from the remaining 147 words in Mr. Anderson's list are deducted those words in which the Nootkah Indians at present differ from the Nitinaht (or Barclay) Sound tribes, and those words in which they may agree, but with which agreement I am unacquainted, it is probable that very little change will be found to have taken place in the Aht language since Cook's visit eighty years ago; perhaps not a greater change than might be observed in the language—say of the south of Scotland, within the last hundred years. It is singular that an unwritten language should have been preserved with so little alteration among tribes so widely scattered, and who have so often opposed each other with deadly hatred.*

* The language of the Indians in the interior of America—commonly called the Indians of the Plain—is constantly changing, owing to their roving habits and intermixture with other tribes. In the case of some of

The curious pronunciation remarked upon by Mr. Anderson as only approximately represented by *lozth* may have been somewhat altered and simplified by lapse of time, or it may be a peculiarity not shared by those of the Aht tribes best known to me. The words spelt by him according to that pronunciation are now pronounced in different instances as *thl*, *lth*, or *lh*, or are at least nearly represented by such a combination of letters; not very different, after all, from Mr. Anderson's pronunciation, only I cannot distinguish the sound of *s* or *z*. I quite recognize what Mr. Anderson means when he says, "It is formed by clashing the tongue partly against the roof of the mouth with considerable force, and may be compared to a very coarse or harsh method of lisping." I do not, however, recognize an actual lisp, which would, of course, imply the presence of a sibilant. In Mr. Anderson's vocabulary I find, without any very careful examination, a few words either erroneously set down by him, or which have since changed their meaning. The error (if any) in one or two cases may easily be explained. I here give a few words, as set down by Mr. Anderson, and also their present pronunciation and meaning:—

MR. ANDERSON'S WORDS.	PRESENT WORDS.
Nootkah.	Nitinaht (or Barclay) Sound.
Opulszhl, "the sun."	*Hoop-palh*, "the moon."
Onalszthl, "the moon."	*Nas*, "the sun."
Tsechkah, "a general song."	*Tseka*, "to speak, say, or sing."

these tribes, the vocabulary of a missionary is of little use to his successor after the lapse of a dozen years. The Coast Indians, on the other hand, remain for generations—perhaps for centuries—on one spot, and their language, consequently, is less susceptible of alteration, notwithstanding the effect of the coast intercourse before alluded to.

Mr. Anderson's Words.	Present Words.
Nootkah.	Nitinaht (or Barclay) Sound.
Haweelsth, or *Hawalth*, "friendship, friend."	*How-wilh*, "chief."
Eineetl, "goat, deer."	*Ahtoosh*, or, *Moouch*, "deer."
Okumha, "the wind."	*Ennitl*, "dog."
Tchoo, "throw it down."	*Wikseh*, "wind."
Jakops, "a man."	*Tchoo*, "incites to any sort of action."
Nahei, *Naheis*, "friendship."	*Chekoop*, "a husband."
Ta-eetcha, "full, satisfied with eating."	*Ko-us*, "a man."
	Nahay, *Nahais*, "give or to give."
	Teech, "well; not sick."
	Teechah, "I am well."

The present meaning of *tush-she* is "a door-way," the same word being applied to any gangway, and also to a track or road in the woods. *Mooshussem* is "a door or lid." For *klao* or *klao-appi*, a word of likely occurrence in barter with Indians, Mr. Anderson has "keep it," or "I'll not have it," having, I daresay, assigned that meaning to the word from the evident dissatisfaction expressed by the person using it. The real meaning of *klao* is "another," or "something else;" and *klao-appi* means "substitute something else." The expression, therefore, does not convey so much a refusal of the article offered in barter as a request that something else more acceptable should be produced. *Klao*, or *klah-oh*, is a word which enters frequently into the speech of the Ahts, and always with the signification of "another" or "some more." *Ah-ah-tomah-klah-oh Oliver* is a literal rendering of "Oliver asks for more." *Ohkullik*, or *ohquinnik*, set down by Mr. Anderson as the general term for "box," is now used only to describe a box with double sides, the inner ones sliding out. The *innik* or *ullik* gives the idea of duality; *klah-hix* is the common term for "a box;"

klah-haytsoh for one having a lid fitting over the sides. The word *allee*, or *alla*, which Mr. Anderson translates "friend," or "hark ye," is the same as the present Nitinaht (or Barclay) Sound *anni*, and the Chinook *annah*, the transition from *n* to *l*, easy in all languages, being particularly so in the Aht language, in which a sound often lies halfway between two kindred consonants. The exact meaning of *anni* is "look." It is connected with the reply generally made to it, *anni-mah*, "I see;" with *cheh-neh*, "I do not know," or, more literally, "I do not see," or "have not seen;" and also, no doubt, with the Chinook *nanich*, "to see;" and many other words in which the same root may be traced. The word *kaweebt*, applied by Mr. Anderson to the wild raspberry, is now used by the Ahts for a very common and well-known berry-bush, to which the colonists give the name of "the salmon-berry." Though not the wild raspberry, it is of the same order of plants, and not unlike it in appearance, and when in flower might easily be mistaken for the wild raspberry.

Affinity of the Indian Languages on the North-West Coast.

An adequate acquaintance with the Indian languages spoken in Vancouver Island, and on the north-west coast of the continent, would throw a trustworthy and most interesting light on the early history of the different nations of Indians; at least on so much of their early history as consisted in their migrations. On this point, however, I will confine my observations to the people on the outside coast of the island, with whom I happen to be acquainted. A cursory notice is sufficient to prove to the traveller the close similarity of the languages of all the Aht tribes, and, therefore, the relationship of the people; and he is surprised, on going along the coast towards the north of the island, where no great physical obstruction prevents communication between the different tribes, to find a boundary, as it were, beyond which the speech of the Aht people (phonetically, at least,) is so much changed, that even numerals and other radical forms have no appearance of similarity. I hesitate to affirm that the several languages in Vancouver Island are absolutely distinct, for I have not closely studied the whole of them. The contrast I speak of, in reference to the Aht language, appears about Cape Scott, at the northern end of Vancouver Island, where this language meets the language of the Quoquoulth (the Indians of the north and north-east of the island); and the contrast appears again towards the south end of the island at some point between Pacheenah and Victoria, where the Aht language comes into abrupt contact with the Kowitchan, or dialects of the Kowitchan. But though these points, north and south, are the limits of the districts in which the Aht language proper in Vancouver Island is spoken, the same language probably crosses the Straits of Juan de Fuca, and is traceable, with gradual and increasing alterations, through all the tribes along the ocean-coast, from about Cape Flattery to the mouth of the Columbia River. There is a decided resemblance between the Aht language and many words of the Chinook jargon, which is a portion of the language of the now almost extinct Chinook tribes at the mouth of the Columbia River, supplemented by words of other tribal dialects on the north-west coast; also by French, English, Hawaian, and, perhaps (but of these I am doubtful), Spanish words. The real Chinook was the first coast language of the north-west coast languages that was learned by settlers and traders on the banks near the mouth of the Columbia River; and a portion of it was afterwards incorporated into a barbarous jargon, to facilitate communication with other natives.* I know about 100 words of the Chinook jargon, and probably 500 of the Aht language, and among these, without research, I can recall the following parallels:—

Chinook.	Aht.
Mowitch, "a deer"	*Moouch*, "a deer"
Syah, "far away"	*Si-yah*, "far away."
Kloosh, "good"	*Kloothl*, "good."
Chuk, "water"	*Chu-uk*, "water." *Tsu-uk*, "a river."
Kumtax, "to understand"	*Kumotop*, "to understand."
Nanich, "to see"	*Nanetsah*, "to see." *Yetspannich*, "to walk out and see."
Hyas, "great"	*Eher*, "great."
Hy-ya, "a great many"	*Ei-yeh*, "a great many." *Hyemmah*, "a great many." *Hy-yu*, "ten, *i. e.*, the highest number one can count on the fingers."
Chako, "to come"	*Chookwah*, "come."
Klootchman, "a woman"	*Klootsmah*, "a married woman." *Klootchmoop*, "a sister."
Wayk, "no, not"	*Wik, wiklyt, wikah, waykomah*, "no, not."
Wah-wah, "to speak"	*Wah*, "to speak."
Keekilly "low, deep down"	*Keekqulh*, "submerged."

Many other words suggest themselves, not showing such an evident similarity, but still conclusive to one knowing something of the Aht language. The similar ity to the Chinook is contained often in some composite word,

* This is the real origin of the Chinook jargon, in reference to which one writer after another copies the conventional nonsense that the Hudson Bay Company "invented" it. Such an achievement as the invention of a language is beyond the capabilities of even a chief factor.

where the resemblance has been almost entirely lost in the expression of the more simple idea. Thus—to take a partial instance from one of the parallels just adduced—the word *nanetsah* retains, indeed, the radical *nan* found in the Chinook *nanich*, but has a different termination. The Chinook termination, however, has remained in the Aht composite word *yetspannich*, a word which means "to go out and look about," and is applied to any one strolling about without any apparent object. In like manner, the Chinook roots *chuk, tsuk*, enter continually into Aht composite words, and convey a reference to water; *wik* and *wayk*, in composition, imply a negative; and *nan* and *an*, similarly, imply sight; and *kloothl* implies good—thus showing a much more intimate connection between the Chinook and Aht tongues than the mere similarity of a few words, not in a composite form, would suggest. It may be objected that the Aht Indians, a few of whom know something of the Chinook jargon, may have introduced some of the words among their own words; but, with any knowledge of the languages, it seems impossible to hold this opinion. The Ahts know perhaps fewer of the Chinook words than any other Indians in the island, and yet the other Vancouver Indian languages do not, so far as I know, exhibit the same similarity to the Chinook. The Ahts have absolutely no other word for water than *chu-uk*, and it is not likely that they would have adopted the Chinook word, and entirely lost their own term for such a common necessary.

The various tribes of the Aht nation differ a little, but a very little, in their language; each tribe having some few words quite peculiar to itself. One of these differences affords fair evidence of the reality of the relation between the Aht and the Chinook; the difference to which I allude is the variation in the term for deer among different Aht tribes. Those Aht tribes which have, in modern times, seen most of the white man, and, therefore, heard most of Chinook, inhabit Nitinaht (or Barclay) Sound. The name which the tribes in that locality have for a deer is *ahtoosh*, but other Aht tribes more to the north, who have heard less of Chinook than the others—tribes such as the Ahousaht or Moouchaht—call a deer *moouch*, which has a very close likeness to the Chinook *mowitch*. This similarity of an important word in the two tongues existing among those Aht tribes ignorant of Chinook, and which happens not to be found in the language of the tribes who know Chinook, is one proof of an old connection of the Aht and Chinook languages. I have said that, in Cook's list of words, made eighty years ago, a general resemblance of the two languages is found; and I may here add that an intelligent Indian on the west coast of the island has remarked to me upon the similarity of the Aht and the Chinook, without any suggestion from me; also, that the conclusion thus independently formed is confirmed by those traders who are most familiar with the dialects spoken along the coast. Being altogether unacquainted with the neighbouring languages on the nearest American territory, I do not know whether the Aht form of language has kept merely to the ocean coast, or has in any instance penetrated into the interior of the country. I should expect to find that it adhered to the coast; but, no doubt, the course of the language might be altered and directed inland by such a feature as a great river, or a range of mountains. The distance, following the ocean coast, from Cape Scott in Vancouver Island to the Columbia River, which, so far as I know, is the range of the Aht language, is about 400 miles. I have not attempted to trace the language outside of these limits, and I can form no opinion whether the Aht people spread originally from the Columbia River, along the coast towards the north, or whether they spread south from the west coast of Vancouver Island.

Tribal Names.

The Indians relate that Quawteaht gave names to most or all of the things on land, and in the sky, and sea; and that he, also, is the author of their tribal names. The terminal of all the tribal names, namely, *aht*, is the terminal of Quawteaht's own name. This story of the Indians is a myth; the tribal names probably were adopted to describe the principal features of some locality, or in honour of a great chief. It is possible that the affix *aht*, which terminates the tribal names, is identical with *maht*, *mahte*, or *mahs*, which are words respectively meaning "house." The word *mahte* is not only applied to the material building, but also to the settlement or population. *Maht-mahs* (the reduplication being their only way of forming a plural) means "the whole population," or "all the settlements." The word *Ishinnikquaht*, "next door," or "next house," is an instance of *aht* in composition, giving to the composite word the meaning of "house," as *Ishinnik* means "with," "close to," "next to." *Quisaht*, abbreviated compound of *quispah* and *mahte*, signifies "the further settlements"—*quispah* meaning "further," or "on the other side," and *mahte* meaning "house," as above stated.

The natives do not apply the tribal name, with its

terminal *aht*, to the district owned by the tribe, but only to the village and people. The Seshaht territory is called Sesh; that of Ohyaht, Ohy; that of Pacheenaht, Pacheen. It is not unreasonable to suppose that all the names of the tribes were significant when first applied; and, in spite of the legend of Quawteaht, we may be inclined to believe that each new settlement, as it was formed, received its name from some particular feature of the locality, or some notable occurrence connected with the new establishment. When we find in the language *noochee*, "mountain;" *moouch*, "deer;" *klah-oh*, "another;" *koquahowsah*, "a seal;" it seems reasonable to recognise in the tribal appellations of *Noochahlaht*, *Moouchaht*, *Klah-oh-quaht*, *Ahousaht*, names which will bear the simple translations, "mountain-house," "deer-house," "another house," "seal-house." Several other tribal names of the Ahts seem to be significant, though not quite so obviously as the above. The Indian's mode of forming a name is often difficult to trace, as a long word is sometimes represented in composition by only a single syllable, or even a single letter.

CHAPTER XVI.

A GREAT DEER HUNT.

The Waw-win—a great Deer Hunt.

Rare work! all filled with terror and delight.—Cowley.

It is not of much use going out to shoot deer on the west coast without the assistance of an Indian. One may walk alone, day after day, over the rough wooded mountains without raising a deer, while an Indian on the same ground will get several shots. After trying all the usual ways of shooting deer—by stalking them on the hills, by lying in ambush, and by pushing them out of covert, I arranged for a great deer hunt at Alberni in February, 1864.* Nearly

* "*Eheu fugaces, Postume, Postume, Labuntur anni!*" Alas! do not our fleeting years too quickly end! Which of my welcome friends, Anderson, Ker, Connell, Gaskell—men of the right kidney, each one—does not remember the glorious days spent in the chase at Alberni, and the hearth piled with well-dried logs that greeted our return?

"But ye whom social pleasure charms,
Whose hearts the tide of kindness warms,
Who hold your *being* on the terms,
'Each aid the others,'
Come to my bowl, come to my arms,
My friends, my brothers!"

a whole tribe of Indians took part in this *waw-win*, as they call it; as far as I could judge, there were about ninety men in the forest, and half of them were armed with guns. This grand battue is called by the natives *waw-win*, from the word *waw*, which means to speak or shout. The practice is for a number of Indians to spread over a district and drive the deer with shouts through the forest towards some lake or arm of the sea, on the banks of which they are killed, and canoes are kept in readiness to capture or drive back those that are bold enough to attempt escape by swimming. The deer I speak of is the black-tailed deer; I have never known the wapiti to be captured in a *waw-win*. The wapiti is not found in such numbers as the black-tailed deer, nor does the wapiti often come near the coast, where only a *waw-win* can take place, near some large village.

There had been heavy falls of snow, and the Indians were certain that many deer had come down from the higher mountains, and would be found on the side of a great, rugged, wooded hill, which rose steep from the Alberni inlet. A swollen torrent, rising from a source inland, flowed across the back of this hill, and, at the southern extremity of the hill, this torrent fell into the Alberni inlet. The hill itself occupied about two miles of frontage on the inlet. Thus the reader will perceive that there was but one side, the north one, left open for the inland escape of the deer—in fact like the base of a triangle. On this base, if I may so call it, at certain intervals, men were placed to hem in the deer, and then advance and drive them forward into the corner or apex of the triangle, where the torrent fell into the Alberni inlet. When driven into this spot the deer were to be shot. This base was probably about a mile in length. The sloping face of the hill measured about a thousand feet; its surface was broken by ravines and hollows, by precipices and huge masses of rock, all of which were hidden by the forest, and to be seen only as one came upon them in walking. These irregularities of the surface favoured the growth of many clumps of young fir trees, and among these the deer found shelter. It was common to have a *waw-win* hunt on this hill, when deer were wanted for some great intertribal feast.

The Indians spent the evening before the day appointed for the hunt in dancing and singing, and in various ceremonies intended to secure good luck on the morrow. We, on our part, cleaned our rifles, and got to bed soon. About two o'clock in the morning, the Indians assembled on the hill, and occupied the base line above described. They took no dogs with them. I crossed the inlet in a canoe, with three other gentlemen, and reached the ground about two hours later. The Indians did not appear to be under the command of any one, nor did they advance in any order, but straggled forward, beating the bushes and pushing through the clumps of young trees, shouting loudly all the time. It was very cold and very fatiguing work, as we laboured over fallen trees and occasionally sank deep into the snow. I often wished I had left my rifle at home, for it was heavy to carry, and we saw few deer, and could not fire, owing to the danger of hitting the men. I had landed on the north part of the hill, at one end of the base line spoken of, and I had intended to proceed from man to man of the Indians as they advanced, that I might notice their proceedings. This plan would have brought me to some point of the torrent at the back of the hill, but I soon found that the Indians advanced too quickly to allow me to carry it out. If I had persevered in my attempt to do so, I should have been left behind, and have been quite out of the way of witnessing the result when the deer were hemmed in at the south of the hill, where they were to be shot down.

As we went on, the Indians collected into twos and threes and fours, which was a sign that the line was being shortened, and the hunters were pushed one against another. The excitement was now great among all the Indians that I saw; they laughed, and yelled, and redoubled their exertions to start the deer, and we occasionally heard muskets cracking along the line. The effect of all this manœuvring now began to be seen; a herd of twenty or thirty deer came bounding over the snow towards us, and, being greeted with terrific yells, turned and fled. I had never been quite able to keep up with the Indians, few white men could; and now as the noise and excitement and the musketry increased, I decided on not advancing much farther towards the angle we were approaching, lest the fate of William Rufus should overtake me. The surface of the side of the hill was so broken, and the trees were so numerous and large, that one could see only a small bit of ground anywhere. The deer seemed now so desperate as to have lost their timidity; many broke through the line of their enemies and escaped.

From the top of a mass of rock on which I was glad to rest, I saw beneath me a bare patch of the hill-side; beyond that the forest again, and farther down still a low gravelly point without trees, which formed the angle at the meeting of the torrent with the inlet. A few canoes were floating about as if waiting for something. The shouting and yelling, and a confused noise of voices and of feet trampling the branches of prostrate trees, were now heard on every side. Deer leapt wildly across the bare patch and disappeared in the wood beyond, followed by Indians excited as only uncivilized men can be; then first one deer, then a few, then more deer trotted out on the gravelly point, and looked about in all directions, and smelt the water. There was soon a large herd on the point, and, in a few minutes, the pursuers began advancing a little along the point and firing. The shooting was very bad, and the deer trotted about for many minutes without losing more than a few of their number. I loaded and fired my rifle as fast as I could; but, being a long way off, probably did little damage. My friends having now come to me, we descended and joined the Indians, in order to bring the morning's work to as speedy a termination as possible. It was extraordinary to notice the carelessness of the Indians; after all their exertions to bring the deer to this place, they allowed nearly one-third of them to escape. A few deer took to the water, but the canoes pursued them, and they were turned back to the shore by blows of the paddles on their heads. The total number killed during this *waw-win* was fifty-three, that is to say, sixteen during the chase and thirty-seven on the point of land. We sat down for a time after the hunt was over, and the Indians had a long talk among themselves to decide how the deer were to be divided. The man whose hunting ground the hill was considered to be—though not a chief—received the largest share of any. The Indians do not much relish deer-meat, and, on this occasion, seemed to value the skins more than any other part of the animal, except for the chance they had of selling the venison to some of the ships at Alberni. We left them discussing the proceedings and the results of the hunt, and went home to our breakfast.

CHAPTER XVII.

MORAL DISPOSITIONS.

The Savage Character—Vindictiveness—Coldbloodedness—Attack on the Elkwhahts—Murder of a Girl—Human Sacrifice—Custom of the Min-okey-ak—Notions about Stealing—Affection for Children—Habitual Suspicion—Want of Foresight—Absence of Faith—Ingratitude—Sincerity of the Indian's Declarations.

Judge from their own mean hearts, and foully wrong mankind.—Southey.

It is very difficult, for a civilized man, to form in his mind a correct estimate of the moral condition of a savage. In one part of his character the savage resembles the lowest members of a civilized community—such as the outcasts in large cities; but another part of his character, inherited through a long succession of moral degradation, unchecked by any surrounding counteracting influences, is unlike anything that can be witnessed even in the most brutalized individual in a civilized community. There is a resemblance, in many respects closer than one likes to admit, between the promptings and habits of uncivilized man and those of the wild beasts which he hunts. The Aht savage seems to the traveller, on a first observation, very like an animal with a superior instinct and the gift of rude speech. Regarding him in that light, or, at least, not quite as a fellow-man, I have been pleased with his conversation, particularly with his account—given in the easy but striking manner characteristic of narrators who are free from drudgery and live much out of doors *—of the ingenious ways in which he captures fish, wild animals, and birds; and it has been only on turning the talk towards other topics—such as the history and destiny of his race in this world, or after death, and on remembering, in connection with these thoughts, that the untutored Indian was a fellow-being—that I have fully realized his actual benighted condition. The first natural impulse of any civilized observer, who judges by recognized standards for appreciating a social and moral condition, is to turn with aversion from a people so degraded as the natives on this coast; but, in my own case, I found that this feeling gradually changed to one of interest and curiosity, after seeing them in their own villages, where all their ways and doings had, at least, the recommendation of being thorough and of being novel. It then appeared that, together with the rude vices of a man always cut off from every external influence of an improving kind, the savage had some qualities that were of a nature to be commended: he was sincere in his friendship, kind to his wife and children, and devotedly loyal to his own tribe. His hospitality and faithfulness to any trust reposed in him were

* No persons equal in power and manner of graphic oral narration, those gentlemen in the Hudson Bay Company's service who have passed the greater part of their lives in the Indian country, remote from all civilized intercourse.

noticeable virtues. I also found, on visiting his house, that he had much more of what was playful and kindly in his nature towards his relatives and friends, than one would expect him to have. And, of course, the more intimately the savage became known to me, the more clearly man, in man's natural condition and proportions, stood forth, exhibiting a character which owed its peculiarity specially to excess or defect in regard to the moral qualities—qualities which he shared with the rest of the human race. These excesses and defects come up before one's mind, in describing his character, far more readily than any good qualities which the Indian possesses. His virtues do not reach our standard, and his vices exceed our standard; so, in reflecting on his character, we naturally think first of his vices, not of his virtues. The prominent characteristics which I have observed in the Ahts are a want of observation, a great deficiency of foresight, extreme fickleness in their passions and purposes, habitual suspicion, and a love of power and display. Added to which may be noticed their ingratitude and revengeful dispositions, their readiness for war, and revolting indifference to human suffering. A murder, if not perpetrated on one of his own tribe, or on a particular friend, is no more to an Indian than the killing of a dog, and he seems altogether steeled against human misery, when found among ordinary acquaintances or strangers. The most terrible sufferings, the most pitiable conditions, elicit not the slightest show of sympathy, and do not interrupt the current of his occupations or his jests for a moment.

Vindictiveness.

The Aht natives are very revengeful, and appear to cherish rancour for a length of time, sometimes for more than one generation. Disputes between individuals lead to implacable family feuds. Though it is usual to accept large presents as expiation for murder, yet, practically, this expiation is not complete, and blood alone effectually atones for blood. An accepted present never quite cancels the obligation to punish in the breast of the offended person or tribe. Many years after the offence, and, generally, when disappointed in some blood-thirsty expedition, these savages will call to mind an old injury, and make it the pretext for a murderous attack on an unsuspecting tribe. An illustration of this is afforded by an occurrence in the Straits of Fuca a few years ago. The Nitinahts, on the Vancouver Island shore, had mustered for an expedition to attack another island tribe near Victoria, but were deterred by the arrival of several ships of war at Esquimalt. These were English ships of war, which, after the unsuccessful attack on Petropaulovski, went to Vancouver Island to refit. Unwilling to go back without heads for trophies, the Nitinahts determined to attack the Elkwhahts, on the south side of the Straits—a tribe against which they bore a grudge for some old injury, but with which people the Nitinahts had, since the injury, been for years on friendly terms. After nightfall, the attackers paddled across the Straits, and drew their canoes over the rocks, into the forest near the Elkwhaht village. It was the fishing season, and a quiet morning in summer. Before the sun rose, the Elkwhahts were out in their canoes fishing, at some distance from the shore. All at once the eager enemy rushed from the forest, dragging their canoes, and, embarking in them, they intercepted the terrified, unarmed fishermen before they could reach the land. The women and children ran out of the houses and shrieked, but there was no battle. In a few minutes the headless bodies of the Elkwhahts were lying in their canoes, which floated here and there, and the victors were paddling across the Straits, singing a death-song.

Coldbloodedness.

I was told by a trustworthy eye-witness of another bloody act, committed at Klah-oh-quaht Sound by a native who is well known to me. My informant, while trading on the coast, stayed to sleep at the village. While at supper, he heard the death-song; and, on going out of the house, found the natives assembling to meet canoes on their return from a warlike expedition. It was clear moonlight, so that everything could be seen. The men landed and danced on the beach, many holding high in one hand a musket, and in the other, several human heads. A few captives were dragged by the hair towards the village. Amongst these were two children, a boy and girl, of about twelve years of age, who had been captured by the Indian alluded to. This savage had been at San Francisco, and could speak a word or two of English. Anybody on the west coast of Vancouver Island knows "trader George" (the Indian in question), the rich merchant of Klah-oh-quaht. Approaching my informant in a state of great excitement, he repeated, "me strong," "me brave," "me very strong heart," and suddenly drew his long knife, and so quickly severed the girl's head that the blood spouted upwards, and the body seemed to steady itself for a moment before it fell. The demon danced with the head in his hand, and pushed on the boy before him. This infernal crime was committed merely to show to the white man that the native warrior had a "strong heart."*

I may mention another atrocity which occurred within a few yards of my house. As a magistrate, I had to take official cognizance of this act. In December, 1864, the Seshaht Indians, then occupying their village close to Alberni, put one of their women to a violent death. The day before they commenced a celebration of a peculiar character, which was to last several days, and the murder of the woman formed, no doubt, a part of this celebration. The woman was stabbed to death by an old man in whose house she lived, and who probably owned her as a slave, and offered her for a victim. The body was then laid out without a covering by the water-side, about a hundred and fifty yards from the houses. There appeared to be no inclination to bury the body, and it was only after the chief had been strongly remonstrated with that the poor victim's remains were removed, after two days' exposure. I observed that even after this removal, certain furious rites took place over the very spot where the body had been exposed. The chief feature of the celebration, apart from the murder, was a pretended attack upon the Indian settlement by wolves, which were represented by Indians, while the rest

* It may be said that in killing this girl, the Klah-oh-quaht only exercised his right as a victor, according to Aht ideas. This, however, is little more than saying that the rest of his tribe were as infernal as himself.

of the population, painted, armed, and with furious shouts, defended their houses from attack. The horrid practice of sacrificing a victim is not annual, but only occurs either once in three years, or else (which is more probable) at uncertain intervals; always, however, when it does happen, the sacrifice takes place during the Klooh-quahn-nah season, which lasts from about the middle of November to the middle of January. The Klooh-quahn-nah or Klooh-quel-lah is a great festival observed annually by all the Aht tribes, after their return from their fishing-grounds to the winter encampment. It is generally a time of mirth and feasting, during which tribal rank is conferred, and homage done to the chief, in a multitude of observances which have now lost their meaning, and cannot be explained by the natives themselves. I was not aware until this murder was committed under our eyes, that human sacrifices formed any part of the Klooh-quahn-nah celebration. I should think it likely that old worn-out slaves are generally the victims. The Seshaht Indians at Alberni represent the practice as most ancient, and the fact that the other tribes of the Aht nation (about twenty in number) observe it, favours this supposition. Their legends somewhat differ as to this practice, some saying that it was instituted by the Creator of the world; others that it arose from the sons of a chief of former times having really been seized by wolves.* To some

* These Indians imitate animals and birds extremely well, such as wolves or crows. At this Klooh-quahn-nah celebration they had their hair tied out from their heads, so as to represent a wolf's head and snout, and the blanket was arranged to show a tail. The motion of the wolf in running was closely imitated. More extraordinary still was their acting as crows; they had a large wooden bill, and blankets arranged so like wings that, in

extent it is a secret institution, the young children not being acquainted with it until formally initiated. Many of them during the horrid rite are much alarmed; the exhibition of ferocity, the firing of guns and shouting, being calculated, and probably intended, to excite their fears. Part of a day is given up to an instruction of those children who are to be initiated, and it is impressed upon them that the Klooh-quahn-nah must always be kept up, or evil will happen to the tribe. The tendency, no doubt, and probably the intention of this human sacrifice, and the whole celebration, is to destroy the natural human feeling against murder, and to form in the people generally, and especially in the rising generation, hardened and fierce hearts. They themselves say that their "hearts are bad," as long as it goes on. In the attendant ceremonies, their children are taught to look, without any sign of feeling, upon savage preparations for war, strange dances performed in hideous masks, and accompanied by unearthly noises, and occasionally, at least, upon the cruel destruction of human life. Although I have no direct evidence of the fact, I believe that part of the course of those to be initiated would be to view, howl over, and perhaps handle, or even stick their knives into the dead body of the victim, without showing any sign of pity or of horror.

A strange belief, of which I could get no explanation, nor learn its origin, existed lately among these people connected with an instrument called min-okey-ak, made of a stone or other hard substance, fastened to the end of

the dusk, the Indians really seemed like large crows hopping about, particularly when, after the manner of these birds, they went into the shallow water, and shook their wings and "dabbed" with their long bills.

a long string. This instrument was supposed to be thrown from an unseen hand, and the person struck by it sickened and died. No one was allowed to live who knew how to make the min-okey-ak. The last person possessing this knowledge among the Ohyahts—the tribe from which I derived this information—was a young man of a family of eight men, and it was resolved at a meeting of the chiefs, that the whole family should be extirpated. On an appointed day, four of the doomed men were asked, one after another, by different individuals to go fishing or hunting, and each was killed by his companion unawares. The other four, on the same day, were invited to a feast, and murderers sat beside them with concealed knives, who, at a given signal, stabbed them to the heart. The women were sold into slavery, and the house and property of the family were destroyed. Since this tragedy, no one among the Ohyahts has known how to make the min-okey-ak.

But enough of these terrible and repulsive scenes! They are atrocities of which it is painful to read, but which, nevertheless, should be placed before the reader, in order to show to him what savages really are, and how blessed are the influences of Christianity and civilization. I turn from these harrowing details to a more general account of various characteristics of the people, which were observed by me during a somewhat lengthened intercourse with them. And, first, as to their notions on the subject of stealing.

Stealing.

Stealing is not sanctioned by public opinion among the Ahts, but they all have a tendency to sympathise with some forms of theft, in which dexterity is required. Chiefs and heads of large families very seldom commit theft; they know the value of a good name, and prefer inciting their poor men to the unlawful act. A chief who himself steals is a very bad chief indeed. Larceny of a fellow-tribesman's property is rarely heard of, and the aggravation of taking it from the house or person is almost unknown. When the thief and loser are of the same tribe, the loser either retaliates, or, by feeing the chief, induces him to use his offices in recovering the property. In cases of theft from another tribe, the chief of the tribe to which the offending native belongs, on receiving a remonstrance, either compels him to make restitution, or himself pays the value for the honour of his people. On the other hand, anything left under an Indian's charge, in reliance on his good faith, is perfectly safe; he takes a pride in returning every separate article that was given to him. I must not, however, be understood to say that thieving from other tribes is unusual among the Ahts; on the contrary, it is a common vice where the property of other tribes, or white men, is concerned. But it would be unfair to regard thieving among these savages as culpable, in the same degree, as among ourselves. They cannot understand the considerations on which we desire to protect among ourselves the rights of property. Nor have they any knowledge of a moral or social law forbidding the act. Thieving, that is, intertribal thieving, has been commonly practised among the tribes for many generations. In addition to which, we should consider how strong the temptation to steal must have become when articles of civilized manufacture—curious tools of iron, saving the wearied arm many months of labour—were first introduced to their sight, and left about carelessly before them. I think that discriminating laws should be made. It is unjust, and therefore, in the long run, useless, to punish the Aht savages according to our law for some offence which they do not regard as an offence, and which, at all events, is committed under conditions not contemplated by the framers of the law. The efficacy of human punishments lies, in a great degree, in the public opinion concerning them; and certainly the savages on this coast think that our imprisonments and hangings are nothing but the arbitrary and harsh exercises of superior power. Men whom they think innocent are hanged, and those whom they consider guilty often escape.

Affection for Children.

I have been pleased often to notice the affection of the Indian fathers for their children, and how proud they are in remarking any skill in their childish amusements. Undoubtedly they have, in general, strong love for their relations, most of all for their children. They never beat them, and I have known many instances of fathers taking home for their children little dainties which it required an exercise of self-denial to abstain from. Should they suffer the loss of those they love, the women howl and lament; the men nurse their sorrow, and show, by altered demeanour, and even loss of flesh and health, their inward affliction. At the same time, this love is not connected with thoughtfulness and care for the sick, who, as is described in a chapter of this book, if not neglected, are often treated with utter disregard to their comfort.

Habitual Suspicion.

Like other wild men, the hand of the Aht Indian has been against every man—so far as he has felt it consistent with his own safety; and, as a natural consequence, his eye is ever on the watch against the hostility of others. His thought, when he comes in contact with any but the few who are within the circle of his bosom friends, is, "How can I turn this person to my own account, and how can I defend myself from his design against me?" For, to his credit (as far as it goes), it must be allowed, that he does not for a moment believe that he is sacrificing a confiding or honest person, but sets down all appearance of unguardedness either to folly or simulation. The Indian is educated by his necessities, by his fears, and by his experience of human nature within the range of his own observation. His countenance apparently of studied self-command, his watchful concealed glances, his suspicions developed upon every occasion, show a character lying, as it were, in ambush. The power of self-command possessed by savages seems to me to have been over-estimated. It is great up to a certain point, both over the countenance and over the emotions; but in reality it is much inferior to that of civilized men, though a first acquaintance with the stern manner of savages would lead one to believe the contrary. When their composure is once broken through by the assault of feeling, all their self-possession is gone, and they become the sudden slaves of fear, anger, or the like. Their nerve, under ordinary, and perhaps even under extraordinary, circumstances, is naturally strong; but, when once it gives way, they have no adequate counteracting moral power to sustain them.

Want of Foresight.

I may mention, also, deficiency of foresight as a leading and evident component of the moral habit of the Aht savages—a deficiency which weakens their virtues, and partially palliates many of their vices. The possessor of a civilized education and an enlightened conscience does not act without bearing in mind, in a general way, the probable consequence of his deeds, both to himself and others; in the main, his actions, whether good or evil, are deliberate and wilful. But, with the exception of following certain inherited habits necessary for very existence, the Indian does not appear to exercise to any adequate extent his power of reflecting on and acting for the future; impending dangers, and near and sensible advantages, of course exercise their influence; but the advantage of acting strenuously for a result which he considers uncertain, is altogether unrecognised. Even his cunning calculations and attempts at deception, most clever and complete in themselves, are simple and short-sighted, and remind one almost as much of the instincts of the animal, as of the exercise of human powers. In this want of inclination and ability to prepare for and mould the circumstances of the future, we find, perhaps, not so much a characteristic of the people on this coast, as a leading cause of the long-continued uncivilized condition of barbarous nations generally.

Absence of Faith.

Another great impediment to these natives advancing as a people, by ameans very conducive to their progress,—that is, by their becoming tillers of the soil,—exists in their impatience of delay or any long expectation. If they could only learn the lesson of trustfulness and hope taught to the farmer by seed-time and harvest, the improvement of their moral condition would have begun, probably on a good foundation. The almost entire absence of faith and hope is, indeed, among these natives a striking and painful defect. They will work hard as long as the goal of their efforts is almost, or quite, within sight and as long as they have no sort of hesitation as to the adequacy of their strength or skill. They have no faith in any kind of help but their own, and none of the hope which often enables civilized men to contend to the last against circumstances, and sometimes to pull through against all likelihood. In sickness and approaching death, the savage always becomes melancholy. The prospect of Chay-her, the land of departed spirits, has no comfort or relief for the Aht savage then; the only good thing he has ever felt sure of is the life which he is about to part with, and consequently his only desire is, to meet with some one who will restore him to health.

Ingratitude.

Ingratitude is a vice which is commonly attributed to these Indians by those who know them well. It is unpleasant to have to deny, even to a savage fellow-creature, the possession of such a virtue as gratitude, which is shared by many of the inferior animals; but it must be stated that those persons best acquainted with the character of the Aht Indians agree in no respect more completely than in complaining of their ingratitude. I have concurrent testimony on this point from Indian agents and traders who spoke their language tolerably well, and who have been a good deal among them. Their belief is, that you may feed a hungry Indian, tend him when sick, or save his life, and he will afterwards ridicule or rob you, as if you had never been kind to him. The sensibilities of the natives, they say, are so rude that what, according to our notions, is kindness, does not seem to the savages to demand any acknowledgment on their part.

To this strong general testimony I will not offer a decided opposition; but I think that, generally, civilised men are apt to expect too much from a savage, and, being disappointed, are ready to deny the good which, perhaps, really exists in his nature. As I have said several times in this book, it is a most difficult matter, even for observant and thoughtful men, to understand the character of a savage, or to gain so much of his confidence as to induce him to lay aside his habitual reserve. A particular feature of the character of the Aht Indian is the manner in which he gives or withholds the expression of his affections. Great weight is attached to a declaration of friendship, and still more, perhaps, to that of sorrow for another's misfortune or death. Among civilised people, announcements of friendship or sympathy are accepted as matters of form, and people look for signs of reality in something beyond these ordinary expressions. But in the Indian's declaration of personal feeling, every syllable is weighty; you are not supposed for a moment to doubt his word, nor he to be capable of falsifying. Such earnest expressions, it is true, may not uniformly be followed by constancy, but, at the time they are made, they are generally sincere; the Indian, in such a declaration, lays aside his usual pride and caution, and this sacrifice is the pledge of his sincerity.

The Ahts have, it is true, no word for gratitude, but a defect in language does not absolutely imply defect in heart; and the Indian who, in return for a benefit received, says, with glistening eyes, that "his heart is good" towards his benefactor, expresses his gratitude quite as well perhaps as the Englishman who says, "Thank you." The measure of the Indian's gratitude, I think, should be taken by more accurate means—by a study of the immediate working of his heart, so far as one can reach it, and from observation of his conduct after gratitude has been expressed. Two points of character throw light upon the subject. The Indian's *suspicion* prevents a ready gratitude, as he is prone to see, in apparent kindness extended to him, some under-current of selfish motive. His *reserve* prevents a frequent expression of gratitude—such expression being kept for great occasions. Again, his mind, occupied much with the present, and what is immediately useful to him, makes him judge another, and treat him according to his own interpretation of that other's behaviour, without much consideration either of past kindness or past hostility. Further, the Indian is not, in general, very grateful for assistance which, in his view, costs the giver nothing—however useful or necessary the assistance afforded. A person may keep an Indian from starving all the winter through, yet, when summer comes, very likely he will not walk a yard for his preserver without payment. The savage does not, in this instance, recognise any obligation; but thinks that a person who had so much more than he could himself consume might well, and without any claim for after services, part with some of it for the advantage of another in want. This view, considered from an abstract point, is true; still the recipient of kindness, either savage or civilised, ought to entertain feelings—strong feelings of gratitude towards the benefactor who has thus acted out right principles. The savage's judgment is right—his feeling is deficient. In justice it must be said that the Indian would often similarly succour any one in need of his help, and not look for any ulterior benefit. His gratitude shines best—and in this he shows his discernment—when he thinks that behind the kindly act he can discern a really friendly heart. He is accustomed, among his own people, to gifts made for purposes of guile, and also to presents made merely to show the greatness and richness of the giver; but, I imagine, when the Aht ceases to suspect such motives—when he does not detect pride, craft, or carelessness—he is grateful, and probably grateful in proportion to the trouble taken to serve him.

CHAPTER XVIII.

SORCERERS.

Some account of the Sorcerers or "Medicine-men."

Go to!
You are a subtile nation, you physicians.—BEN JONSON.

THERE is a class of persons among the Ahts who pretend to possess extraordinary powers, and who, without having any tribal rank, are extremely influential. I have not been quite able, in my own mind, to assign a position to these sorcerers, nor to determine exactly the connection of their practices with the religion of the people. I think these sorcerers may, in many respects, be called devil-priests; that is to say, their influence is supposed to be with those spirits which the natives believe to be evil rather than with those which they believe to be good. The general practice of the people is to address the good deities direct, without the agency of the sorcerers; for instance, standing alone in the forest, they pray to the moon for abundance of food or for health, or security, but when the powers of evil—the avenging deities, who are supposed to bring misfortune, sickness, and famine—have to be propitiated, the natives always seek the intervention of the sorcerers. I do not say that they never employ the sorcerers in addressing the good deities, but only that the influence of these impostors is believed to be more efficient with the evil spirits. This employment of agents to deal with evil spirits is found amongst savage men generally. Of course the savage, as every human being, is now by nature an alien to God, and the peculiar circumstances surrounding his daily life lead to the development of this innate feeling of alienation. He discerns faintly the phenomena which produce good effects, but sees and feels with terrible distinctness the ravages of cruelty, suffering and death; and being unable to conceive that Quawteaht, the beneficent spirit, permits such evils to afflict mankind, the savage turns with instinctive terror to propitiate the demons by which he believes these miseries are inflicted.

The sorcerers among the Ahts, in their pretensions and practices, seem to me to have a greater general resemblance to the inferior Lamas in Tartary than to any other class of which I have read. The Mongolian belief in the transmigration of souls, in the cause of sickness, in the power of the Lamas to expel the visiting demon *Tchutgour* (query, the Aht *Chay-her*,) by incantations and yelling; the duplicity and imposture of the Lamas, and their horrible ceremonies, might indeed be almost transferred without alteration from M. Huc's narrative to these pages. The common doctor of the Ahts is called *Ooshtuk-yu*, the "worker," and the sorcerer *Kau-koutsmah-hah*, the "influencer of souls." The "worker" and the old women act as doctors in ordinary cases, but the "influencer of souls" is required in times of great bodily or mental trouble, and in fact, on every unusual occasion, whether individual or tribal. The sorcerer professes and undertakes to bring back truant souls into bodies that have been bereft of them; also to effect interchanges of souls, to interpret dreams, to explain prophecies, to cast out demons, and to restore the body to health. The sorcerer seldom gains tribal rank, but appears to be content with his actual power, and with the fees which he extorts from his dupes. There is not, so far as I could ascertain, among these sorcerers, as there is said to be among those of some other savages, any peculiar sorcerers' dialect, or set of terms unknown to the rest of the people, in which they can converse together on the subject of their professed art, nor are their supposed personal gifts dependent on family descent. Practically they vary their ceremonies and treatment to suit their own purposes; but there must be some prescribed rules of action in which the young sorcerers are instructed. The sorcerers are obliged, for their own sake, to do extraordinary things, or they would soon be looked upon as ordinary persons. For some reason they have less power among the Ahts than among the tribes farther north on the coast of British Columbia; in several tribes known to me there is no *Kau-koutsmah-hah*, (influencer of souls), but only a common *Ooshtuk-yu* (worker). I have seen the sorcerers at work a hundred times, but they use so many charms, which appear to me ridiculous,—they sing, howl, and gesticulate in so extravagant a manner, and surround their office with such dread and mystery,—that I am quite unable to describe their performances. The ceremonies of the sorcerers formed the only phase of savage life—marked as it is by repulsive features—which I could not bring my mind by any effort to study; the whole thing was so foolish, meaningless, and pretentious. It is undoubtedly a fact, however, that many of these sorcerers themselves thoroughly believe in their own supernatural powers, and are able, in their preparations and practices, to endure excessive fatigue, want of food, and intense prolonged mental excitement. Their practices among the tribes most under their influence comprise almost everything which subtle wickedness can devise for the purpose of terrifying and controlling the ignorant. The whole gamut of the most frightful noises which the human voice, the collision of hard substances, and the beating of bearskin drums can produce, is run up and down by them with ease. The howling of the Aht sorcerers is perfectly demoniacal; no wild beast could utter sounds so calculated to strike sudden terror into the heart. While in perfect security, I have shuddered at the yells of these savage men. One of their practices is to absent themselves from the encampment of the tribe, for a time, to fast in the forest, and suddenly to appear, naked and almost fleshless, with lacerated bodies, and foam on their lips, uttering cries and sounding rattles and drums. Their heads are, on such occasions, covered with frightful masks. The natives rise from their occupations on seeing the sorcerers approach, and run from their presence to seek the shelter of the houses, where they cower in silence. Outside, the demons howl, and leap through the village; then, on a sudden, all of them make a rush and close together, like wolves over a prey;

sometimes it is a dead human being, or a living dog, which is torn asunder by their hands and carried off in their teeth. Excepting, perhaps, the human sacrifice at the Klooh-quahn-nah season (see pages 155 to 157), which horrid custom is supported by these impostors, the devilry just described is one of the worst practices of the sorcerers. They have milder methods, however, of keeping up their influence and filling their boxes; and having described one of their worst ways, I will mention another of a less objectionable nature.

As all the people are credulous, they are easily deceived by any shrewd fellow who desires, by some exercise of his wits, to obtain increased wealth and higher consideration. A clever practitioner, just before the herring, salmon, or berry season, will get it spread about that he has dreamt there will be great quantities of berries or fish at some particular places, the knowledge of which he keeps secret. By various ceremonies, such as abstaining from ordinary food, washing himself unusually well, and walking in lonely places at night, he will manage to persuade the ignorant and weak-minded members of his tribe that he is doing a great work, that he is inducing the berries to grow and the fish to come to be caught. This he will make the ground for levying a species of tax; and the curious part of it is, that, whether the berries and fish are plentiful or not, this "Artful Dodger" gets, not only higher social consideration, but douceurs of berries and fish throughout the season. I have known him get two-thirds of a canoe-load of the fish that were first caught in the season.

Any account of the Aht sorceries would be incomplete

which did not mention the old women, with their coarse skins, blear eyes, and shambling gait.

> . . . Dire faces, figures dire
> Sharp-elbowed and lean-ankled too.

They are generally employed in the care of the sick, but also practise the arts of sorcery, in unimportant cases, with considerable success. Prophecy is their particular department. They foretel wars, deaths, good seasons, and other events bearing on the interests of individuals and of the tribe, who, for the information, give them presents. The apparition of ghosts is especially an occasion on which the services of the sorcerers, the old women, and all the friends of the ghost-seer are in great request. Owing to the quantity of indigestible food eaten by the natives, they often dream that they are visited by ghosts. After a supper of blubber, followed by one of the long talks about departed friends, which take place round the fire, some nervous and timid person may fancy, in the night time, that he sees a ghost. A child will dream that his deceased parent is standing at one end of the house. Waking with a scream, the dreamer starts from his couch, and rends his blanket. Friends hurry round, rake up the fire, and the old women begin to sing. The dreamer snatches feathers from his pillow, and eats them, and covers his head with them. His nearest relative approaches with a knife, and scores the ghost-seer's arms and legs till the blood comes, which is received into a dish, and sprinkled on his face, and on the part of the house where the spirit seemed to be. This scoring the limbs reminded me of the ancient Viking practice of marking warriors, on the bed of sickness, with the point of a spear. After the operation, the wounds are dressed with blackberry leaves. If the vision continues, the friends throw articles belonging to the dreamer on the fire, and cry "more! more!" till all his property (including clothes, mats, and even his boxes,) is heaped upon the fire. The greatest excitement prevails, and young girls are often sick and exhausted for many days after such an unfortunate dream.

There are, I think, several beliefs, held formerly by the Ahts, originating how or when I shall not conjecture, that would materially contribute to assist the sorcerers in retaining power—particularly their belief in the transmigration of souls, and in the reality of dreams. I will mention first their ideas concerning the transmigration of souls. Like other rude Indians, these people have no intellectual conception of the soul, other than as a being of human shape and human mode of acting. They imagine that the soul, like the inhabitant of a house, may wander forth from the body and return at pleasure. It may pass from one man into another, and also enter into the body of a brute. Stories are told of men who, going into the mountains to seek their "medicine,"—which means choosing a guardian spirit, on attaining manhood,—have associated with wolves, like the Arcadian mentioned in Pliny's legend; and, after a time, body and soul have changed into the likeness of these beasts.* If the soul has

* What is called the "medicine" of the natives, is something which they seek after arriving at manhood, and which is only to be got by hard trial of privation or exposure. The Indian, taking with him neither food nor water, and only a single blanket to cover his body, ascends to the summit of a high hill not far from the encampment, and there remains for several days. He keeps a fire burning to show to the people that he is actually at the place. The longer he endures the more efficacious

migrated, and entered any other form or body, and the soul of this other form or body does not in turn migrate to the one which has been bereft, this latter first becomes weak, and then sickens, and finally dies if the soul is not brought back. A similar notion (*See* chapter on "Religion") prevails respecting a soul's visit to *Chay-her*, or the inferior world after death. The natives often imagine that a bad spirit, which loves to vex and torment, takes the place of the truant soul during its absence. What anguish must be endured by these wretched creatures when possessed by this idea! I may add that the souls of dead friends are believed to reappear in human shape, or in the form of some beast or bird; and they are generally supposed to presage evil, and are regarded with fear. Sometimes, however, it is thought they visit the earth with good intentions; and it is the practice of many families, on retiring to rest, to place a meal of dried fish and potatoes beside the embers of the fire, for the refreshment of such ghostly visitors. These notions about the soul, it will be obvious

"medicine" is he supposed to obtain. As might be supposed of a people whose life and thoughts are bound almost within the limits of their bodily perceptions, this medicine generally comes through a dream in the form of an animal, as a wolf or eagle, when the sufferer's body and mind are enfeebled and disordered by hunger and exposure. Occasionally the medicine-seeker loses his reason, and wanders about and dies, and he is then believed to have gone in further search, and his return to the village is looked for month after month. The animal, thus supernaturally revealed to the natives as his "medicine," is supposed, throughout his life, to be connected with him as only an untrained imagination could conceive or explain, and finally, as is believed by some of the natives, to receive into its body the Indian after his departure from the earth. A multitude of stories concerning the adventures of men who have gone forth to seek their "medicine" are told by the natives.

to the reader, would open to the sorcerers a ready path to power, after the people's belief in their supernatural influence was established.

The other belief I mentioned, as aiding the sorcerers, the belief, namely, in the reality of dreams, is strongly held by the natives. The soul, as already said, is supposed to have the power of leaving the body during sleep, and of conversing with distant people, and visiting regions and places in remote parts of the world, and in the land of spirits. Dreams are regarded by the people, as the explanations of the movements of their vagrant souls; also as premonitions from the dead, and, in some sense, as intimations from an unknown greater power. An unlucky dream will stop a sale, a treaty, a fishing, hunting, or war expedition. Dreams are both good and bad, but oftener forebode evil than good. Almost equal to dreams in importance is the influence of omens. An eagle flying near the houses, the appearance of many seals, a watery moon, the presence of a white man, are the fancied causes of innumerable events; in fact, hardly a day passes in a native house without some fear being caused by dreams or omens. All the people live in constant apprehension of danger from the unseen world.

> No natural exhalation in the sky,
> No common wind, no 'customed event,
> But superstition, from its natural cause,
> Construes awry, and calls them prodigies,
> Signs, fatal presages, and tongues of heaven
> Plainly denouncing vengeance.

CHAPTER XIX.

TRADITIONS.

An Account of a Few of the Primitive Traditions of the People.

By sundry recollections of such fall
From high to low, ascent from low to high.—WORDSWORTH.

IT is extraordinary how many stories the Aht natives have to tell about every curious rock, hill, valley, and lake in their district. One must have been a long time amongst them, and quite possess their confidence, before they will speak to him freely on such matters; but, when assured of the listener's character and friendly disposition, there is no end to the stories which an old Indian will relate. An account of the innumerable original traditions and legends current among the Aht people would be very interesting and useful; but the matter is sufficient for a large book, and I shall, therefore, content myself with recording a few selected traditions, which, I am sure, have not been in any way derived from the teaching of priests or travellers.*

* There is a common story, I may here mention, of an ascent by a rope to a region above the earth; and a host of other stories which I hardly like to leave unrecorded, for such savage myths are, in many respects, interesting

How they first came to this Coast.—One of their stories is that they came in old times from the west, in numerous canoes, and, being caught near the shore by a storm, they fastened their canoes to the long kelp. The gale increased, and in the morning the canoes were scattered, a few survivors being able to land at different points on the coast, from whom the present separate tribes are descended. This tradition partly agrees with the story also told of two Indians having come from an unknown country (*see* chapter on "Religion"), on whose approach the various creatures fled, and left behind numerous Indians who had been contained in their bodies. In plain words, both stories mean that a few Indians originally came to the coast, and afterwards increased in number.

Of the great Bird or Deity Tootooch.—Tootooch is a mighty supernatural bird dwelling aloft and far away. The flap of his wings makes the thunder (Tootah), and his tongue is the forked lightning. He is the survivor of four great birds which once dwelt in the land of the Howchuklisahts in the Alberni Canal, three of which were killed by Quawteaht. These mighty creatures fed upon whales. Quawteaht one day, desiring to destroy them, entered into a great whale, and gradually approached the Howchuklis shore, spouting to attract attention. One of the birds swooped down upon him and caught him with

to the student of early history, and probably would illustrate the mental peculiarities of a people more satisfactorily than the general description of any traveller. It is to be hoped that some account of the primitive mythology of all the Indians in Vancouver Island will be published before it is much farther intermixed and distorted. The Rev. A. C. Garrett, of Victoria, Vancouver Island, and the active and observant traveller, Dr. Robert Brown, lately commanding the Vancouver Island Government Exploring Expedition, possess extensive information on this subject.

his talons, when Quawteaht dashed down to the bottom of the water, dragging with him his adversary, who was quickly drowned. Another Tootooch, and another, came to the attack, only to be served in the same way; and the last remaining one spread his wings and fled to the distant height, where he has ever since remained. According to Quassoon's tradition, related in this chapter, Quawteaht and Tootah—if the same as Tootooch—had once been better friends. The natives, I may remark, get confused about the gender of many of their divinities. So far as I know, the Indians neither worship Tootooch, nor believe that he has any great influence over their affairs. I have sometimes thought that Tootooch was the malevolent spirit whose power they fear, as is described in Chapter xxi., but I have not been able to satisfy myself on this point. The Chinooks and other tribes at the mouth of the Columbia river call their evil spirit "Ecutoch," which word somewhat resembles Tootooch.

How Fire was obtained.—Quawteaht made the earth, and also all the animals, but had not given them fire, which burned only in the dwelling of the cuttle-fish (Telhoop), who could live both on land and in the sea. All the beasts of the forest went in a body in search of the necessary element, (for in those days the beasts required fire, having the Indians in their bodies,) which was finally discovered and stolen from the house of Telhoop by the deer (Moouch), who carried it away, as the natives curiously describe it, both by words and signs, in the joint of his hind leg.

The narrators vary slightly in this legend; some asserting that the fire was stolen from the cuttle-fish, others that it was taken from Quawteaht. All agree that it was not bestowed as a gift, but was surreptitiously obtained.

Of the Origin of the Indians.—The following account of the origin of the people was given to me by Quassoon, of the Opechisahts, a famous hunter, but rather a stupid man on general subjects. The first Indian who ever lived was of short stature, with very strong hairy arms and legs, and was named Quawteaht. Where he came from was never known, but he was the forefather of all the natives here. Before his time fishes, birds, and beasts existed in the world (this is a most common Indian notion). Quawteaht killed himself—why the narrator could not say—but he lay covered with vermin, when a beneficent spirit, Tootah (their word for thunder), in shape a bird, came and put the vermin into a box, and Quawteaht revived and looked about, but saw no one, as the bird had flown away. Bye and bye, the bird returned, and Quawteaht married her, and had a son, who was the forefather of all the Indians.

How the Head of the Alberni Canal came first to be Settled by the Ahts.—A very long time ago the Ahts lived only on the coast, and never entered the singular inlet known as the Alberni Canal already described. At length, three adventurous spirits determined to explore the close and unknown waters. They started up in their canoe, and the first strange phenomenon which struck them was that, as they advanced, the mountains closed in upon them, shutting off all possibility of return. They went up the unknown inlet without meeting with any appearance of habitation; but they noticed fragments of salmon floating upon the tide, which seemed to imply that people lived at some place further up. When they turned the point which brought them close to the head of the inlet, a novel prospect burst upon their view. They beheld a most admirable dwelling, better, say present narrators, than any Englishman's house that was ever built. They touched the shore, and entered the house. It was plentifully supplied—venison, elk meat, salmon, berries, oysters, and clams (the last two they noticed particularly) were there in abundancc. But what astonished them most was that the inhabitants consisted entirely of women. Two of the men stayed in the house that night; the other slept outside, under the trees. In the morning, he was horrified to find that his two companions had been killed, and their bodies cast out of the house. Making the best of his way back, the mountains opened for his return, and he again found himself among his own tribe. He told his story; and now many were eager to go to this land of plenty, and desirous also to be revenged on the murderers of their friends. They put boards across several canoes (a usual practice when they have to carry much with them), and went up in a large body. As they turned the final promontory, all eyes were strained in the direction of the beautiful house which had been described to them. Instead of the house, they saw nothing. There was no house,—not a log nor a board to show that a house had ever stood there. There were no women, no inhabitants of any sort, and the sea there produced neither oysters nor clams. Evidently these weird women had taken their houses on their backs, and had flown off to the mountains, taking the oysters and clams with them; and the proof of the whole story is that, from that day to this, neither oysters nor clams are to be found in the head waters of the Alberni canal. This, in fact, arises from a fresh-water stream entering the inlet at this place, and making the water unsuitable for those shell-fish.

This story, there is little doubt, is founded on fact. The exaggerations are just such as might be expected. The mountains closing in upon the canoe, and opening again for its return, is the narration of men accustomed to the open coast, and not to narrow, land-locked waters. The beauty of the house at the head of the canal is a traveller's wonder, resting upon the evidence of only one pair of eyes, and, therefore, exaggerated with impunity. In describing the abundant supplies seen in the house, and in enumerating them, the surviving Indian would not be particular, but would name, probably, every article of food which himself and tribe were accustomed to find upon the coast. Among these, he would mention oysters and clams. It is probable that, when the three Indians arrived, the men were out hunting and fishing, and that the house presented the appearance of being occupied by women only. The husbands, on their return, put to death the two men found in the house; and then the whole tribe placed the boards of their house across their canoes, put their women and children and moveables upon these, and went up the river to one of the lakes, or to some other place of security. So readily, by Indian lips, may the marvellous be produced.

Concerning the Loon.—The commonest of all the Aht stories about animals and birds is the story which accounts for the cry of the loon. Two Indians, a long time ago, went out to fish for halibut in different canoes, and one was successful, but the other did not catch a fish. The fortunate fisherman laughed at the other, who got angry, and said to himself, "I am stronger, and will take his fish, and make him ashamed." Then he thought that his successful companion had many friends, and that, if he harmed him, they would retaliate. While in this mind, his eye caught the small wooden club with which the halibut is killed before being dragged into the canoe, and with this instrument, while his companion was pulling up a fish, he knocked him on the head. He then took his fish, and was going away, when he thought that, to prevent the deed being known, he would cut out his companion's tongue, so that he should not be able to speak. This being done, he returned alone to the village, and his wife took the fish. On being asked by the other man's friends where the missing man was, he said, it was some time since he had seen him; but when he last saw him, he had no fish: the weather, however, being fine, he would, no doubt, be home by-and-bye. While thus speaking, the other canoe arrived, and the man's friends went to ask how many fish had been caught, to which the mutilated fisherman could only reply by making a noise like the cry which the loon now utters. The great spirit, Quawteaht, was so angry at all this, that he changed the injured Indian into a loon, and the other into a crow; and the loon's plaintive cry now is the voice of the fisherman trying to make himself understood. How strangely this savage story often came back to my mind in crossing the wild, silent lakes, where the stillness was unbroken but for the melancholy note of the loon!

This story is frequently told, and with unusually little

variation, by the natives along the whole coast; but they cannot explain why both the assailant and his victim were punished.

Of a great Ebb and Flow of the Sea.—Generations ago, the Seshahts, who live now during part of the year in Nitinaht Sound and the remainder of the year at Alberni, were unacquainted with the head of the Alberni Canal. They had two houses on Nitinaht Sound, and used to migrate from one to the other.

At that time a most curious phenomenon of nature occurred. The tide ebbed away from the shores of the Sound and left it dry, and the sea itself retreated a long distance. This continued for four days, and the Seshahts made light of the occurrence. There was one, however, Wispohahp, who, with his two brothers, did not do so. After a mature consideration of the circumstance, he thought it likely that this ebb would be succeeded by a flood-tide of corresponding height and power. Accordingly, he and his brothers spent three days in the forest collecting material for a rope of cedar inner bark, which, when made, was so large as to fill four boxes. There was a rock near the Seshaht village, from the base of which sprang a group of bushes, of a sort well known for its toughness. Round these bushes Wispohahp fastened one end of his rope, attaching the other to his canoe. In his canoe were placed all his moveables, his wife, his two brothers, and their wives; and thus prepared they waited for the result. After four days the tide began to flow, and crept slowly up to about half-way between the point of its furthest ebb and the Seshaht houses. At this point, its pace was suddenly quickened, and it rushed up at fearful speed. The

Seshahts ran to their canoes. Some begged to be attached to Wispohahp's rope; but to this he would not consent, lest it should be broken. Others would have given him several of their women; but he would not receive them. They were all soon caught by the rising water; and while Wispohahp rode safely at anchor, the Seshahts, unable to resist its force, were drifted in their canoes to distant parts. Finally, the water covered the whole country, except Quossakt, a high mountain near the Toquahts, and Mount Arrowsmith (Cush-cu-chuhl). The Toquahts, another tribe living near the Seshahts, got into a large canoe (Eher Kleetsoolh), and paddled to the summit of Quossakt, where they landed. At the end of four days, the flood-tide began to abate. As it did so, Wispohahp hauled in his rope, and as the waters descended to their usual level, found himself afloat near the site of the former Seshaht dwelling. He built himself a small house, having two chambers, with a passage in the middle. One of the chambers he occupied himself, while the other was used by his brothers.

Some time after a Klah-oh-quaht canoe, manned by three Indians, approached the shore where the house was situated. One of the three had with him in the canoe a quantity of the medicine which they use for making fishermen successful in the capture of the whale. They brought their canoe close to the land, and when asked what they wanted, said, that they had come to see Wispohahp's house. Wispohahp, after some consideration, invited them to land, and, as the Indian manner is when friendship is intended, helped to pull up their canoes, and offered them sleeping accommodation. One of the Klah-oh-quahts, to show his goodwill, made a present of his medicine. After this, Wispohahp proposed to make him chief of their small household. This was finally agreed to, and the Klah-oh-quaht took a Toquaht wife—for that tribe had returned from Quossakt; and this is the origin of the present tribe of the Seshahts. The Klah-oh-quaht who thus became a chief was the great-grandfather of Hy-yu-penuel, the present chief of the Seshahts, and the friendly terms upon which the Klah-oh-quahts and Seshahts live is owing to this circumstance.

CHAPTER XX.

USAGES IN WARFARE.

Usages in Warfare—Description by an Eyewitness of an Indian Attack on a Village—Admiral Denman's Brush with the Ahousahts.

Man, only, mars kind nature's plan,
And turns the fierce pursuit on man.—Sir W. Scott.

Like a fiend in a cloud
With howling woe;
After night I do croud,
And with night will go.—W. Blake.

Though the members of an Aht tribe live together in much social harmony, there are many wars between separate Aht tribes along the coast. The motive for a war is oftener a spirit of revenge than a wish to obtain additional property or land. As previously observed, a trifling cause, such as an unavenged or an imagined affront—offered, it may have been, in the time of a preceding generation—is considered a sufficient pretext for an attack on another unsuspecting tribe. Arrangements for war are made secretly, and a declaration or notice of the intention to attack is not given. No individual, nor body of persons in a tribe can engage the tribe in war; the matter is debated and settled in a full meeting of all the members of the tribe. The question never is whether the proposed war is just or unjust, but whether there is sufficient force, and what are the chances of success. If victory is likely to be doubtful without assistance, another tribe is invited or compelled to join the attacking force. The appointed war-chief of the tribe, who is always chosen by the people, and retains his office until displaced in popular favour by a more vigorous aspirant, assumes command of the party, as a matter of course, in virtue of his office. The subordinate military positions in an expedition are generally assigned by the people to chieftains of acknowledged bravery and skill in war. Attacks are made during the night. Notwithstanding their propensity to warfare, the Ahts are not remarkable for bravery. They seldom meet openly a foe equal in strength, and a slight repulse daunts them. If prisoners are taken, they are either put to death immediately, or kept as slaves. I never heard of an instance of captives being tortured by the Ahts. They do not take the scalp of an enemy, but cut off his head, by three dexterous movements of the knife, from the back of the neck, and the warrior who has taken most heads is most praised and feared. The natives do not eat human flesh, and deny that the horrid practice existed among their forefathers. The presence of so many animals, and the abundance of easily caught fish on the coast, fit for human food, incline me to disbelieve that the people ever were cannibals. I think it probable that the old navigators too hastily inferred the existence of cannibalism, from the dried human hands that were offered to them for sale at Nootkah. These may have been trophies, or charms, preserved by the natives under some superstitious feeling. The Indian interpreter and trader, J. Long, who published a book on the North American Indians, in 1791, records, as a custom of the Mattaug-wessawauks—a tribe on the eastern side of the continent—that, if one of the people was killed by accident, they kept a dried and salted hand or foot, as a charm to avert calamities. I have also read somewhere that, in our own country, during the reign of Charles II., and down to a later time, the hands of criminals who had been executed at Newgate were thought to be of great efficacy in the cure of diseases and the prevention of misfortunes.

I shall probably best convey an idea of the native mode of warfare to the reader, by describing an expedition of the Klah-oh-quahts against the Ky-yoh-quahts, a large tribe living on the coast, about eighty miles north from Klah-oh-quaht Sound.* A bad feeling had existed for some time past between the two tribes, which had been fostered by the chief warrior of the Klah-oh-quahts—a restless, ambitious man, who was always on the look-out for a cause of quarrel. The tribe debated the question of peace or war for several months, and at last agreed to attack the Ky-yoh-quahts, provided that Shewish, the chief of the Moouchahts, which tribe lived between the expected belligerents, would join the expedition, with his warriors. An envoy was sent to Shewish, in a light canoe, to invite his co-operation, and, before leaving on his mission, the diplomatist was instructed to use various arguments that were likely to be effective. After five days

* In Commander Mayne's book on Vancouver Island, there is a brief erroneous account of this war.

had passed, the messenger returned, with the intelligence that the Moouchahts would join the Klah-oh-quahts in exterminating the Ky-yoh-quahts; or, at least, in reducing them to the position of a tributary tribe. There was immediately great excitement in the Klah-oh-quaht village. Not an hour was lost in commencing preparations; the war canoes were launched and cleaned, and their bottoms scorched with blazing faggots of cedar to smooth them; knives were sharpened; long-pointed paddles, pikes, and muskets were collected; fighting men and captains of canoes chosen, who, during the night, washed themselves, rubbed their bodies, and went through ceremonies, which, they supposed, would shield them from fatigue and wounds. In the forenoon of the next day, twenty-two large canoes took their departure from Klah-oh-quaht, with from ten to fifteen men in each, under the command-in-chief of Seta-kanim, the great advocate for the war. Part of the crews were natives of small neighbouring tribes dependent on the Klah-oh-quahts. The women on the beach, before the canoes left, sang a spirited song, and urged the men to be bold, and support the honour of the tribe. After proceeding for twenty miles through an inner water, the canoes followed the sea-board for about the same distance, and reached the village of the Hishquayahts—a tributary tribe of the Klah-oh-quahts—which had to furnish six canoes, manned. The fatigued warriors slept in their canoes that night, and Seta-kanim ordered the Hishquayahts to be ready in the morning with their contingent. Leaving Hishquay at dawn, on a fine morning in June, the whole force, increased now to twenty-eight canoes, arrived, during the afternoon, at Friendly Cove, Nootkah Sound, near the principal village of their allies, the Moouchahts. Before approaching the village, the canoes were formed into three divisions, eight of the largest canoes in the middle and ten in each wing division, in which order they proceeded slowly towards the shore. As they raised their war-song, and stopped now and then to beat time with paddles on the gunwales of the canoes, a change could be noticed in the appearance of the warriors. The savage blood in them was up; their fingers worked convulsively on the paddles, and their eyes glared ferociously from blackened faces besmeared with perspiration; altogether they were two hundred murderous-looking villains. When within fifty yards of the shore, all the canoes, which had been going at the rate of six knots at least, came to a dead stop, not one of them a foot ahead of another. The Moouchahts by this time had come out of their houses, and the two parties, according to the native custom, looked at each other in silence for a considerable time. At last Seta-kanim rose in his canoe to address the people on shore. He was a tall muscular savage, with a broad face blackened with charred wood, and his hair was tied in a knot on the top of his head so that the ends stood straight up; a scarlet blanket was his only dress, belted lightly round his loins, and so thrown over one shoulder as to leave uncovered his right arm, with which he flourished an old dirk. Such a voice as he had! One could almost hear what he said at the distance of a mile. The speech or harangue lasted forty minutes, and seemed rather a violent address. Strange to say, Seta-kanim spoke to the Moouchahts, his allies, not in terms of civility, but imperiously as if he were bullying them. Very likely he ventured to do so from the notion that, as they had gone too far now to withdraw from their engagement, he, as the leader of the Klah-oh-quahts, might safely assume a tone befitting the greatest man in the joint expedition. Only a short reply was made by Shewish to the visitor's speech, and then all the Klah-oh-quahts landed, and, having drawn their canoes above high-water mark, went to the chief's house, where they found piles of herring spawn and dried salmon collected for a repast. Their hunger being satisfied, speaking began; and one chief after another expressed opinions as to the best mode of attacking the Ky-yoh-quahts. Finally, on the motion of Seta-kanim, the meeting adjourned to a smooth untrodden sandbeach in the neighbourhood. Here Quartsoppy, a Klah-oh-quaht, whose wife was a Ky-yoh-quaht woman, was directed to describe on the sand the Island of Ocktees, on which the village of the Ky-yoh-quahts was placed. He immediately set to work and drew an outline of the island, then showed the coves, beaches, tracks; next the village with the different houses, divisions, and sub-divisions—referring now and then for confirmation to other natives who also knew the locality. Small raised piles of sand represented houses, one of which was Nancie's, the chief of the Ky-yoh-quahts, another belonged to Moochinnick, a noted warrior; others to chiefs of inferior repute. Quartsoppy, referring to his drawing, also showed, or otherwise informed his audience of the usual number of men in each division of the camp, their arms and supposed ammunition, the characteristics of the principal men, as their youth, age, courage, activity, or strength.

All this time the warriors of the two tribes and the Hishquayaht tributaries stood round the delineator in a large circle, and qestions were asked and eager conversation held. After several speeches had been made, a general plan of attack proposed by Seta-kanim was adopted: fifteen Klah-oh-quaht canoes were to form the centre; the Moouchats, with fourteen canoes and one hundred and fifty men, to attack from the right; and seven Klah-oh-quaht canoes, with the Hishquayaht auxiliaries, to compose the left attack—the whole force to approach secretly, and to land and advance at one time, and a man from each canoe to be detached to set fire to the enemy's houses with matches and prepared gumsticks. This general plan being adopted, the two tribes, Klah-oh-quahts and Moouchahts, separated for the purpose of arranging the details of their respective duties; for instance, Seta-kanim for his people assigned to subordinate chiefs their positions in the attack, according to his own knowledge of their capabilities and according to Quartsoppy's information as to whom they might meet. Notwithstanding his influence, however, a violent dispute arose between two of his best men as to who should attack the lodge of the famous chief Moochinnick, and the rivals would have come to blows but for the interposition of several old men. Towards nightfall, when every preparation was completed, both parties of the natives returned from the sandbeach to the village, and ate another meal, after which criers went round to notify that the starting hour would be at early dawn. The weather continued fine, and before sunrise on the appointed day, the Klah-oh-quahts started in their canoes in the same order in which they had entered the bay, working their paddles to the beating of a drum and the shouting of a war song. Their allies, the Moouchahts, under the command of their war-chief, Nisshenel, a man of gigantic stature, followed at a distance of two hundred yards, in two divisions, each of seven canoes. Crossing Nootkah Sound, the expedition came out on the seaboard, after three hours' paddling; and now precautions were taken to prevent discovery of their approach. Orders were issued that the canoes should form a single line, and keep within paddle's-length of the rocks. During the forenoon the small village of another Aht tribe, the Ayhuttisahts, was reached, and the warriors landed and re-blackened their faces. The coming night was the night of the attack. Having proceeded all day cautiously in a single line, winding close round the rocks like a great sea-serpent, the canoes succeeded, just after nightfall, in reaching undiscovered, a deep cove within two miles of the Island of Ocktees, where the Ky-yoh-quaht village was. The men now rested on their paddles until midnight without speaking a word. There was no moon, and though the stars were bright, the haze on the water and the deep shadow of the forest favoured their approach. The hour at last came; the canoes, urged forward by long stealthy strokes, hurried on their fearful errand, and the line of the Ky-yoh-quaht village, extending in a curve round the head of an indentation, was soon seen.

Four hundred well-armed savages, under their own leaders, and with a concerted plan of attack, sprang on the beach, and rushed towards the village. Fortunately, a minute sooner, as afterwards appeared, two stray Ky-yoh-quahts, coming from the north, had reached the landing-place, and were carrying their blankets and paddles towards the houses, when the hostile canoes emerged from the fog and swept rapidly towards the shore. "Wéena! wéena! strangers! danger! danger!" resounded through the air before the canoes touched the beach, and the cry was answered instinctively by a hundred half-waked sleepers, 'Wéena! wéena! Klah-oh-quaht! Moouchaht! Wéena!" and already the crack of muskets and the noise of running and shuffling within the houses were heard. The torches and the blaze from several houses that had been set on fire now lighted up the front. The Ky-yoh-quahts had retreated into the house of their chief, which they had barricaded with boxes and loose planks, and they kept up a quick but not destructive fire on the assailants. Seta-kanim, with the two bearers of his muskets and the party under his immediate command, was well forward in the centre. The canoemen on the left were inside the Ky-yoh-quaht houses, and were killing the inmates, and had set several houses on fire; stragglers, shouting and gesticulating, but evidently not relishing the fight, were between the advanced parties and the shore, and a large body of Moouchahts was collected near their canoes on the beach, as if they had fallen back immediately after the first rush. The attack was a failure; that could be seen at a glance. Still, for ten or fifteen minutes the fight continued, both where the Klah-oh-quahts tried to enter the chief's house in the front, and also inside the houses which the canoe-men on the left had attacked. By-and-by the fires became duller, and what went on could not be so well seen. Batches of excited savages came towards the canoes, and shouted and fired their muskets into the air; finally, Seta-kanim, who had fought in the front, out of cover the whole time, finding himself left with about a dozen men, retired sullenly to the shore. The enemy did not follow, and the discomfited assailants paddled away in confusion; Klah-oh-quaht and Moouchaht canoes mixed together, and every warrior in a savage humour. The confidence of the advance was changed now in the retreat to fear and suspicion. Passing Ayhuttis, Hishquay, and Nootkah, the Klah-oh-quahts reached their own village two days after the fight, and, as they did not raise on their approach the victorious song, all the women met them with loud lamentations. They brought in the canoes thirty-five Ky-yoh-quaht heads, and thirteen slaves, chiefly taken by the canoe-men on the left of the attack; and this detachment, and the party under Seta-kanim, had lost altogether eleven men killed and seventeen wounded. The heads were placed on poles in front of the village, and the spoil taken from the Ky-yoh-quahts was apportioned to the captors. The distinction of a change of name, denoting some act of daring, was awarded to a few who had been forward in the attack.

The result of this war expedition was not satisfactory to the Klah-oh-quahts, who had looked forward to the extermination of their powerful rivals, instead of which they had been repulsed with loss; and, having offended the Moouchahts by reproaching them as the cause of failure, the Klah-oh-quahts were now apprehensive that the Ky-yoh-quahts and Moouchahts would unite against them. Their fears increased daily, till every one in the camp was in a feverish and unhappy state of mind. No one could sleep without expecting to be waked by a knife in his throat. Winter, too, was at hand, and the stock of provisions low; yet it was thought necessary to stop all trade to the north in the direction of the Ky-yoh-quahts. Few Klah-oh-quaht canoes would venture half a mile from the shore to fish. A large stockade with only one gate was built, and the whole tribe lived within the enclosure. The night was divided into two watches, and sentinels were posted. False alarms, devised on purpose by the chiefs, exercised the people in defending the camp. Such a state of matters soon produced discontent, and turned the anger of his own tribe against Seta-kanim, whose restlessness had caused the war. So strong a feeling was manifested against this chief that he shut himself up in his house for more than three months, and did not once venture out of doors for fear of being shot; and it was only by thus keeping out of sight, and by giving all his property away as presents, that he managed to escape without further punishment. Many wars, and a train of calamities to all the tribes concerned, followed this untoward attack upon the Ky-yoh-quahts.

To illustrate the bearing of the Aht natives in presence of a superior force of white men—whose random shooting with great guns, and practice of attacking by daylight, they ridicule as contrary to correct notions of warfare—I give here an extract from a despatch of Rear-Admiral Denman, dated on board the frigate *Sutlej*, in Klah-oh-quaht Sound, the 11th October, 1864, and addressed to the Governor of Vancouver Island. A trading schooner, the *Kingfisher*, had been decoyed near the shore by Cap-chah, an Ahousaht chief, who told the captain that he had a quantity of oil to dispose of. Cap-chah killed the captain, and two other Ahousahts killed the sailor who was on board, as well as a Quoquoulth Indian, who was one of the crew. The bodies, after being cut open, were thrown into the sea, and the schooner was plundered and burned. Admiral Denman's object in visiting Klah-oh-quaht Sound with H.M.S. *Sutlej*, was to demand delivery of the murderers; and, on arriving at the Sound, he found that H.M.S. *Devastation* had preceded him, according to orders. The following extracts from the official despatch describe the further steps that were taken to punish the Ahousahts for refusing to deliver the chief Cap-chah:—

"Finding Matilda Creek and Bawden Bay deserted by the natives, I proceeded up the North Arm to a village called Sik-tok-kis, on the right bank, and sent Mr. Hankin with the Indian interpreter Friday, *alias* Thomas Robert, on shore in a canoe to endeavour to open communication with the natives, and to demand that the twelve principals in the murder and piracy of the *Kingfisher* should be given up.

"No natives would answer them, though they were heard talking in the bush; but after some time one Indian came down to speak with Mr. Hankin, who, desiring Friday to keep him in conversation, ran to the beach, and calling up four of the covering boat's crew, seized him and brought him on board.

"The man seized acknowledged to having been on board the *Kingfisher* at the time of the murder, and has afforded much valuable information. I enclose a copy of his deposition.

"At the same time I had sent the *Devastation* to Herbert Arm, where all communication was refused, and a large body of Indians in their fighting paint fired upon the boat and ship. In conformity with my orders Commander Pike confined himself to self-defence, and returned to report proceedings.

"From the information obtained from the captured Indian, I found that three of the actual murderers were at Moo-yah-kah in Herbert Arm, who had fired on the *Devastation;* that Cap-chah, the chief of the tribe, and the murderer of the captain, resided at Trout River, in Cypress Bay, or in Bedwell Arm, both of which belonged to him. That Sik-tok-kis was the residence of Ayah-kahchitl, and that others, parties to the crime, were to be found at Obstruction Inlet, and at two villages at the head of Shelter Arm.

"On the 3rd, I proceeded up Herbert Arm to Moo-yah-kah, and sent the *Devastation* to Sik-tok-kis, Obstruction Inlet, and Shelter Arm, with orders to destroy the canoes, houses, &c., but not to fire on the natives unless resistance were offered. Commander Pike was not able to find the village in Destruction Inlet, but he destroyed Sik-tok-kis and those in Shelter Arm, and found in each of them letters, accounts, and other property belonging to the *Kingfisher.*

"I sent Friday into Moo-yah-kah under the ship's guns. A number of Indians came down and held a palaver with him on the beach; he told them that I promised not to fire on them if they delivered up to me all the men concerned in the affair of the *Kingfisher*, three of whom I knew were there. Friday, on his return, brought a message from the Indians saying, that if I wanted the men I might come and take them, if I destroyed the village they would soon build it up again, and that if I attempted to touch the canoes they would shoot every man who came near the shore.

"I then ordered a heavy fire to be opened on the

village, and on the surrounding bush, to clear it, and sent in the gigs to complete the destruction of the village under cover of the ship's guns, and those of the heavy boats.

"Notwithstanding these precautions, several musket shots were fired at the boats, but were instantly silenced by the boats' guns, which replied to them with admirable precision.

"Having brought away twelve canoes, I returned to Matilda Creek, where the crime had been perpetrated, and the *Kingfisher* sunk, and next day I ordered the remains of the village, which had been abandoned and dismantled, to be fired.

"The *Devastation* had, on the 5th, been ordered to destroy the villages of Cap-chah, in Cypress Bay and Bedwell Arm, and to bring away his canoes; the boats were fired on, and Cap-chah himself was seen at the head of his men in Cypress Bay, dressed in one of the blue jackets which had formed a part of the *Kingfisher's* cargo.

"Finding that all these measures had failed to bring the Ahousahts to terms, I was obliged to strike a yet more severe blow, directed against Cap-chah himself in such a manner as to impress the Indians more deeply with the idea of our power, and with the impossibility of escaping punishment due for such atrocities against unoffending white traders.

"On the morning of the 7th October, forty seamen, and thirty marines, with one Ahousaht and six Klah-oh-quaht Indians, to act as guides, were landed at White Pine Cove in Herbert Arm, under the command of Lieutenant Stewart, the senior lieutenant of this ship. Lieutenant Stewart was ordered to march across the trail to Trout River (about three miles), and to endeavour to seize Cap-chah and any of his people.

"The Ahousahts were completely taken by surprise, and they must have been all captured in the temporary huts which they had constructed in the bush, had not the alarm been given by the barking of a dog when our party was within a few yards of them. The Indians had barely time to rush into the thick cover, from whence they opened a heavy fire upon our men, which was returned with such effect, that in a few moments they took flight, leaving ten men dead. Cap-chah himself, who did not fight, was wounded in two places as he ran away.

"The success of this affair is due to the excellent conduct of Lieutenant Stewart, and the officers and seamen and marines under his command, while the defeat of the Ahousahts by an attack after their own fashion, has produced profound alarm and astonishment.

"Cap-chah is in hiding, and his people, having abandoned all idea of resistance, look upon him as responsible for all the calamities which have befallen them. He has effected his escape to Moo-yah-yah, and I am now on my way to Herbert Arm with a party of his own people aboard to promulgate the terms which I have demanded to obtain the person of Cap-chah and others actually concerned in the murder.

"In consideration of the severe punishment which has been inflicted on the Ahousahts, I have now limited my demand to the delivery up to me of Cap-chah and the six persons who took part in the murder, although the cargo and effects of the *Kingfisher* we have found in every place destroyed, prove how very extensively the tribe at large was implicated in the piracy.

"It is with great pleasure that I inform you that the service, in which sixty-nine canoes have been destroyed, and about fifteen men killed, has been performed without the slightest injury on our side.

"I hope soon to return to Esquimalt with some of the murderers on board, and I have promised that no further measures shall be adopted against the Ahousahts for one month from this time; but if the six murderers are not given up by that time, I shall be obliged to order forcible measures to be resumed."

Having had several Ahousahts in my employment subsequently to this attack by the ships, I learnt from them that the destruction of their canoes was felt as a misfortune, but the loss, as they described it, of half a war-canoe of men, was thought to be of no consequence whatever. The want of canoes prevented them from obtaining and laying in a store of their usual food for the winter, and the tribe consequently dispersed and lived among other friendly tribes, until the fishing season commenced in the spring. During the winter they were busy preparing new canoes, and it was expected that they would be pretty well supplied with them before the autumn of 1865. For some reason the ships of war did not return at the end of the month's grace allowed by Admiral Denman for the delivery of Cap-chah, nor at any later time; consequently the Ahousahts now believe that they gained a victory over the ships, and, in consideration of such a triumph, all the trouble of making new canoes has been forgotten. Cap-chah has added to his reputation; he is the great chief who defied and baffled the English or King-George war-vessels. Owing to the curious distinction drawn by the natives between the crews of the Queen's ships on the one hand, and the great King George tribe on the other,—believing the people in the ships to be a separate tribe by themselves—my Ahousaht informants told these particulars to me as if I were an indifferent person, and the affair had been, not between them and my own countrymen, but between the Ahousahts and some other tribe. The extent and composition of a great society of civilized men are beyond their comprehension.

CHAPTER XXI.

RELIGIOUS PRACTICES.

The Religious Practices of the Ahts.

Rather with the Rechabites we will live in tents of conjecture.
FULLER.

No subject connected with the people could possess a more general interest than that of their religion, but it is one as to which a traveller might easily form erroneous opinions, owing to the practical difficulty, even to one skilled in the language, of ascertaining the true nature of their superstitions. This short chapter is the result of more than four years' inquiry, made unremittingly under favourable circumstances. There is a constant temptation—from which the unbiassed observer cannot be quite free—to fill up in one's mind, without proper material, the gap between what is known of the religion of the natives for certain, and the larger less-known portion which can only be guessed at; and I frequently found that, under this temptation, I was led on to form, in my own mind, a connected whole, designed to coincide with some ingenious theory which I wished might be true.

Generally speaking, it is necessary, I think, to view with suspicion any very regular account given by travellers of the religion of savages; their real religious notions cannot be separated from the vague and unformed, as well as bestial and grotesque mythology with which they are intermixed. The faint, struggling efforts of our natures in so early, or so little advanced a stage of moral and intellectual cultivation, can produce only a medley of opinions and beliefs—not to be dignified by the epithet religious—which are held loosely by the people themselves, and are neither very easily discovered nor explained. In a higher stage, accurate systematizing, in a more or less acceptable and reasonable form, of the undefined notions which frequently accompany and form a part of human appreciation respecting objects supposed to be more than human, is the work, not of barbarous, but of intellectual and civilised minds. Religious system, in its highest character and plan, has, in the Scriptures of the Old and New Testaments, been embodied in these divine revelations to mankind. I refer to the three eras of the savage—the civilised, the heathen, and the savage.

In speaking of the religion of the Ahts, I use the word simply for want of any other; what I refer to is among them rather a certain form of worship or propitiation of deities according to old usages, and not, of course, a system of religion in our sense of the word, containing a body of moral and spiritual truths. No attempt is made by any class of priests, nor by the older men, to teach religion to the people,—there are no doctrines of religion in which they could instruct the people. If the sorcerers are considered to constitute a priestly class, all that they do in the way of teaching is to introduce to a knowledge of ceremonies and usages the youths who are destined to be their successors.

I can say thus much of the religion of the Aht Indians, that it clearly is an influential power among them, and extensively governs their affairs.

The people are extremely unwilling to speak of what is mysterious, or akin to the spiritual in their ideas; not, it appears, from a sense of the sacredness of the ideas, but from a notion that evil will result from any free communication on such subjects with foreigners. Even after long acquaintance, it is only now and then, when "i' the vein," that the sullen, suspicious natures of these people will relax, and permit them to open a corner of their minds to a foreigner who possesses their confidence.* They generally begin by saying that no white

* *I was two years among the Ahts, with my mind constantly directed towards the subject of their religious beliefs, before I could discover that they possessed any ideas as to an overruling power or a future state of existence.* The traders on the coast, and other persons well acquainted with the people, told me that they had no such ideas, and this opinion was confirmed by conversation with many of the less intelligent savages; but at last I succeeded in getting a satisfactory clue to such information as this chapter contains. Is it not possible that many otherwise observant travellers have too hastily assumed, after living a few months among savages, that they had no religion? It is no easy attainment to know the language of savages conversationally; and to get their confidence—particularly the confidence of the intelligent Indians—is a still more difficult task. *A traveller must have lived for years among savages, really as one of themselves, before his opinion as to their mental and spiritual condition is of any value at all.* The fondness of the Ahts for mystification, and the number of "sells" which they practise on a painstaking inquirer going about with note-book in hand, are unexpected and extraordinary on the part of savages whom we regard as so mean in intelligence. They will give a wrong meaning intentionally to a word, and afterwards, if you use it, will laugh at you, and enjoy the joke greatly among themselves.

man is able to understand the mysteries of which they will speak. "You know nothing about such things; only old Indians can appreciate them," is a common remark. And in nine cases out of ten, so many lies and mis-statements are mixed up with the account, either directly for the purpose of mystifying the inquirer, or owing to the unenlightened confusion of the savage in thinking upon religious subjects, that little reliance can be placed upon it. Also, the opinions expressed by some of the natives are found, on examination, to differ on so many points from those of others, that it is hardly possible to ascertain the prevailing opinions of any tribe. Still, speaking of the tribes of the Ahts together, as a nation, I have satisfied myself as to one or two facts in connection with their religion. They undoubtedly worship the sun and the moon, particularly the full moon (*hoop-palh*), and the sun (*nas*), while ascending to the zenith. Like the Teutons, they regard the moon as the husband, and the sun as the wife; hence their prayers are more generally addressed to the moon, as being the superior deity. The moon is the highest of all the objects of their worship; and they describe the moon—I quote the words of my Indian informant—"as looking down upon the earth in answer to prayer, and as seeing everybody." The great Quawteaht himself, who made everything, and who first taught the people to address the moon and the sun in times of need, is, in their estimation, an inferior divinity to both these luminaries.

Prayer is common among the Aht natives—among men, women, and children. There is a word in their language, *queel-queel-ha*, meaning "to pray," also *klah-quay*, "to beseech;" these words are more urgent words than *na-nash* "to beg, or ask for," or than *ah-ah-toh*, which means simply "to ask." I could not find that they have any, as it were, recognized chief worshipper, or any class of priests, except the sorcerers, but I have noticed that the prayers of old men are thought to be specially efficacious. For different wants the Ahts have different modes of prayer. When working at the settlement at Alberni, in gangs by moonlight, individuals have been observed to look up to the moon, blow a breath, and utter quickly the word *Teech! teech!*—their word for "health" or "life." This opinion of the moon's power over human affairs is wide-spread. I remember that we boys at school in Scotland used to turn over the money in our pockets for luck on the appearance of a new moon. *Teech! teech!* "life! life!" this is the great wish of these people's hearts—even such a miserable life as their life seems to a civilized observer. So true is it that

> The weariest and most loathed worldly life
> That age, ache, penury, and imprisonment
> Can lay on nature, is a paradise
> To what we fear of death.

"*Teech! teech!*" is their common and almost constant prayer. On one occasion the tribe of Seshahts, at Alberni, being dissatisfied with a friend of mine—the late Mr. George Reid, from Fraserburgh, Scotland, who was also one of the best friends the natives ever had *—resolved to

* George Reid was originally a working cooper in my service, but was promoted to the position of superintendent of Indian affairs at Alberni. He died in Victoria in October, 1865, at the early age of thirty-nine. I esteem it a privilege, and valuable lesson, to have known one who was so remarkable, intellectually and morally, who was so modest, manly, and good—

kill him; but their design was betrayed to us by a friendly native, who, on disclosing his danger to the intended victim, urged him to pray to the new moon for life, and he would be secure.

The usual manner of praying is for the suppliant to retire alone into the woods, if possible, near to a running stream, and having rubbed his face with a prickly bush, he lays aside his blanket, stands erect naked, with extended arms, and looks towards the moon. Set words and gestures are used, according to the thing desired; for instance, in praying for salmon, the native rubs the backs of his hands, looks upwards, and utters the words "Many salmon, many salmon;" if he wishes for deer, he carefully rubs both eyes; or if it is geese, he rubs the back of his shoulder, uttering always, in a sing-song way, the accustomed formula. Bears are prayed for only during the last moon, before the snow appears; and it is usual for the suppliant, in praying for bears, to rub his sides and legs vigorously with both hands, and to wear round his head a piece of red blanket, adorned with feathers. All these practices in prayer no doubt have a meaning; for instance,

in every respect so fine a pattern of what a man ought to be. Many hundreds, now scattered here and there, of all nations, who also knew him, and were his friends, would repeat my words without envy or grudging, and would acknowledge, that among all of us at the settlement, Reid's character was the type which showed to the savages the high civilization our countrymen had reached in comparison with themselves. The savages saw amongst us a man, not of the church, not set apart, but a man hard at work all day like other labourers; and this man, having authority over them, was in all things just and sternly consistent; was patient of their talk; seldom answered without a smile. Yet they could not flatter nor outwit him. They could understand an ordinary white man's impatience, selfishness, and partiality; but this Christian life was a mystery to them.

in reference to the above-named practices, we may see that a steady hand is needed in throwing the salmon spear, and clear eyesight in finding deer in the forest.

So far as I know, the Aht Indians do not possess the knowledge of one supreme and beneficent Being; but there are indications, as before said, in some of their legends and usages of a belief in a superior Being, not acknowledged distinctly as good or bad, which presides over their destinies. This great Being is known to all the Aht tribes by the name of Quawteaht, and if there is any clear conception of him in the minds of the people, I should say that he is generally regarded as a good divinity. There is a large body of floating tradition among them as to Quawteaht, which appears, however, to be very confusedly held, and is certainly very differently related by different Indians. Quawteaht is not a local or tribal deity, but is known in every village. Perhaps the most prevailing notion is that he is the chief of an extensive and beautiful country, situated somewhere in the sky, though not directly over the earth, in which everything is found that the savage mind can conceive as ministering to man's sensual comfort and satisfaction. Everything there is beautiful and abundant. There a continual calm prevails, and the canoes float lightly on the sleeping waters; frost does not bind the rivers, and the snow never spreads its white blanket over the ground. In this pleasant country, where there is continual sunshine, and warmth, and gladness, it is believed that the high chiefs, and those natives who have been slain in battle on the earth, find their repose; the chiefs living in a large house as the guests of Quawteaht, and the slain in battle living by themselves in another house. No Indians of a common degree go to the land of Quawteaht; like Odin, he drives away the pauper and the bondsman from the doors of Valhalla.

My first idea was that the Aht legend of Quawteaht might have reference to some superior chief or white man among themselves, who had in former times been a benefactor, and who had left the memory of his genius and goodness behind him. I now feel comparatively sure that they look upon Quawteaht as an entirely supernatural being, although, of course, their idea of him is a material one. He is undoubtedly represented as the general framer —I do not say Creator—of all things, though some special things are excepted. He made the earth and water, the trees and rocks, and all the animals. Some say that Quawteaht made the sun and moon, but the majority of the Indians believe that he had nothing to do with their formation, and that they are deities superior to himself, though more distant and less active. He gave names to everything, among the rest to all the Indian houses which then existed, although inhabited only by birds and animals. Quawteaht went away before the apparent change of the birds and beasts into Indians, which took place in the following manner:—

The birds and beasts of old had the spirits of the Indians dwelling in them, and occupied the various coast villages, as the Ahts do at present. One day a canoe manned by two Indians from an unknown country, approached the shore. As they coasted along, at each house at which they landed, the deer, bear, elk, and other brute inhabitants, fled to the mountains, and the geese and other birds flew to the woods and rivers. But in this flight, the Indians, who had hitherto been contained in the bodies of the various creatures, were left behind; and from that time they took possession of the deserted dwellings, and assumed the condition in which we now see them. I may remark that Quawteaht, in the widely spread and apparently primitive Aht tradition of the Loon, (*see* Traditions), is represented as knowing—as a matter of course, yet evidently only as an all-seeing divinity could know—the particulars of the dispute between the two fishermen; and it is further stated in the tradition that Quawteaht inflicted punishment upon the offender. This shows that Quawteaht occasionally becomes displeased; but whether they consider this divinity, when in an angry mood, as their evil spirit, or whether their evil spirit is an entirely separate being, I do not know; it may perhaps be Tootooch, (*see* Chapter XIX.). Certain it is that the Aht people believe in a malevolent power of some sort, which frightens the salmon and deer, sends dreadful storms, overturns canoes, and brings sickness and death. I could never get any clear notion as to who this destructive being was. Sometimes the Indians relate that this being is Quawteaht enraged; at other times Tootooch; then Chay-her, which latter, as will be seen farther on, is a personification of death, and the name also of the inferior of the two worlds after death. Neither Quawteaht nor the evil spirit, whether Quawteaht or not, is acknowledged by the natives, so far as I could discover, in any private and, so to speak, bodily form of worship, such as is offered to the sun and moon. Each deity, however, is supposed to have minor spirits connected in some way with itself, which the people frequently symbolise and represent under the form of different creatures; and those of a benign character are believed to have the power, if not of shielding, at least of making things lucky for, the individual who trusts in them. The evil spirits, on the other hand, are regarded with fear, especially if they have been the subjects of a dream; and a very large part, indeed, of the superstitious practice of the Ahts consists in efforts to deprecate the wrath of these avenging deities. This propitiation or devil-worship is carried on by the assistance of a class of devil-priests or sorcerers, commonly called "medicine men," and is accompanied by many foolish ceremonies, by atrocities and revolting festivals. Some account of the medicine men has been given in a previous chapter. I do not think that the belief in the existence of these two opposing powers, the good and the evil god, is in any way derived by the people on this coast from the teaching of missionaries: it is probably the old belief which has been everywhere observed to be a characteristic of heathenism. Perhaps the commonest notion among the Ahts is that, in a former state—as illustrated by the legend of Quawteaht just mentioned—they existed in the form of birds, animals, or fishes. This opinion respecting transmigration, or transformation, mixed up with much that is ludicrous and grotesque, probably would have been the chief characteristic of the religious system that would have arisen among the natives in the course of time, had they advanced intellectually without any contact with Christianity. Some of them believe that, after death, they will again pass into the bodies of the animals which they occupied in a former state; but others have a better notion, that their souls will go to the land of Quawteaht or to Chay-her, which latter is the land of departed spirits for all except the chiefs and the slain in battle—a place described as situated deep down under the earth. Few of the religious beliefs of the Ahts are connected with heaven and the sky: their thoughts of the regions above are confined to Quawteaht's land, and to the fact that the spirit Tootooch (*see* "Traditions") dwells somewhere up there, and to the poetical idea that sickness comes from thence, and may be seen by the sharpsighted floating in the air. My-yalhi is the Aht word for this principle or personification of sickness. Chay-her is described as a country much like the earth, with inferior houses, no salmon, and very small deer. The blankets are small and thin, and therefore when the dead are buried the friends often burn blankets with them, for by destroying the blankets in this upper world, they send them also with the departed soul to the world below. Chay-her, as just said, is generally regarded as the place to which all the common people and slaves (unless slain in battle) go after death; and there they remain, as there is no passage thence to the martial and aristocratic elysium of Quawteaht's land. Chay-her is sometimes personified as an old man with a long grey beard, and a figure of flesh without bones, and is believed to wander at nights seeking men's souls which he steals away, and unless the doctors can recover them the losers will die. In wishing death to anyone, the natives blow and say, "Chay-her, come quick." A corresponding belief is that, when a person is dangerously sick, his soul (*Kouts-mah*) leaves his body and goes down into the country of Chay-her, but does not enter a house. If it enters a house, that is a sign it has taken up its abode below for good, and the sick man dies. The common medicine man (*Ooshtuk-yu*) has no power over a soul descended to Chay-her, but the sorcerer (*Kaukoutsmah-hah*) has the power of sending his own soul in pursuit of the descended soul of the sick man. If the mission be successful, the truant soul is brought back to the sorcerer, who throws it into the sick man's head ; for the soul, as they believe, dwells in the heart (*lebuxti*) and also in the head (*Weht*, brain). My informant asked me if I had ever seen a soul, and said he had once seen his own, when, at the close of a severe illness, it was brought to him by the sorcerer on a small piece of stick, and thrown into his head.

CHAPTER XXII.

USAGES IN FISHING.

The Aht mode of Fishing, with Descriptions of several Fish—the Salmon —Herrings—Halibut—Whale—Cod.

Whatsoever swims upon any water belongs to this exchequer.—J. TAYLOR.

I WILL now mention a few of the fish that are caught by the natives, beginning with the salmon. It is not likely that the accounts of any two travellers will agree as to the salmon in these waters, or that any trustworthy comprehensive information will be obtained until some means exist on the spot of collecting and comparing proved facts about salmon. I entertain this opinion on account of the extent of uninhabited coast in this part of the world—uninhabited, I mean, by any civilised observers—and the number of streams, rivers, and lakes; also the many kinds of salmon, and the different appearances which these fish present at various seasons, and at several stages of their ascent from the sea. The reader will have observed how important to the natives are the periodical migrations of the salmon, and how much human life, and life also of beast and bird, is sustained by this precious visitor. Depending mainly on this fish for their means of subsistence, any change in its habits, or serious diminution of its numbers, would reduce the Aht people to great straits. The bear, marten, mink, racoon, and other animals, together with several birds of prey, would also suffer greatly without the salmon. This fish is, to man, here what the corn crop is in England, or what the potato crop was in Ireland.

"Are there many salmon?" is the common inquiry from canoe to canoe. "The salmon are scarce, and many people will die," is occasionally the disheartening answer. The natives believe that their forefathers knew always how to fish,* but some great personage in the old time taught them how to capture land animals. The hunters among these tribes are more intelligent than the fishermen, or perhaps they seem so to a stranger imperfectly acquainted with their language. The hunters have a better opportunity of noticing, and, consequently, greater readiness in describing the appearance and habits of the objects of their pursuit. So far as I have learnt by particular separate inquiries, made at various points on the west coast of Vancouver Island, seven kinds of salmon visit the Aht streams, and these seven kinds are considered by the natives to agree in nearly all essentials. One kind remains in the sounds, and six kinds ascend rivers. This is the positive statement of the Indians, but whether any

* On the coast of Kerry twenty years ago—in 1845—the people were so ignorant and untaught that they did not know how to fish. When they had nets prepared for fishing, they did not follow the fish, but waited till the fish approached, and they had a good place to make a haul. (See *Foster's Letters on the Condition of Ireland.*)

of these seven kinds are fish of different ages, or males following females, I have not definitely ascertained. Of the six kinds that go up streams, two are unable to leap waterfalls. There are two kinds of salmon trout (*Ne-neech-nuck*) in addition to these seven kinds of salmon. Salmon can be found during the whole year in the sounds, or in the long natural canals, or in the rivers. But there are special seasons, during which more salmon, and salmon of a better quality, can be got. For many years this valuable fish has come and gone with great regularity, though not always in similar numbers. It arrives in some rivers earlier than in others, though the soil traversed by the rivers in their course and the warmth of the water, are in all respects the same.*

I will here simply give the statement of the natives about the salmon, and, for sake of clearness, will use the native names. One kind of salmon in going down towards the deep salt water, meets another kind on its way up, which inquires as to the state of matters in the rivers. The Klaywailth, which is about thirty inches long, ascends from the sea in December, for the purpose of spawning, and remains with the spawn till it becomes very thin. Returning towards the sea in the middle of January, it meets the Kliklimeesoulth—the largest of all the kinds, being on an average over three feet in length—on its way up. This large fish does not stay long after depositing its spawn, but returns to the sea

* It is a curious fact that while the river Doon in Ayrshire is one of the earliest salmon rivers in the west of Scotland, the river Ayr, which is close at hand, is characterised by the lateness of its produce, few salmon being captured in it before the beginning of June.

about the beginning of March, and when in the brackish water near the mouth of rivers, where fresh and salt water mingle, is accosted by the Hissit—the smallest of all the kinds, but a good fish for eating—which asks if there is a clear channel. Next comes the Tsoo-wit, the common salmon in British rivers, and about the same average size. This fish arrives in the inlets and rivers about June, and swims up the rivers without stopping, and afterwards remains for a considerable time. There are more of this fish than of any of the other descriptions. The Tsoo-wit is succeeded by the Satsope, which in size nearly equals the Klaywailth, and has large teeth. The latest salmon is the Enaköus, a fish as large as the Satsope, and remarkable for its hook-nose. The Indians say that this peculiarity is caused by the fish rubbing its nose on stones and gravel, in making its way against the strong streams in shallow rivers, swollen by melting snow. They laughed when I asked them if this peculiarity of the jaw existed only for a short time in male salmon, when the reproductive system was active. The former they evidently considered the real reason. The two last-named salmon cannot leap waterfalls, though they are able to pass small rapids. I thought that the Satsope and Enaköus might be the same fish, as the latter has large teeth, as well as a hook-nose, but the natives affirm that these two fish are different species, one being distinguished by its hook-nose and the other by its long teeth. They say that the nose becomes of a right shape on the return of the fish to the sea, and that both males and females have hook-noses; but this latter statement, from my own observation, I am inclined to doubt, as I have seen female fishes with well-formed jaws or noses, but in other respects resembling those called by the natives Enaköus, going up the rivers in company with the males. The only remaining kind of salmon, as the natives class it, is the Sōha, a large flat-sided fish, which appears in the sounds in winter, but is not often caught. This kind never goes up rivers, and the natives have not discovered its spawning ground. Of all these salmon the Hissit and Tsoo-wit are the best food. They all look better when caught in the sounds than in the rivers. When caught in salt water, small fishes are found in the stomachs of the salmon, but in rivers their insides are quite small, and never have any contents. You do not see many flies skimming on the surface of the Aht streams, and I do not remember an instance of a salmon rising to catch them, but fine trout are caught by fly-fishers. Many of the salmon become tired by rubbing against the stones in swimming up the rivers, and finally die, and are cast upon the beach. The natives say that it is the old salmon which die thus by the way, in endeavouring to reach the spawning ground. They certainly cannot be fresh strong fish on leaving the sea, for in a stream within six miles of salt water I have seen numbers of salmon quite emaciated, and so worn that their fins were almost dropping off. The spawn of the salmon is deposited among the gravel in deep water, at the bottom of the river, where there is little current. It is put into holes which the fish cover by means of their tails and fins, the female doing it first, and the male afterwards.

The water is so clear here, that probably the necessary light for quickening the eggs penetrates to a depth of ten feet. I have not observed any preference given by the fish to shallow waters in seeking a spawning-ground. Sometimes, after spawning, the salmon return to the sea, but swim so fast, and keep so much in deep water, that they are rarely seen. At this time they are very thin and poor-looking. The Indians have no more certain notion where they go to, than that they go into the sea, and, as they suppose, do not swim far away. The young fry (*ta-tooin*), most of which are spawned at various times during the middle and latter part of the year, are seen swimming about the river in winter, and they leave for the sea in five months after attaining the length of an inch. It takes them about a year to grow to this length; * and after attaining this size they grow quickly. All the fry go to the sea; none of them stay behind in their native river.

The most usual modes of capturing salmon by the Ahts are as follow:—close to the sea, with the hook; with the spear, off the mouths of rivers; and with traps, as well as the spear, when the fish are ascending streams. The steel hook is now in general use, with an anchovy or small herring for bait; formerly the salmon-hook was wooden, with two bone barbs, and was fastened to a maple bark line of native manufacture. When the fish are numerous in deep water, a long stick, armed with several bone or iron upward spikes, as long as a little finger, and placed about two feet apart, is thrust down into the water,† and quickly drawn up among the fish, in order to rip

* It is a common practice among the few tribes whose hunters go far inland, at certain seasons, to transport the ova of the salmon in boxes filled with damp moss, from the rivers to lakes, or to other streams.

† The Newfoundland fishermen employ, in the capture of cod, a plummet of lead, armed with hooks, which is let down into the sea and moved to and fro. This practice is called "jigging" the fish.

them. The net is not used at all by the Ahts in taking salmon. Their most picturesque mode of capture is spearing by torchlight from canoes, off the mouths of streams where the salmon linger in the cool, brackish water, before going up the river. Dark nights are preferred for this mode of fishing. Two natives go in a canoe, one steering, and the other standing with his spear in the bow, where a fir-torch flares. I have seen the lights of thirty canoes at one place moving on the water, and have known a canoe to bring in forty good salmon for a night's spearing. Such success, however, is unusual, and is only obtained at particular times under favourable conditions. Before leaving the shore to spear salmon, it is a common practice for a native to enter the water, and to rub his face hard, in the hope that this will induce more fish to come—quite as sensible an act as that of the English fisherman, who spits on his anchor; and with the same idea, at the commencement of the season, men and women go into the water on a moonlight night, and lie quietly on the surface, floating here and there, without speaking a word, now and then crossing one another's arms and spreading the backs of their hands towards the moon. (*See* Chapter on "Religion.") The salmon-spears are made of pine, and are rounded and smoothed by being rubbed on watered stones, and are afterwards straightened by warmth in the ashes of the fires. The spear, with two heads and two finger-places in the handle, is about fifteen feet long, and is used in the deeper water off the mouths of rivers, when the two heads double the chances of hitting a fish at one stroke. The single-headed spear is used in the shallow water in rivers. The spear-head is made of elk-bone, glazed with resin, and becomes detached from the spear on the fish being struck, but remains fastened to the line. The fisherman lays the spear down in the canoe, and hauls in the fish with the line. If the salmon is very large and troublesome, a few small bladders are tied to the line as near to the fish as possible, and he is left to weary himself by the effort of dragging these under the water. In the rivers and mountain streams, in which the water generally is shallow and flows rapidly, the natives place stones across the channel, and with the single-headed spear strike the fish as they pass. It is a pretty sight indeed to see an Indian, with his blue blanket flung carelessly round him, standing on these stones in a vigilant, graceful attitude, poising his long spear. Another mode of salmon river-fishing is by the trap which is used in all the streams on the coast. On each side of the trap, in some instances extending as far as the bank, a wall, or fence of stones or small stakes, slants down the stream, so as to lead the fish, in swimming up, towards the spot where the trap is placed. This consists of three or four long circular baskets, of uniform diameter, made of cedar splinters tied neatly together, a space of about two inches being left between each splinter. The up-stream end of the baskets is closed, and the down-stream end is left open. The length of the baskets is from ten to twenty feet, and their diameter from three to five feet. They are placed lengthwise down the stream, and small stakes stop the passage between each basket, without leaving even the pig-length passage which Monkbarns would have looked for, as by Scottish statute allotted. Inside each basket is a rather shorter basket of the same material and make, except that, while the down-stream end of both baskets is the full size of the cylinder, the inner basket, which in shape is like a long candle-extinguisher, decreases till its open up-stream end is just of the size through which a salmon can pass. The down-stream ends of both inner and outer baskets being lashed together, form the entrance to the trap. The fish enters the inside basket in swimming up the stream, and on getting out of the small up-stream end of it, finds himself imprisoned between the two cylinders. These salmon traps are very neatly constructed, and catch a great many fish.

Herrings.

Herrings are numerous on the coast, but they have not so good a flavour as the British herring. The finest I ever got were caught in December in a bay near the head of a long inlet. Their appearance in that place at the end of the year was, however, unusual. Herrings are caught in the beginning of March close to the seashore in great numbers, and they enter the inlets, creeks, and bays, in the two following months for the purpose of spawning. As far as the Indians know, the herrings have only one spawning ground, and they never spawn, as the Indians describe it, "when snow is on the ground." They avoid places where the water runs fast. The spawning ground is generally the rough, stony bottom of a bay which becomes shallow towards the shore. At the Seshaht islands in Nitinaht (or Barclay) Sound, immense quantities of spawn are deposited by the herrings every year. I have seen many acres of herring-spawn at this place. The natives put cedar branches or stalks of long grass into the water, and press them to the bottom with stones—each person having his own piece of ground—and when the herrings have deposited their spawn, the pieces of grass or the branches are lifted, and the egg-bed is found firmly adhering to them. It is dried in the sun and kept as a delicacy to be eaten with whale oil. After spawning the herrings stay near the place for about a month, and then return to the deep sea. The fry grow quickly,—the natives say at the rate of an inch in a month,—and in the first summer of their existence depart for the sea, on the way to which many of them are eaten by the salmon. The fry return full-grown next spring. The herring is not a difficult fish to catch; many are caught by the Indians in a net similar in appearance to the "scum net" used in the north-east of Scotland. This net is made of nettles, which grow here to the height of eight or ten feet. The outside of the stalks is stripped off, and the inner portion is afterwards steeped in fresh water for four or five days during cold weather—a material thus being formed which makes a light strong net that will last for twenty years. Another mode of fishing herrings is with the fish-rake—a flat-sided pole ten feet long, armed for two feet from one end with sharp bones a few inches long and not far apart. This instrument is moved quickly through a herring shoal with a wavy motion, and the fish are transfixed and deposited in the canoe. For a considerable time after the first appearance of herrings for the season, the rake can only be used on dark nights, when every now and then the water near the canoe is lighted up as the fish approach the surface. At spawning time, being less alert, they can be caught with the rake in the daytime.

Halibut.

The next fish I will mention is the halibut—a very common fish on the coast. The mode of fishing for halibut is by "long-lining." For some reason or other, the natives will not use a steel hook in fishing for halibut. Their own halibut-hook is curiously shaped, and is made of a stringy tough part of the Douglas pine or the yew, which is steamed until it is flexible, when it receives its proper shape. The hook is of bone and has no barb. The sides of the hook must be kept tightly bound together until the time of using. The lines are made of seaweed except for six or eight feet from the hook, where they are of twisted twigs or deer sinew. To make seaweed into a line it is soaked in a fresh stream, and the water being afterwards squeezed out with the hands, the line is rubbed with an oily cloth and afterwards dried in the sun. Clams or small fishes are used for bait in fishing halibut. The fishing season is during March, April, May, and June. Thousands of halibut, some of them weighing more than two hundred pounds, are caught by the natives, and are exchanged for potatoes, gammass, rush mats, and other articles. The best fishing-grounds are about twelve miles off the land, but the halibut is also caught near the shore. The fishing tribes on both sides of the Straits of Fuca would drive away any other tribes which had not been accustomed to fish on the halibut banks. The mode of fishing is to trail the line slowly after the canoe, the hook being sunk in deep water. Hundreds of canoes, with two or three men in each, start at midnight for the fishing-ground, so as to arrive there in the morning. After half a day's work, if the sea is moderate, the canoes are quite laden and the fishermen return. If the sea should rise during their progress to the shore, rather than throw any of the fish overboard, the natives tie large inflated sealskins to both sides of the canoe to increase its buoyancy. The hairy side of these skins is turned inside and the skinny side outside, and various rude devices are painted on the outside, such as the sinking of a canoe, or the capture of a great fish. To get so large a fish as a halibut into a canoe at sea is rather a difficult matter. Accidents, however, rarely happen, and the fish seldom gets away after being hooked. By using bladders attached to the line, and spearing the halibut when he appears on the surface, the largest fish is finally towed alongside the canoe, where he is killed by being struck on the head with a club.

Whale.

A whale chase is an affair of some moment. The kind of whale commonly seen on the coast was described to me by an old whaling skipper as a "finner," in which there is not much oil. The season for fishing whales commences about the end of May or in June. Many whales are killed every season by the Nitinahts, who live principally on the seaboard near Barclay or Nitinaht Sound. This tribe has a custom, which I have not observed elsewhere, of separating during spring and summer into small parties, each under a separate head, but all still continuing under the chiefship of the principal chief of the tribe.

Months beforehand preparations are made for the whale-fishing, which is considered almost a sacred season.

I particularly noticed this circumstance from having, in boyhood, heard of the Manx custom, in which all the crews of the herring fleet invoke a blessing before "shooting" their herring-nets. The honour of using the harpoon in an Aht tribe is enjoyed but by few—about a dozen in the tribe—who inherit the privilege. Instances, however, are known of the privilege having been acquired by merit. Eight or nine men, selected by the harpooner, form the crew of his canoe. For several moons before the fishing begins these men are compelled to abstain from their usual food: they live away from their wives, wash their bodies morning, noon, and night, and rub their skins with twigs, or a rough stone. If a canoe is damaged or capsized by a whale, or any accident happens during the fishing season, it is assumed that some of the crew have failed in their preparatory offices, and a very strict inquiry is instituted by the chief men of the tribe. Witnesses are examined, and an investigation made into the domestic affairs and the habits of the accused persons. Should any inculpatory circumstance appear, the delinquent is severely dealt with, and is often deprived of his rank, and placed under a ban for months. When the whales approach the coast, the fishermen are out all day, let the wind blow high or not. The canoes have different cruising-grounds, some little distance apart. The Indian whaling-gear consists of harpoons, lines, inflated sealskins, and wooden or bone spears. The harpoon is often made of a piece of the iron hoop of an ale cask, cut with a chisel into the shape of a harpoon blade—two barbs fashioned from the tips of deer-horns being affixed to this blade with gum. Close to the harpoon the line is of deer sinews. To this the main line is attached, which is generally made of cedar twigs laid together as thick as a three-inch rope. Large inflated skins are fastened to this line about twelve feet from the harpoon. The weapon itself is then tied slightly to a yew-handle ten feet long. On getting close, the harpooner, from the bow of his canoe, throws his harpoon at the whale with his full force. As soon as the barb enters, the fastening of the wooden handle, being but slight, breaks, and it becomes detached from the line. The natives raise a yell, and the whale dives quickly, but the seal-skins impede his movements. Very long lengths of line are kept in the canoes, and sometimes the lines from several canoes are joined. On the re-appearance of the whale on the surface, he is attacked from the nearest canoe; and thus, finally, forty or fifty large buoys are attached to his body. He struggles violently for a time, and beats and lashes the water in all directions, until, weakened by loss of blood and fatigued by his exertions, he ceases to struggle, and the natives despatch him with their short spears. The whale is then taken in tow by the whole fleet of canoes—the crews yelling, and singing and keeping time with their paddles. Sometimes, after being harpooned, the whale escapes, and takes ropes, harpoons, sealskins, and everything with him. Should he die from his wounds, and be found by another tribe at sea, or on the shore within the territorial limits of the finders, the instruments are returned to the losers, with a large piece of the fish as a present. Many disputes arise between tribes on the finding of dead whales near the undefined boundaries of the tribal territories. If the quarrel is serious, all intercourse ceases; trade is forbidden, and war is threatened. By-and-by, when the loss of trade is felt, negotiation is tried. An envoy is selected who is of high rank in his own tribe, and, if possible, connected with the other tribe by marriage. He is usually a quiet man of fluent speech. Wearing white-eagle feathers in his head-dress as a mark of peace, he departs in a small canoe. Only one female attendant, generally an old slave, accompanies him, to assist in paddling, as the natives never risk two men on such occasions. The envoy's return is anxiously awaited. As a general rule, the first proposition is rejected. Objections, references, counter-proposals, frequently make three or four embassies necessary before the question can be settled. By that time the blubber must be very rancid.

The Cod.

The existence of banks of the real bearded cod on the west coast of Vancouver Island is not yet quite established. I have seen, however, codfish at Barclay or Nitinaht Sound which were unmistakeably of that species. There is a productive bank on the west coast of Vancouver Island of an excellent fish, called by the Ahts, "Toosh-ko," which is very like the "Tusk" of the north of Scotland, and almost as good to eat as the true cod. Being a fatter fish, it becomes slightly yellow during the process of drying; but in other respects the Vancouver Island "Toosh-ko," when well prepared, is equal to the best dried Boston cod. It sells in Victoria at from 10 to 12 cents. a pound. In the deep sea off shore, instead of being caught by "long-lining," these fish are enticed to the surface and speared by the natives in a singular manner. They tie a line to the head of a small herring or anchovy, which is thrown alive into the water, and after descending several fathoms, is rapidly drawn back towards the surface. The "Toosh-ko," in following this prey, approach the surface, and are speared from the canoes. A bit of wood fifteen inches long—generally decayed wood, on account of its lightness—is sometimes used in smooth water as a decoy-fish, instead of the herring or anchovy bait. It is made thin at one end for three or four inches, and a piece of heavier white wood, representing an elongated spoon bait, is fixed on each side of the thin part. This instrument is thrust down into the water on the end of a long spear, and being detached by a jerk, spins upwards, and attracts the Toosh-ko, which, on approaching the surface, is speared, and the decoy is picked up and again used. This may seem a strange way of fishing cod, but I have seen it practised with success.

CHAPTER XXIII.

USAGES IN HUNTING.

The Aht mode of Hunting; with Descriptions of Several Animals—the Panther—Wolf—Bear—Wapiti or Elk—Blacktailed Deer—Indian Dogs—Marten—Mink—Racoon—Beaver.

And what's worse,
To fight the animals, and to kill them up,
In their assigned and native dwelling place.—SHAKSPEARE.

THE outside coast of Vancouver Island offers good sport to those who take pleasure in hunting wild animals, the pursuit of which involves little danger to the hunter; but the mere partridge-shooter, who always expects his dinner to be ready for him at an appointed hour, should not try this Far West sporting-ground. Whoever visits this coast at present for the purpose of hunting must possess the spirit and endurance of the sportsman, or his expectations will be disappointed. The traveller who lands from a ship to shoot a few ducks in a bay, or a deer near the shore, has only an imperfect notion of the sport which the country affords. To find what game there is really in the country, he should leave the shore and traverse the interior at proper seasons, carrying his shooting gear, food, and blankets through intricate woods and over broken ground, where a mile-and-a-half an hour will be good walking; now and then wearing snow shoes, and sometimes prepared for rain; and at all times satisfied with a native hut or a spreading cedar-tree as shelter for the night. It is advisable to take with one a native hunter, who understands the habits and peculiarities of the wild fowl and the animals which are found in the district. And I may remind the untravelled sportsman, who would exchange the anxieties of life for an interval of interest and adventure in these pathless woods, that in the Aht district he must live for the time remote from civilized man, among a savage people, whose language he does not know, and who will be quite ready to take advantage of him. This is, indeed, the chief difficulty at present in the way of the sportsman; but by-and-by, when settlements are formed along the coast, wild sports in Vancouver Island will be more generally followed. *

The Aht natives, distinctively, as before stated, are a fish-eating people, but one or two good hunters are found in most of the tribes. The hunters of those tribes which

* I may mention here that the Indian hunter is certainly inferior to the experienced white man in the best qualities of a sportsman, whatever quickness of sight, or knowledge of the habits of animals he may possess. The Aht savage has not yet learned how to shoot game, running or flying, and under unexpected circumstances he wants the coolness and judgment of the civilized hunter. If deer spring from cover on both sides of him the Indian becomes flurried, fires hastily, and misses his aim; but the white hunter retains his self-possession, and perhaps knocks a deer down right and left. I have noticed also that the Indian has fired a long shot when it was certain that by waiting he would get a nearer one. He is too excitable, and acts on the first impulse in discharging his gun, particularly when the powder is not his own.

go inland only at certain seasons in pursuit of salmon, and hunt along the stream from which they obtain their fish, are, of course, less informed respecting the habits of the wild animals than the small tribes which, living inland along lakes and rivers, spend more of their time in hunting. I took up my quarters forty miles from the sea-board, near the village of one of these latter tribes, in which were two noted native hunters—Quicheenam and Quassoon—who were familiar with the rough mountains and wild lakes of the interior. They showed me their traps, and explained their modes of hunting the various beasts of chase. They also described several animals which I am sure never existed but in their lying imaginations. I will relate what they told me, and what I myself saw here and elsewhere upon the coast. On my return now to civilization, it will be curious to notice how far this account agrees with the conventional statements in books of natural history.*

PANTHER.

The most dangerous wild beast in this part of the island is a species of panther (*ky-yu-men*), which occasionally enters the deer traps of the natives. It is not so numerous as might be expected from the number of elk and deer in the district on which it might prey. The largest panther that has been killed near Alberni measured eight feet from the nose to the end of the tail, and was over three feet high at the shoulder. The tail was two feet long, The colour of

* I may record that I have seen a whistling marmot, and only one, on the West Coast; and in 1863, an Indian brought me a small tortoise from Sproat's Lake, which Dr. R. Brown thinks probably was the *Actinemys Marmorata* of Agassiz. I could not find that the tortoise was regarded as a sacred animal.

this formidable animal was a light brown, with a dark-brown streak all the way down the back, and a black tip to the tail. His skin was measured by Captain John Henderson, of the steamer *Thames*, and myself, at Alberni, in 1865. The panther is of a solitary disposition, and is rarely seen by the native hunters. They do not pursue it, but rather endeavour to get out of its way. Hardly anything is known by them of this animal's habits, except that it prowls at night, and captures the deer by springing suddenly upon them. On one occasion I saw a young panther shot, which had betaken itself to a tree, and it looked a dangerous beast, lying on the ground wounded, and gnashing its strong teeth. It was of a brownish yellow colour, with dark tips on the hairs, and a lighter line down its back. In the full-grown animal this line, as has been observed, turns to a dark colour. During the last few years several flocks of sheep have been disturbed by panthers in the neighbourhood of Victoria, but it is not thought that there are many of these animals in any part of the island.

Wolves.

Wolves (*sah-ook* or *kannatlah*) of different colours are numerous along the whole coast, but are seldom shot, as these wild and savage beasts are of little use to the natives, and besides are regarded with superstitious fear. Occasionally, however, a wolf is shot which has approached too near a village on a misty night, and its fat is then melted down for a medicine to be applied outwardly to wounds and bruises. As the animals which form the prey of the wolves abound in the woods—retreating inland in summer to the mountains, and in winter coming nearer the shore—the wolves do not assemble in large packs under pressure of a common want of food, but hunt in couples, or four or five together. I have often heard their dreadful howls at night. Deer are the favourite prey of the wolves, but they will eat almost anything—putrid fish, or carcases of animals left by hunters in the woods, and when pressed by hunger, even the refuse that lies about the temporarily deserted native encampments. The traps for marten, racoon, and deer, also the bear traps—when Bruin is helpless under the treacherous mass of wood—are harried by the wolves, who devour the captured prey. The dogs of the natives fly, and crouch near their masters, when the wolves' howls are heard; but an old mastiff bitch of mine, which I brought from London, came off not very much the worse from several stiff encounters. No instance is known of wolves having attacked the natives.

Bear.

The common black bear (*chimmus*) is frequently met with, and makes excellent sport. He sometimes reaches a size of three feet high at the shoulder, and six feet long, not including the tail. The latter end of the autumn, just before the bears go into their winter quarters, is the best season for hunting them. Three or four hunters—one carrying a lance, and the others armed with guns—enter the woods with half-a-dozen dogs, and separate in search of game. When a bear is seen, a whoop is sounded to bring the hunters together. The dogs follow, barking loudly, but cannot always overtake the bear; he sometimes turns on the dogs, and drives them back. On seeing the men, the bear again runs, and finally climbs a tree, commonly a cedar, as the branches come low down the trunk, and the foliage affords cover. A bear, however, by grasping the bole of the tree between its paws, can readily climb a full-grown pine-tree, which has no branches to a considerable height from the ground. His fate, on being discovered, is no longer doubtful, though many shots may have to be fired before he is dislodged. A bear, desperately wounded, will not relinquish his position while he has power to support himself. He hangs sometimes, for a time, by one paw, until at last, weak and dizzy, he falls to the ground and is despatched by a lance thrust. Another plan of getting a bear is by marking the end of his track, commonly at a drinking place on a river bank, and by shooting him from a canoe or an ambush on shore. The bear is also shot or speared in his winter hiding-place, which is usually the decayed body, or under the root, of some large tree in a retired part of the forest. Here the female bear brings forth her young, and makes a bed for them at the bottom of her den. The large bears generally have two young ones at a birth, and the small bears only one. Four months is about the time during which the bear remains in retirement; but the animal does not sleep during the whole winter, for I have seen bears (probably males) walking about in January, when the snow was a foot deep. In the month of February I have seen their tracks towards water. Bear cubs are often seen about the native villages which have been taken from the mother's den at an age when the skin was of no value, and there was consequently no inducement to kill them. The food of the bear consists of grass, leaves, berries, and salmon. He is a great fisher, and will repair at night to the bank of a shallow river or stream, and there patiently sit on his haunches, looking downwards, until a rippling of the water, touched brightly, perhaps, by a ray of the moon, shows an approaching fish; by a clever scoop of his large paw he lands the fish on the bank, seizes it with his mouth, and retires into the forest. This is not a difficult feat with tired salmon in a shallow stream; I have thrown them upon the bank with the paddle of a canoe. Another fishing station of the bear is on a tree blown down and lying across a brook; with his paw near the surface of the shallow water he catches the fish swimming up, as they appear from under the tree.

The natives frequently catch wild animals in traps. One description of trap is generally used, and is simple and effective. It is made larger or smaller, as required for bears, deer, beaver, racoon, marten, or mink. Since guns were introduced trapping has been little practised, and few skilful native trappers can now be found. It is still, however, followed, especially by the marten hunters, as gunshot injures the skin of small animals. Pitfalls are seldom used on the West Coast for the capture of wild animals. The bear-trap succeeds best when snow lies on the ground. A few sticks, two or three stones, and a bit of rope made of cedar-bark, are all the materials necessary in making the trap. A thick piece of timber, or the trunk of a small tree, is heavily weighted with stones for about the length of five feet from one end, and the extremity of this weighted end rests on the ground. The unweighted end of the piece of timber is then raised about eight feet above the ground, and is kept thus suspended by a strong rope of cedar-bark which is attached to it, and also tied to the end of a cross-piece, which has been placed immediately above the raised end of the piece of timber. The other end of this cross-piece, which at its middle or centre rests upon a convenient support—perhaps the stump of a tree, or other suitable object—is then depressed to within about two feet of the ground, by a slender rope slightly attached to it. This rope is made to cross the animals' track, and on his touching it, it slips off this depressed end of the cross-piece, and this end of the cross-piece itself immediately flies up so much above the level that the other end is depressed, and the whole cross-piece slips off its resting-place, and the whole affair—cross-piece and piece of timber —of course falls to the ground. The latter falls heavily, both on account of its own weight, and also from the weighty pressure of the stones on the other end, and thus the bear is, in fact, crushed by it. Of course, for smaller animals, slighter materials are employed. Placed in the accustomed track of the bear to his feeding or drinking-place—generally at a spot where a stump or upturned root for supporting the cross-bar allows the trap to be set without disturbing the usual appearance of the path—the bear walks against the slender rope, and a heavy log falls on his neck or back, and presses him to the ground.* This stick-trap is also used by the natives in capturing deer (but not elk) when ammunition is scarce.

Elk.

So far as I know, there are but two kinds of deer in the country—a black-tailed deer (*ah-toosh* or *moouch*), and

* A small trap, made on this principle, is used for capturing martens by the Indians who inhabit the woody district around Hudson's Bay.

what is called the American elk (*kloh-nym*). This name of elk is the name given to the animal by the colonists, but it must not be confounded with the moose of the United States. The deer meant by me is similar in general appearance to the stag of Europe, and is probably the wapiti, or *Cervus Canadensis*. I may note, however, that it is stated in some books that the branching horns of this animal are no incumbrance in forcing its way through the woods, and that it lays them flat on its back before plunging among the trees. Neither of these remarks is true of the wapiti of Vancouver Island.

The other deer, which I call "blacktail," may be the *Cervus Macrotis* or *Virginianus*. The reader may judge for himself by the description.

Both these species of deer are numerous, owing to the smallness of the population and the absence of large carnivorous wild animals in Vancouver Island. The wapiti deer have not been much seen by the colonists, but they are numerous in the interior of the island. In summer, they frequent the mountains, and in winter, they come down to the lower ground. A man and boy at Pacheen, on the West Coast, killed seven elk in two days, in 1864. The body of the wapiti is round, and as large as that of a good-sized ox, and the height of a full-grown buck is sometimes above five feet at the shoulder. The male elk is the larger. The legs and hoofs are shaped like those of a deer, but seem longer and thinner in proportion to the weight of the animal's body. The head is flat on the sides, like the head of a horse, which it somewhat resembles, except that the nose of an elk is much sharper, and the upper lip is somewhat prominent, and well adapted for grasping. The tail is quite short, and is kept down in running. The ears are less broad, and less finely shaped, than the deer's, and stand straight up. The hair, in winter, is long and coarse; but comes off towards summer, beginning at the flanks. The colour of the head and of the body of the elk is the same, viewed as a whole, namely, a light brown, with a little yellowish tinge at the end of the lower lip and round the eyes, along the back it is of a somewhat fainter colour than the body, and has a sandy-coloured rump and tail. In summer, when the hair is short, the elk becomes of a light red colour, the hinder part, including the tail, then being white. His swiftest pace is a trot, and he never bounds, except in leaping over fallen trees. For a short distance, the elk runs, on clear ground, as fast as a dog; but is soon overtaken, especially if snow lies on the ground. He has tracks of his own through the woods, as he cannot go freely through the forest, owing to his great size and his spreading antlers. The largest pair of elk horns that I have seen weighed forty-six pounds; the length, twenty-seven inches; they measured across between tip and tip, twenty-five inches. The females have no horns. As the elk, in this island, has never been domesticated, no one has had an opportunity of observing the progressive growth of the antlers; but the natives say that the brow antler comes at the fifth year, and an additional point every year afterwards. The horns fall off and are renewed annually. Previously becoming soft and hairy, they are dropped about March or April, and for two months the reproductive growth is hardly perceptible; but after that interval, the horns grow quickly for the remainder of the year. The lower jaw teeth of the deer and elk are the same—eight teeth in the front of the jaw, with grinders near the throat; but the upper jaw of the two animals is differently furnished. The deer has no teeth in the upper jaw in front of the grinders, whereas the elk has one large conical tooth on each side of the upper jaw, about two inches back from the point of the nose. Both have facial slits, or supplementary breathing organs, under the eyes. The female elk brings forth in May or June, and generally produces one, but sometimes two young ones at a birth. The flesh of the elk is good to eat, indeed is finer in flavour than that of the black-tailed deer. His food consists of grass, bark, and leaves. He loves to retire into the thick parts of the forest, from which he comes out in the early morning and in the evening for the purpose of feeding. The natives hunt the elk both in summer and winter, and find them fattest in October and November, at which time they have been feeding long on good pasture. So quick is the native hunter's practised sense of hearing that, in walking through the woods, he will first discover the near presence of deer by the slight noise they make in feeding. Two or three elk generally go together; but as many as nine females and young, with one king or leader, are occasionally seen. I knew an old native hunter—Quicheenam, of the Opechisahts—who, with his whole family, was accustomed to go every summer for two months about thirty miles from his village, for the purpose of shooting elk and deer on a large rocky mountain. There being no wood on the mountain, except a scrubby fringe at its foot, a hut was made of stones, and wood was carried up for fire. Knowing well the haunts and habits of the animals, and approaching them warily behind masses of rock, the hunter and his sons killed many elk and deer every season; and, as the animals were too heavy to be removed to any distance, they cut the flesh into long strips, which they dried in the smoke, and carried in bags to their village. On this excursion, no dogs were taken; but in chasing elk in winter, the dog is a useful ally of the hunter. Three dogs are sufficient to pursue and harass a small elk; but it is better to have four or five to surround a large elk. Every Aht tribe has several dogs, short-haired, sharp-nosed, thin-tailed, sour-natured animals, of middle size, with a wheezy bark, and which howl as if howling were natural to them.

The more inland tribes say they got their dogs from the tribes dwelling on the seaboard. They may have been originally left by voyagers, and may have degenerated; or the dogs of the Ahts may be indigenous. Mr. Joseph Dean, an intelligent settler at Komux, told me that he, on one occasion, saw dogs—half-bred between dogs of the Indians and dogs of the colonists—playing with wolves, the wolves chasing the dogs, and the dogs chasing the wolves. As has been already stated, the wolves at Alberni several times attacked my mastiff bitch. Following by scent the track of the elk in the snow, the dogs bark on seeing him, and the courageous animal, on hearing the voice of the dogs, stops and turns round to butt them. As long as the dogs harass him, the elk will not fly, even on the appearance of the hunter.* It is common for half-a-dozen natives to go out

* An old chief, Kal-lowe-ish, not more given to lying than his neighbours, assured me that an elk will approach and stand still, looking at a blue blanket spread upon the snow, but will not be attracted by a red or white blanket, and that he has lured elk in this way in hunting without dogs.

elk-hunting. They make a small hut of branches in the forest, hunt in the morning and evening, and sit round the fire during the day. On killing an elk, they search for his marrow, and eat it as a precious morsel; in this, resembling the Danish "Kitchen-middeners," who also seem to have liked marrow. A wounded elk sometimes attacks the hunter, who, for his protection in such an event, carries a knife, made of sharpened iron hoop (formerly of mussel shell), fixed into a wooden handle three feet long. The natives formerly made many weapons and instruments of elk-horn; but, since the introduction of iron, elk-horn has not been much used for such purposes.

Black-tailed Deer.

The other species of deer I have called the black-tailed deer, as the tail is always black for about two inches at the end on the upper side, the under side being white. The tail is not over four inches long, and is turned up in running. This is a much smaller animal than the elk, seldom exceeding 150 lbs. in weight, but its shape is beautiful. The flesh, however, is inferior in flavour to that of the elk, and also to the flavour of the English deer. It is in best condition about the end of the year. All that I have seen were of the same colour—a lightish brown, but not so light as the elk—with a slightly darker shade along the back than on the body. The hair at the end of the nose, the forehead between the eyes, and the top of the head round the root of the horns, is black. In the males the parts between the nose and eyes, and round the eyes, are ash-coloured, with darker shades towards the cheeks.

The ears are long and flexible, and are of the same colour as the body. The hair of this deer is shorter, closer, and finer than the coarse, spongy hair of the elk. It becomes thin and short in summer, at which time it is of a lighter colour than in winter. When dropped, the young are beautifully marked along the back with round spots, but these soon disappear.

In running, the black-tailed deer bounds with every foot from the ground at the same time. The hunter finds it singly, or two or three together, in ravines or thickets, or in the morning and evening browsing in the open forest. As many as forty have been seen in one day. When numerous in the mountains, the black-tailed deer are often caught with dogs, which are able to gain upon them among rocks or in thick wood; but nearer the shore the natives generally shoot them. Traps are also set in their tracks near drinking places, and sometimes dogs chase the deer into the water and enable the natives to capture them. In this way I captured two deer from a boat one forenoon at Alberni. They do not swim quickly, and are easily taken. The horns of the black-tailed deer are not large; the brow antler is wanting, and five points are the most I ever saw on the horns of an old animal. The natives say that the horns "fall with the grass"—about December—and "grow again with the leaves." The young are brought forth about May. The average number at a birth is two; this number is rarely exceeded.

Marten.

Of the remaining land-animals hunted by the natives, the marten (*Kleekklayhy-yeh*) is one of the most valuable, as its fur is prized by white traders. The fur of this active and graceful little animal is in its best condition in winter, but the marten is most easily caught in the autumn and fall, when it approaches the waters in search of salmon. The marten makes its house among stones on the ground, but more commonly inside decayed trees on which the bark is loose. It will climb up between the bark and wood of a decayed tree to its nest many feet from the ground. The marten sleeps during the greater part of the day, and comes out to feed in the early morning, and afterwards runs about for a few hours before returning to rest. The hunter at this time watches to shoot it, but trapping is preferred because the shot injures the skin. The trap is a small stick-trap, exactly like the bear-trap already described. It is baited with a bit of salmon and placed near where the tracks of the marten have been seen, or where a tree has been playfully scraped with its claws, as is its wont on a bright forenoon. As many as forty traps are set at one time by a hunter, and if by the whole number one marten is caught in a week, it is fair sport. There is but one kind of marten on the island. The natives do not know that the marten eats anything but salmon or salmon-trout. They do not think that it eats birds or eggs. It does not go into the water, but feeds on dead salmon washed upon the beach, or on portions of fish left by the bears in the woods. The remains of deer killed and abandoned by the natives also furnish it with food. The marten breeds during summer in the stump of a decayed tree, and the female has generally three young ones. The hunter never sees more than two old martens, with their young, together. The only apparent difference between the female and male is that the male is of a darker colour on the breast. I could not find what the marten was likely to feed on when fish or deer was not obtainable; perhaps it may be able to get one or the other all the year round, or it may feed on birds.

Mink.

The mink (*chastimit*) is a small animal, not unlike the marten in shape, but with a less bushy tail and an inferior fur of a darker colour, and white instead of red under the throat and on the breast; it is more independent than the marten in the matter of food, being able to dive under water and fish for itself. The natives kill numbers of mink all the year round for the sake of the skins, which they sell to the traders. They are shot, taken with stick-traps, or caught by dogs. Dogs can catch them on a clear beach, but not in the forest. The mink does not climb trees. Morning or evening is the best time for getting them. This animal lives among the stones on the beach, and keeps near the sea-coast, where it feeds upon clams, oysters, mussels, fish, and also birds. It sleeps during the afternoon and night, and hunts for its prey generally in the early morning. The natives say that the mink also eats salmon-berry leaves, but that the marten does not. As many as five mink are sometimes seen together. Summer is their breeding time, and the female generally has four young at a birth.

Racoon.

Another common wild animal hunted by the natives is the black-footed racoon (*Klapesim*), the skin of which is also sold to white traders. I have forced a racoon in the day time from under the root of a fallen tree, and killed him with a stone. He is generally found up a cedar tree, which he easily climbs, and he spends the day in sleep on one of its branches, coming down in the night time to feed. The locality he prefers is the neighbourhood of small shallow streams that run into a river. More racoons are found near the sea-shore than away from it. Like the mink, he is fond of mussels and shell fish, or a dead deer, but roots, berries, and leaves, are also favourite articles of food. He will not enter the water, yet the bear himself is not a keener fisher. When twilight comes, the racoon, who has passed the day rolled up in the form of a ball on the thick branch of a cedar tree, descends to the ground, and stations himself upon his haunches, by the side of a stream, in which there may be only a few inches of water. His round eyes, specially adapted for seeing well in the dark, glisten as the tiny fish sport before him, and, suddenly extending at the same time his two fore-feet into the water, he presses the little captive between them and conveys it to his mouth. The racoons seem to be sociable animals, as four or five are sometimes seen together. The female breeds in summer, and has as many as five young ones at a birth. When taken young, the racoon is easily tamed, but it is always of rather a capricious temper. The common native stick-trap, baited with a small fish, and placed near a track of the racoon towards the water, is used by the natives in capturing this animal. They sometimes succeed in shooting him from the bank of a stream in the morning, while fishing, as described. Though proverbially wary, the racoon is more easily captured by the natives than either the marten or mink. His gait is heavy and awkward, and when discovered on the ground he rarely escapes.

Beaver.

The beaver (*Attoh*) which, in some respects, is the most interesting of all the wild animals hunted by the natives, is the last I shall mention. The skin of the beaver, formerly, was very valuable in trade. What the natives told me of this animal was rather disappointing, after all my boyish respect for the sagacity which it was said to display. They think the beaver is a commonplace animal, which any ordinary hunter can capture. A chief might be proud of the name of Kill-bear, or Kill-elk, or Kill-whale, but Kill-beaver would hardly be valued as an honorary title. I confess that I have seen many beaver-dams both in the streams and lakes of the Aht district, and they never struck me as anything extraordinary. The most noticeable effort on the part of the beavers that I could hear of was, biting through and felling a willow tree seven inches in diameter; but the stupid creatures could not move the tree when it was down, so all their labour was lost. Perhaps as the winters are mild in Vancouver Island, an inferior instinct suffices on the part of the beaver, compared with the instinct required by the animal in a severer climate. No large community of beavers has been seen by the Indians. Their dams are formed both in lakes and streams, and are made of trunks and branches of trees, sticks, mud, and stones huddled rudely together. Their oval houses are built of the same materials, and are about six feet in diameter, and five or six feet in height. Four old beavers and six or eight young ones are the most that have been seen in one dwelling.

The beavers lie in these houses—as the Indians express it—"like boys;" but when the female has young ones she goes into a separate bed, or chamber, I could not ascertain which. There is no storey in a beaver's house for convenience of change in case of floods; the waste-way is generally sufficient to carry off any extraordinary quantity of water. The beaver breeds at any season when there is no snow on the ground, and has three or four little ones at a time. The houses of the beaver on the banks of lakes are abandoned when the water is very high; and the beavers go to small streams, which they form into a succession of diminutive lakes. These dams are connected, in case of a flood, by a sufficient watercourse through the middle of the dam, and down the centre of the stream; and on, or rather in, the dams, the beavers build their houses, and provide themselves with an entrance by means of a hole under water. It is in these houses on small streams that the beavers generally breed. The principal food of the beaver in this district is grass, and the leaf and bark of the willow and alder, and roots at the bottom of the lake. It is not necessary for him to lay in a stock for winter. He sleeps during the day, and comes out at nights to feed; the only difference in his habits being that he sleeps a little longer in the winter—still, however, appearing at nights for the purpose of feeding. His eyes are small, and he cannot see far, but his nose is very keen. He swims in the water with a part of his head above the surface like a seal. The natives approach to leeward at night, and spear the beaver from a canoe, as he floats eating a branch taken from the shore; or they shoot him when he is in shallow water, but not in deep water, as he sinks on receiving the shot. They also block up the opening into his house, break through the wall, and shoot or spear him. It would be no use waiting at his house to shoot the beaver as he went out, for the entrance is under water. Trapping is perhaps the favourite mode of capturing the beaver, as it leaves the skin uninjured. The common stick-trap is used without bait, but with the addition of a side or wall made of cedar sticks, which projects into the lake for ten or fifteen feet, so as to lead the animal towards the trap as he approaches the shore. The beaver generally lands at one place, and the trap is set in the track, almost the whole of it being in the water. The deceiving string is placed just about the water line.

CHAPTER XXIV.

DISEASES.

Diseases—Medicines and Medical Practice.

And at their heels, a huge infectious troop
Of pale distemperatures and foes to life.—SHAKSPEARE.

THE commonest diseases among the Ahts are bilious complaints, constipation, dysentery, and consumption, produced, I suppose, by their coarse oily food, irregular meals, and frequent personal exposure. Fevers and acute inflammatory diseases are also common, and these often end fatally, as the natives do not understand the proper modes of treatment. Rheumatism and paralysis are rare maladies. I have been told by traders that syphilis was unknown among them twenty years ago. I think this is a mistake, and that it is probably indigenous, as the natives have herbs which they use in curing this disease. It is now quite common, and is almost invariably followed by consumption. Many of the old people, particularly the women, suffer from ophthalmia. Being totally ignorant of the pathology of diseases, and believing that bodily ailments are caused, either by the temporary absence of the soul, or by the presence of the spirit of some animal or demon in the sick person, the natives treat every disease nearly in the same manner, and direct their efforts towards the recovery of the soul or the expulsion of the evil spirit. They have no knowledge of anatomy, nor any distinct knowledge of the circulation of the blood. Sprains and contusions are cured by the plentiful application of cold water. In cases of breakage of the arm or leg, the limb is straightened, and four deep incisions, several inches long, are made lengthwise through the flesh, round the limb, at the place of fracture. Into these cuts the doctor spits, after chewing leaves. No splints are used except when a leg is broken; a piece of delicate white pine bark cloth is then tied round the limb, in many folds, and allowed to remain till the bone has become re-united. I have seen several cases of broken legs that had been cured by the natives, but there was always some shortness of the limb afterwards. They possess sufficient skill to set dislocations in a rough way, which probably causes much pain to the patient. In gunshot wounds the ball, when buried, is never removed, but operations with a knife are performed for the extraction of bullets lying near the skin. Amputation and blood-letting have never been resorted to by the natives as a means of cure.

Perhaps no people more extensively believe in the assisting of nature, by means of medicines and extraordinary operations. These appliances, as might be expected, consist more in jugglery and sorcery than in legitimate allopathics. The natives use many plants in their medicines, and some of these may perhaps be worthy of the attention of more civilized practitioners. They understand the best season for getting the different kinds, so as to preserve their virtues for medicinal purposes. The Oregon grape, a shrub which grows plentifully at some parts of the coast, is a favourite medicine, and an article of barter among the tribes—as I learnt by noticing the native lads in a vessel collecting it, for the purpose of sale, at any village on the coast which the ship might stop at. It is largely used both by the natives and colonists, for the cure of venereal diseases. This grape makes an excellent tonic, and I have been assured that its virtues, in the complaints mentioned, are undoubted. The astringent qualities of the blackberry, and the value of the dogwood root, as strengthening medicines, seem also to have been discovered by the Ahts. A common tonic is a powder made of comb from a wasp's nest, burned and mixed with cold water. Hemlock bark is used as a sticking plaster. There are many other plants known to the native doctors for their curative virtues, and a still greater number of empiric medicaments, which they use as favourite specifics in different diseases. None of the natives possess sufficient knowledge to compound medicines, with any appreciation of their properties, though the sorcerers pretend to make valuable mixtures. Their most common way of using leaves, roots, or bark medicinally, is to make them into a kind of tea, which is allowed to cool before being taken. No metallic medicines are used. An infusion of the soft young cones of the pines is taken by women for various purposes, particularly, I think, to keep them from bearing children—an object which is also thought to be secured by a medicine made of the scrapings of the inside of a human skull. There is a small three-leaved plant, with a white flower in May, from which a medicine is made that is said to have a sure effect in producing abortion. The women mash the roots in water, and drink the solution, occasionally, once or twice a day. So far as I know, the natives are not acquainted with many poisons, though some of them pretend to such a knowledge, in order to frighten others of their tribe. They poison deer with the roots of a climbing species of convolvulus. Of all the medicines used on the coast—and these are beyond enumeration, for the Indians seem to have a medicine for everything—the love medicines are by far the most numerous. Every doctor or doctoress has a favourite specific, which is rubbed on the body as a means of attraction, or placed on the garments of those on whom it is intended to operate. Among the medicines is a decoction that will make a man cry, and a well-educated half-breed woman, who disbelieved the superstitions of her mother's people, candidly declared to a friend of mine that she had faith in this medicine. The different medicines used by the Ahts are kept secret, and it is most difficult to get any information from them with respect to their medical practice. If you ask the old women or doctors, they will either not answer, or will intentionally mystify you. They will speak on such a subject only to those for whom they have the highest respect, and who they believe will not take advantage of the information to damage the practice of those possessed of the secret. We laugh at such things, but have we nothing of the same kind among ourselves? Are not English physicians as jealous? How often are rural druggists asked for love powders? And do not herbalists believe in the virtues of certain herbs as fully and sometimes as absurdly as the neglected and untaught Vancouverian? In all the tribes, as before mentioned, the old women are the ordinary nurses and doctors, but in serious cases the sorcerers are sent for to expel the evil spirit, which is supposed to have occupied the patient's body.

Many observances are connected with the giving of medicines, and greater efficacy seems to be attributed to the mode of administering than to the medicine itself. I saw a case of bowel complaint treated in a curious way. Having drank a decoction of some leaf, root, or bark, the sick person sat naked on his couch, and the doctor, firmly pressing his hands on each side of the body, rubbed with his thumbs till the patient became pale and sick, accompanying the work with a low song; then, finally, raising his hands so as to join the fingers above the patient's head, he blew through them, and the sickness, or the evil spirit, was supposed to be blown away. An English trader on the coast told me afterwards that he attributed the preservation of his life on one occasion at Pacheen to this mode of treatment, when the usual remedies for constipation had failed to relieve him. Among the Ohyahts, a few years ago, there was a young woman, deformed and of diminutive stature, who had a high medical reputation. A native presented his leg to her, which she grasped at the knee, and rubbed, as would a Malvern doctor. On its being remarked that she did not cry nor groan, as usual with native practitioners, the patient explained aside that she was quite skilful in her work, but that if in his case she cried or groaned during the operation of rubbing, her charge would be a blanket, instead of a fathom of small beads, and he could not at that time afford a blanket. As long as patients are not hopelessly sick the women seem to treat them kindly, but their singing and howling must distress a sick person's nerves. Work in the house goes on as usual, and no attempt is made to lessen noise. The cracked voices of the old nurses produce a very effective discord; but, to make matters worse (though they believe they are bettering them), friends occasionally join in a dreary, piteous song, and keep time to it with sticks on the sides of the house. It is characteristic of a savage to want fortitude in bodily sickness; he never fights against disease, but sinks at once languid and helpless; and it is amidst bad smells, smoke, laughter, and the crooning of hags, that his stricken body is expected to regain its health. The sorcerers rely partly on the actual means of cure already mentioned, but principally on incantations and the necromantic influence which they are supposed to exert through the medium of small bits of bones, metals, and feathers contained in their pouches. Their most absurd requirements are superstitiously observed. A patient will travel fifty miles to consult the sorcerer or doctor of a friendly tribe, if he has a good name, and will pay him handsomely if he succeeds in his cure.

The practice of abandoning aged persons, or those afflicted with lingering disease, was lately quite common among the Ahts. Before satisfying myself on this point, I had believed that this inhuman custom was confined to those savage tribes which, being forced to wander over extensive districts in pursuit of game for food, and obliged to be at all times ready to fight an enemy, were unable to carry with them, in their rapid marches, persons infirm from age or sickness, and children of defective formation. But the practice is common among the tribes on this coast, who are seldom in want of food, and who never move their encampments but for short distances, and the custom, I think, rests simply on the unwillingness of the natives to be troubled with the care of hopeless invalids. It is not much worse, as a proof of the insensibility of the human heart, than the manner of treating insane persons was in Scotland, and other civilized countries, before lunatic asylums were established. The victims among the Indians, as stated above, are not always aged persons; young and old of both sexes are exposed when afflicted with lingering disease. A father will abandon his child, or a child his father. In bitter weather a sufferer has been known to have been taken to a distance from the encampment, and left unsheltered, with a small quantity of water and dried salmon. No one is permitted to add to the allowance, or to show attention to the miserable invalid; his own relatives pass him by in the woods with perfect indifference. Individuals thus abandoned occasionally recover and return to the village, but more often they perish wretchedly, and the wild beasts devour them. In opposition to this indifference, an eyewitness told me of the frightful manner in which the parents of a young girl who died showed, on that occasion, their excessive grief. As soon as life had departed they screamed, and frantically seizing the body by the hair, arms, and legs, threw it about the house till they were quite fatigued; then, after a time, they placed it on a couch in a sitting posture, to await burial.

CHAPTER XXV.

USAGES IN BURIAL.

Usages in Burial—Appearance of the Aht Burying-Grounds—Burial of a Chief.

Let not that ugly skeleton appear!—DRYDEN.

THE Aht tribes differ somewhat in their modes of burial. They have no stone tombs, and neither burn nor inter their dead. The usual practice is to place deceased men of rank and young girls in rudely constructed boxes, which are fastened upon trees at a height of about twelve feet from the ground. A white blanket is thrown over the box, and four or five blankets, or pieces of calico, are hung upon a neighbouring tree. These blankets are torn in many places —either for the purpose of showing grief, or of spoiling them so that they should not be worth stealing. Another tree is draped with strips of blue blankets. The coffins of the highest chiefs, and sometimes also those of well-born infants are hoisted to a great height from the ground. A child which has only the name given to it at its birth is buried differently from a child which has received a second name. The one with two names is put higher up the tree than the others. Old women, and men and boys of no rank in the tribe, are wrapped in worn blankets or mats, and simply left upon the ground. No grave is dug to receive their bodies; a little of the earth is removed, and they lie there covered with sticks and stones; occasionally a worn-out canoe is used for a coffin. As among the people in remote parts of our own country at present, the days of mourning among the Ahts often end in a festival. A poor man of rank, wishing to bury his wife or child with the usual ceremonies, has been known to postpone the funeral for many months, until he obtained the means of giving a feast and distributing property. When a death becomes known in a native village, all the women begin to wail and continue lamenting for several hours. The near relatives of the deceased blacken their faces, and put on mean apparel. Little time is lost in conveying the body to the grave. Every tribe has a burial-place or places—generally on an islet or point of land—set apart for this special purpose, and these are never desecrated even by hostile tribes. The corpse, wrapped in a blanket and placed in a canoe or box, is conveyed to the burial-ground by the deceased person's friends, who are accompanied by many or few canoes, according to his rank or popularity during his lifetime. The whole of the dead man's personal effects that have not been given away before his death are deposited with him—except his best canoes, his house-planks, and fishing and hunting instruments, which, with any slaves he may have had, are inherited by the eldest son. If his friends are very superstitious they burn the dead man's house with all its contents, or they remove the materials, and build the house in another place. These usages in burial among savage tribes may be supposed to spring from sentiment, or some strange imagination; but, beyond the exhibition of a certain natural regret and instinctive respect for the dead, I think we shall err in investing the burial customs of the Aht nation with much significance. The habit of suspending the remains of young girls and men of rank upon trees originated probably in the desire of preserving the bodies from wolves and other wild animals; and for the same reason islands were preferred as burial places.* The natives bury a man's personal effects with him, and burn his house, in the fear that if these were used, the ghost would appear and some ill consequences would follow. Burning the house may have been practised at the first in order to guard against the spread of infectious diseases. I have not found that any articles are deposited in burying places with the notion that they would be useful to the deceased in an after time, with the exception of blankets (*see* "Religion"). Such a belief, however, exists, I have heard, among the tribes farther north on the coast of British Columbia, and it is possible that the Ahts may have derived the custom from them without any thought of its meaning. An islet used as a native burial-ground has generally a wretched look. The most appropriate idea of a burying ground is associated in my mind with some hill-side far from houses, or among old trees near a rocky shore—the grass being wild and unshorn, not trimmed, nor

* A tradition exists in a district of Sutherlandshire in Scotland, that, owing to the ravages of wolves in disinterring bodies, the people were obliged to use the precipitous island of Handa as a safer place of sepulture.

the place made into a flower-garden by art. But the burying places of the natives on this coast are too forlorn to please even the eye of one who does not care to see the bright flowers blooming in these sad places of rest. Fragments and piles of old canoes, boxes, boards, paddles, blankets, and other articles cover the surface. Here and there, rude coloured wooden carvings are placed near the bodies of chiefs. The labour of carving these images, when a sharp shell or a piece of bone was the only instrument available to the carver, must have been great. You may see a wooden figure which stands grimly contemplating the skull of an enemy placed in his hand; another, famous as a speaker in his lifetime, is represented with an outstretched arm; a third grasps a wolf. I once saw canoes daily visiting at twilight, for several weeks, one of these burying places, where they remained till past midnight. The visitors lighted a great fire and fed it with oil, gumsticks, and other combustible materials, and they wailed loudly at intervals during the whole time. The death and burial of the deceased, who in this case was a person of high rank, were thus described to me :—

The whole tribe had assembled in the house, and a friend of the sick person, in a loud and grave tone, announced that his relative was breathing his last. He then recounted his generous acts and deeds of daring, and intimated that the dying man wished to bequeath all his personal effects to his tribe. There was a contrast between the brave history of this chief and the poor creature who lay on a few mats, breathing heavily, his eyes glazed and his features pinched and pallid, from disease and exhaustion. The distribution next began, in which each person shared according to his rank. About an hour after life had departed, messengers went round to the different houses to give notice of the funeral. All the women in the village began to wail loudly. The men remained stern, sad, and silent. The corpse, wrapped in a blue blanket, was put into a canoe, which moved slowly from the shore, accompanied by about ninety canoes. Having reached an islet, a native climbed a large tree, and after various ceremonies, the body—which, in the meantime, had been placed in a box—was hoisted up and secured to a lofty branch. Long speeches were afterwards made in praise of the deceased, whose death, it was stated, should be honoured by a human sacrifice. A small neighbouring tributary tribe was accordingly visited by an armed party, which returned in a day or two with several heads. These, it was stated, had not been taken by force, but had been demanded and given as a necessary sacrifice on the occasion of the great warrior's death. Such human sacrifices, happily, are now of rare occurrence.

The natives have periods of mourning, but whether definite or depending on the will of the mourner, I cannot say. They cut the hair, as a mark of respect for the dead. The men seek solitude while mourning, but the women display their grief openly. In their houses the women often talk about friends who have died; how they were respected; what great things they did; how good they were: and, as long as four or five years after their death, becoming sad during such conversations, the old women go outside, and sit wailing for days. It seems odd to an Englishman that a woman should sit by herself, crying for so long a time, without any one taking the least notice of her. The men do not indulge in such long drawn-out sorrow; but their grief is sharp, as they have strong natural affections. I remember an old Ohyaht's grieving for his eldest son, who was drowned. The mourner's hair was cut close, the body and face blackened, tattered blankets wrapped round him, (sackcloth, indeed, and ashes!) and all the while he piteously wept. There is a heartrending expression in an Indian's grave hard face distorted by grief. Tears did not come often to his relief, and now and then he ceased his wail, and sat still, all his emotion "contracted in one brow of woe." The body of the son had not been found, and the old man, with a few friends, carried to a resting-place in the forest two cedar boards,—a sort of bier, I suppose,—on one of which was a small porpoise, over which the other board was placed, which bore the roughly traced representation of a man. After the funeral, the bereaved father divided all his own property among those present.

CHAPTER XXVI.

MISCELLANEOUS.

Miscellaneous—Giving Names to Persons—Description of a Feast where a Name was Given—Indians have some Standard of Correct Speech—Aht Names for Different Winds—Few Memorials of an Older Time—Rock Carving on the side of Sproat's Lake—Imperfectness of Indian Traditions—Pipes—Secret Fraternity among the Tribes on the Coast.

But much—much more than this I could declare.—Mace.

At their birth Aht children receive a name, and another name is afterwards given to them by guests brought together by the father for this purpose. Individuals are allowed to change their names when they please. One man in ten years may have ten different names, such as Kill-whale, Take-down-tree, Make-canoe, Shoot-flying-bird. Generally, notice is given by announcing the alteration at a feast, which simple announcement is considered sufficient when the change of name is unaccompanied by any increase of rank; but when so accompanied, the name is conferred, together with the dignity, by the tribe at a special meeting. The name of the principal chief is sometimes changed to mark events of importance to the tribe, and occasionally he assumes the name of a deceased chieftain of another friendly tribe. This accounts for the otherwise curious fact observed by navigators, viz.: individuals of different and perhaps distant tribes bearing the same names, such as Wick-an-in-ish, Maquilla, Hy-you-pen-uel, Makouina. The relinquished name is never mentioned, and if young persons use it unthinkingly they are immediately checked.* On the introduction of a new article which the natives have not seen before—a common occurrence since the colonization of the island—a discussion takes place about a proper name for it, and some person of good judgment in such matters is appointed to settle the name. Every tribe has one or two of these nomenclators. A list of Aht names for persons and places will be found in the appendix.

I was present on one occasion of giving a new name to the son of a man of rank in his tribe. The house was cleared at ten o'clock in the forenoon, soon after which the guests arrived. During the speech which the father delivered, two female slaves sang and rattled on a tin instrument, and at its conclusion a crier announced in a loud voice the names of the guests. To each of these a present was thrown, which was large or small according to the rank of the recipient, and the esteem in which the giver held him. My share was a small basket of potatoes, a fathom of large blue beads and four marten skins. After the distribution the host made another speech, stating the object of the meeting, which was to raise his son in the esteem of

* There is a high mountain, called Kloquiltsah, on the east side of the Alberni Canal, the name of which is never mentioned by the Indians in passing, lest a strong wind should come from the mountain and upset their canoes.

his tribe, and to obtain for him a name and a degree of rank. He then asked the guests to vote this rank—which was of a trifling nature—and to choose a suitable name for his son, which was done after some discussion. I noticed that the name, after being decided upon, was several times repeated by different persons, apparently with the object of settling its proper pronunciation. Correct pronunciation is more esteemed by the natives than might be supposed. That they have some standard of correct speech is evident, from the readiness of the children to ridicule a stranger who mispronounces native words, and also from the care with which a native repeats any word which the traveller seems to be desirous of remembering or noting down.

I will here mention the Aht names for the winds. As the Aht Indian knows nothing of the compass points, he names the winds in a way that is difficult for a stranger to understand. In different places the wind of the same name will not have the same direction. The name is not dependent upon an undeviating direction, but is given for some other cause: for instance, wind might blow at different times in two directions, inland, from the sea or coast; yet the two winds—as they really would be—would be called by only one name by the natives, as coming from the sea or coast. Of course the same inaccuracy would take place if they fixed upon any other natural object—lake, river, &c.,—in relation to which to give a name to any wind. *Ew-uttyh* and *Ew-ahtokuk*, are native names for the same wind—the former name being given when it blows gently, the latter when it blows strongly. These winds blow straight down the upper part of the Alberni Canal, and though the canal before reaching the sea changes its direction, still a wind blowing straight down this lower part of the canal is called by the natives the same name as the wind blowing down the upper end, though the wind is in reality very different. In thus giving the same name to winds from different quarters of the compass, the Ahts seem deficient in that observation of nature which in many respects is so wonderfully developed in savages. If they used the term Ew-uttyh merely to denote a night wind without any reference to direction, they would display no want of savage perception—the latter portion—*uttyh*—of the word meaning night; but they use the word so as to confound diversity of direction. This word probably originally meant a night wind, but as the night breeze is gentle, it was afterwards applied to any gentle wind of a certain direction, whether blowing by day or night.

The generic Aht word for wind is *wikseh*. *Ewkstis*, at Alberni, is the ordinary breeze up the canal, which exhibits its most characteristic phase on a summer afternoon. It is probably the name generally given on the coast, to the landward breeze that sets in from the sea during the daytime in the summer months. *Toochee* is the wind that brings ships down the Strait of Juan de Fuca, and may, therefore, be considered as ranging from east to south-east. *Huch-leetlh* brings vessels from the north end of the island towards Barclay or Nitinaht Sound, and is, therefore, a north-west wind, as the natives have no other idea of a ship sailing except "before" the wind. Their canoes, from deficiency of keel, will not sail "upon" a wind. *Tokseilh* is the name given to a strong wind from the sea, which blows straight towards the shore; it probably ranges from south to south-west. *Ewksah* is the name for a gentle wind from the same direction. This wind is considered by the natives to be distinct from Tokseilh and all other winds. In speaking to a white man, the Ahts would probably call the Tokseilh a great Ewkstis. None of these names correspond with our compass points, except accidentally. On describing to the natives the remoteness of the country I had come from, they inquired if the man who blew the winds from his mouth lived there.

No glyphics, traces, or records of a past people have been discovered on the coast. The historical value of a native tradition disappears after two generations, under a load of grotesque imaginings. Already the destruction of the "Tonquin" is ascribed to Quawteaht, and supernatural beings are described as having been concerned in it. My own memory among the natives is, I daresay, connected in their minds with a chief spearing salmon in the happy land of Quawteaht. The time of their father's father seems to be about the limit of these people's trustworthy traditions. The imperfectness of their traditions may be judged of by their not having among them any knowledge of so extraordinary an event as the building, launching, and fitting out of a large schooner close to a village in Nootkah Sound, by Captain Meares, about eighty years ago. I see that Hall, in his lively book, *Life with the Esquimaux*, states that, in his opinion, the traditions of the Innuits are accurately handed down through centuries. If this is the case, these hyperborean savages must be very unimaginative to keep a true record for so long a time, without a written language. The only rock carving ever seen on this coast is on a high rock on the shore of Sproat's lake behind Alberni. It is rudely done, and apparently not of an old date. There are half-a-dozen figures intended to represent fishes or birds—no one can say which. The natives affirm that Quawteaht made them. In their general character these figures correspond to the rude paintings sometimes seen on wooden boards among the Ahts, or on the seal-skin buoys that are attached to the whale and halibut harpoons and lances. The meaning of these figures is not understood by the people; and I daresay, if the truth were known, they are nothing but feeble attempts on the part of individual artists, to imitate some visible objects which they had strongly in their minds.

The Aht Indians are fond of tobacco, but they have no medicine-pipe, nor do I think they have among them the marked superstitious pipe usages by which most of the North-American Indian tribes are distinguished. They formerly had plain cedar pipes (*kosh-kuts*), devoid of ornament, but there were also to be found in all the tribes the ornamental blue-stone (*Tshimpsean*) pipes, which had been obtained in traffic with the Northern Indians. The present Aht name for tobacco is *quish-shah*, their word for smoke. Tobacco has been so long known to the natives that they can hardly explain what material they smoked before they had it; but they probably, in former times, made use solely of the leaves of the small shrub which is to this day mixed with the tobacco in their pipes, for the purpose of diminishing the intoxicating effect. It is customary, after meals, to pass the pipe round among the guests. This, however, is merely a compliment, arising from the high price of tobacco; and I should not wonder if, to some extent, the sacred associations connected with the pipe, which generally prevail among the North-American Indians, had originally no deeper origin than the scarcity of the smoking material. The Ahts do not smoke through their nostrils, though they are occasionally seen doing so; and they have not the placidity of the Englishman in smoking, but smoke with short laboured puffs. I may remark here, that Dr. Wilson—(*Prehistoric Man*, vol. ii. p. 17)—is wrong in stating that the Clalam Indians inhabit Vancouver Island, and that they have elaborately carved blue claystone pipes of their own manufacture. No such people live in Vancouver Island; but there is a tribe called the Tsclahllams, on the south side of the Straits of Fuca, which probably is meant. This tribe speaks a kindred language to the Ahts, and is a cedar-using tribe, which probably would only possess carved stone pipes as articles of traffic received along the coast from the powerful Tshimpsean tribes inhabiting Queen Charlotte Island, and the shores of British Columbia to the north of Vancouver Island.

At the risk of being thought too critical, I may say here that I doubt if the "Tawatin Indians on Fraser River" (whoever they may be) ever executed as an original work the ivory carving of a whale copied into Dr. Wilson's second volume, at page 22. The outline is too simple and truthful for an Indian work of art; it is superior to any representation of a whale which I have observed among those tribes most devoted to whale fishing. Indians living near the mouth of Fraser River may possibly enough have seen whales in the Gulf of Georgia, but none of the gentlemen in the Hudson Bay Company's service recollect them as great whale-fishers. The carving, probably, either came to the Indians of Fraser River from some of the whaling tribes on the outside coast, or was copied by the "Tawatins" from the "Jonah-picture" of some priest.

I should not omit in this account to notice that there is a secret association or fraternity among the Aht natives, composed of persons who are united for some purpose which has not been discovered. Meetings are held at different places about once a year, in a house covered round in the inside with mats. All non-members and women are excluded. As many as seventy natives from various tribes on the Vancouver shore, and also on the American side, have been known to attend one of these meetings. It is not a tribal affair, chief's affair, nor a medicine man's affair; these persons may or may not be members of the association, but unless they are members, they are not permitted to enter the house, and seem to be quite ignorant of what is going on. A meeting sometimes lasts for five days. The members wash and paint themselves, and wear their best clean blankets, and now and then come out of the house to wash and put on fresh paint. The proceedings inside the house are conducted in silence; there is no singing nor noise during the meeting of this secret association. Is this fraternity likely to be in any way connected with freemasonry? Freemasonry has been displayed in quarters least suspected.

CHAPTER XXVII.

EFFECTS UPON SAVAGES OF INTERCOURSE WITH CIVILIZED MEN.

Effects of Intercourse between Civilized and Uncivilized Races—Real Meaning of Colonization as regards Aborigines—Want of Definiteness in the English Colonial Policy—Moral and Physical Agencies concerned in Disappearance of Native Races—Decay of Tribes in their Isolated State—Evidence from my own Experience and Observation; —Inconsiderateness of Untravelled Writers—Aborigines, as a rule, not Harshly Treated by English Colonists—What are the Diseases and Vices of Civilization ?—Course of Operation of the Destructive Agencies following Intercourse with the Whites.

" *They had heard it said that it was a law of nature that the coloured races should melt away before the advance of civilization. He would tell them where that law was registered, and who were its agents. It was registered in hell, and its agents were those whom Satan made twofold more the children of hell than himself.*"—Dr. Selwyn, Bishop of New Zealand, at Manchester, October 7, 1867.

In this chapter I will offer some remarks—the result, as before mentioned, of long-continued and close observation —on the subject of intercourse between civilized and uncivilized races. The Bishop of New Zealand must use other language than the above, if he desires to influence the opinions of reasonable men on this most difficult subject. One would not expect that, in a colonizing country like England, there would be such differences of opinion among practical statesmen—as Parliamentary debates show—with respect to the real effect of colonization upon aborigines. There is, in my mind, little doubt that colonization on a large scale, by English colonists, practically means the displacing and extinction of the savage native population. By the expression "savage native population," I distinguish between the rudest untutored races and aboriginals of finer native races more capable of civilization; with these latter, or with an improved remnant of them, it is not yet shown that English colonists, or their descendants, will not intermix. I hope it may be shown in New Zealand that such intermixture is possible. But, as far as experience has taught us, it is extremely improbable that any large population of English descent will mingle their blood, and grow up side by side, with any race that differs widely from them in character and in civilized culture. In all dominant races, indeed, there is, to a large extent, an aversion to intermixture with other people—whether civilized or uncivilized. For instance, the English colonists have not yet shown any tendency to amalgamate with the descendants of the French in Canada, who live close to them in the same country, and are on almost the same level of civilization, and whose women are most attractive.

It is important that correct ideas should prevail as to the effect, in all its bearings, of colonization upon native races, for difference of opinion on this subject leads to various evils in our colonial policy, of which not the least is recrimination between the English and Colonial

Governments. The theory of an inevitable extinction of aborigines is regarded by many with repugnance, from the fear that such a theory must involve the harsh and neglectful treatment of the natives. But I do not think there need be any such apprehension; a clear view of the impending extinction of the inferior people would probably rather stimulate English settlers to acts of justice and humanity towards them. It would also give a much-needed definiteness to the imperial policy as regards native races in the colonies.

Several agencies—moral as well as physical—are concerned in the disappearance of aborigines before intruding civilized settlers, and these agencies must be properly estimated by the inquirer who seeks to form a right opinion on the subject. The problem he has to solve is a difficult one, which requires facts, and not theories, for its solution, and, unfortunately, we possess few accurately observed facts that bear on the question. These, indeed, will always be hard to obtain, owing to the want of opportunities by travellers, and the difficulty of observing precisely the particulars of change which accompany the continual intermixture of two different races—the one civilized, the other not.

Perhaps the first question of all, in reference to savages of a low class, will be, whether there are not in them—as races—the elements of natural decay leading to the extinction of the race, which elements, with increased speed and intensity, work out their destructive tendencies, if the people consort habitually with a greatly superior nation? West of the Rocky Mountains, it is certain that the experience of the Jesuits in California, and of the earliest settlers in the American and British territories on the North Pacific, affords proofs of the tendency of the savages to extinction, even before white people went amongst them. It was observed by the first fur-traders who entered different parts of New Caledonia—the present British Columbia—as I have heard from their own lips, or from those well acquainted with these pioneers—that the natives were rapidly decreasing in numbers.* This was before any number of civilized men had visited the country, and also before the introduction into it of ardent spirits, or the diseases produced by a mixture of races. The natives were decaying, and had been decaying, in their isolated state. Similar evidence is furnished by the history—so far as it is known—of the Aht people themselves. In 1778, Captain Cook rated the population of Nootkah village, in Vancouver Island, at 2,000; and Captain Meares, ten years later, confirmed this estimate in the main, and stated that the population of all the villages in the Sound at Nootkah amounted to between 3,000 and 4,000. The aggregate of the latter is now hardly 600 souls, yet the natives have remained in almost a primitive state, only visited occasionally by a ship of war or a trading schooner; they have had plenty of food and better clothes than they possessed prior to their knowledge of blankets, and their number has not been lessened by any epidemic, nor by the

* "Only a fur-trader," is a depreciatory phrase that has been heard in the colony in connection with gentlemen in the Hudson Bay Company's service. I must speak of the class as I found them, during a long acquaintance; cheerful and hospitable, and uncommonly well read and intelligent. Not to mention names, many a happy, long-to-be-remembered evening I have spent in their houses, for which I can make no return but this passing acknowledgment.

division or emigration of any portion of the tribes. The people have not abandoned themselves to the use of intoxicating drinks, though, no doubt, ready enough to do so; nor have their women—unchaste though they are—ever visited any of the settlements for the purpose of prostitution. These are instances of native races having decayed quickly, though possessing abundant means of food and shelter, living removed from civilized settlements, and left undisturbed to follow their own customs.

My own experience on this point may be added, as regards native tribes who decayed in the presence of white men, though well treated, and though ardent spirits were not introduced among them. I refer to the tribes among whom I lived in Nitinaht (or Barclay) Sound. Probably these people would have declined in number had the settlement never been formed near them. As already stated, I was the resident head of a large civilized settlement, established on the west coast of Vancouver Island, among savages who had seen only a few passing white men before my arrival. Having founded the settlement, in the face of opposition on the part of the Indians, as described at the beginning of this book, I had an opportunity of knowing them from the first, and of becoming acquainted with their fierce and rude natures. During the whole time that I was among these savages—a period of over five years—no instance of wanton ill-usage by the settlers occurred; on the contrary, the natives were treated kindly, and their condition was at first improved by the establishment of the settlement. Their houses, food, and clothing were better than they had formerly been. They fished and hunted as had been their wont in the old time. For any work which they did, they were well and regularly paid. The use of intoxicating liquors was forbidden to every one in my employment, and though it was impossible altogether to exclude ardent spirits, yet owing to the remoteness of the place and the peculiar approach to the harbour—as I was legally authorised and even bound to prevent the introduction of spirits—I was able to make the settlement as nearly a temperance settlement as any village of two hundred colonists of English descent could be made, under the best regulations and most favourable conditions for making the attempt. A clergyman resided in the place, who, though he did not succeed in establishing school-instruction on a large scale, yet learnt the language of the aborigines, and visited among them for the purpose of administering the simple medicines and comforts which the sick natives required, and were willing to receive. Taken as a whole, the settlement at Alberni probably was one in connection with which the Indians, not being compelled to abandon their old ways of life, enjoyed nearly all the advantages of a neighbouring civilization, with a comparative exemption from the distressing evils which are supposed necessarily to attend it.

What was the effect on the aborigines of the presence of this settlement? At first no particular effect was observable; the natives seemed, if anything, to have benefited by the change in their circumstances. They worked occasionally as labourers, and with their wages bought new blankets and planks for their houses. As a rule, the Indians did not abandon the blanket as an article of dress, though some of them took a pride in wearing, for a short time, the white men's cast-off clothing. They acquired a taste for flour, rice, potatoes, and other articles of food that were sold to them at low prices, and thus, on the whole, probably spent the first winter after the arrival of the colonists more comfortably than usual. It was only after a considerable time that symptoms of a change, amongst the Indians living nearest to the white settlement, could be noticed. Not having observed the gradual process—my mind being occupied with other matters—I seemed all at once to perceive that a few sharp-witted young natives had become what I can only call offensively European, and that the mass of the Indians no longer visited the settlement in their former free independent way, but lived listlessly in the villages, brooding seemingly over heavy thoughts. Their gradual shrinking from association with us, when first observed, caused a little alarm; but I found, on inquiry, that it did not arise from ill-will. The fact was that the curiosity of the savage had been satisfied; his mind was confused and his faculties surprised and stunned by the presence of machinery, steam vessels, and the active labour of civilized men; he distrusted himself, his old habits and traditions, and shrank away despondent and discouraged.* Always suspicious, it now became the business of the Indian's life to scrutinise the actions of the whites, and speculate apprehensively as to their probable intentions. He began soon to disregard his old pursuits, and tribal practices and ceremonies. By and by it was noticed that more than the usual amount of sick-

* The same feeling, in a comparatively small degree,—a beaten, cowed feeling, with a sense of some loss of self-respect,—must have been experienced by most men, at some change of their work or condition in life which has brought them suddenly among men, vastly their superiors in general, and also in special intellectual ability and force of character.

ness existed among the Indians, and particularly among the Indians who lived nearest to the white settlement. This increased ill-health was not caused by spirits, syphilis, or any of the other destructive agencies which are, I think, often erroneously described as the peculiar accompaniments of a high state of civilization. The disquiet produced in the mind of the natives by the presence of the settlers perhaps had something to do with it; at all events sickness increased during the second winter after our arrival, and many of the natives died from dysentery, and from a species of small-pox. Though no trustworthy anterior death-rate can be referred to for the purpose of comparison, I believe that mortality among the natives began to increase soon after the formation of the settlement, and a high death-rate continued during the five years that I was there. I may repeat that this did not result from ill-usage, nor from the excessive use of ardent spirits, nor from debauchery; but from other causes, among the chief of which, according to my observation, I would name—the effect of a change of food, and the despondency and discouragement produced in the minds of the Indians by the presence of a superior race: the latter being the principal cause. Nobody molested them; they had ample sustenance and shelter for the support of life, yet the people decayed. The steady brightness of civilized life seemed to dim and extinguish the flickering light of savageism, as the rays of the sun put out a common fire.

The conclusions to which these observations point, if correct, ought to modify in some degree the opinions of untravelled persons who attribute the decline and extinction of native races in our colonies, to the injustice and cruelty of the intruders, and to the diseases and vices which they carry with them. On these opinions, which appear to be generally entertained, I will comment, but shortly only, as my space is limited. I will take them in the following order :—1. Injustice and cruelty. 2. Diseases. 3. Vices.

As regards the first point, alleged cruelty on the part of colonists, it may, I think, be affirmed, as an historical fact, that very little violence has been used by English settlers generally in superseding weaker races. This will appear to any one who, laying aside prejudice, studies impartially, as I have endeavoured to do, the dreary records, from the earliest time, of actual life upon the frontiers of our different colonies, including those now comprehended within the United States of America. Many instances of harsh treatment by English settlers can no doubt be proved, and such instances occur at the present day; still, the history of the intercourse of our countrymen with aborigines, taken altogether, is creditable to us. Sufficient allowance is not always made for the circumstances in which settlers in savage countries are placed. Their situation is widely different from that of the mercantile emigrant or clergyman, who goes to the colony upon a salary. The poor, self-dependent emigrant, after disembarkation, finds himself in a position from which he cannot retire, for he has little money, and a wide sea extends between the new land and his mother-country. The English settler acts in this emergency according to the instinct and vigour of his race. Not content—like the lazy savage—to be a fisherman or hunter, he takes a firm hold of some object for his labour that presents itself to his grasp, and is prepared immediately to defend his acquisition, and to protect his family, if assailed. When the acquisition, as often happens, is a piece of waste land, unvalued and really unowned by any individual, the intruder generally feels, in defending it, that he is in a different position from that of a mere labourer. His duty and work are peculiar, as he is one of a body of men by whose efforts the surface of a neglected country has to be redeemed. The wrong of intrusion, if it is a wrong, is quickly turned into a right, under these circumstances. But I almost think, as already stated in Chapter II., one may reasonably say that civilized settlers have a right to occupy the land of a savage people on certain conditions, and that, therefore, they are justified in defending their occupation against the original so-called occupiers, now transformed, by the course of events, from patriots into aggressors. Now, as no authority nor law could prevent the peaceful, though determined, progress of these intruding settlers, after having gained a footing, they must, in all cases, be permitted to spread and cover the surface of the country, according to their increase and characteristics. Roads, fields, villages, towns will appear. And the savage—who all the time may have been kindly treated—will disappear.

Then, with regard to the second point—the diseases of emigrants, which are said to destroy aborigines—these, no doubt, will be the diseases of the mother-people, changed somewhat in their manifestations and effects by the mixture or contact of different races. To speak plainly, on a matter of great concern—bodily diseases—I doubt if many writers have clear ideas in their minds as to what they mean by diseases which, they say, "are carried among savages by civilized men." What are these diseases thus carried from England by emigrants—diseases, contagious in their nature, yet harmless in a crowded ship—destructive on shore to the aborigines only? Phthisis, small-pox, syphilis—what? I believe the last-named disease alone is meant; but, as this disease prevails among savages generally in their primitive condition, though in a milder form than among civilized men, the introduction of it, even if it occasionally happens, cannot be charged against the colonists as a race. Syphilis, and several other diseases, assume a peculiarly virulent character when the two races commingle. More than this cannot, I think, in relation to this subject be said of it.

Let us now consider the third point, the "vices" of an intruding people, which, as alleged, destroy a native race. Here, again, I think, writers err in not stating their meaning with sufficient distinctness. The vague expression, "vices of civilization," so frequently used, must refer (in addition to the particular vice which, in its effects of disease, I have, in fact, discussed under head two,) to the English vice of drinking, and its pernicious example; for no other of our too many vices would be likely to cause the rapid disappearance of aborigines. The use of ardent spirits is not a vice; it is the excessive use—the abuse of them—that is vicious; and I doubt if the mere example of drunkenness on the part of colonists, bad as it is in itself, is greatly injurious to the natives, though, under special circumstances, it might become so. To some extent it may be injurious, as confusing their moral sense by the spectacle of a superior man degrading himself; but practically, the example of drunkenness on the part of the white man is not so decisively the cause of vice on the part of the natives as is often supposed. If every white man in a settlement abstained wholly from intoxicating liquors, still the savage, when once he had tasted spirits, would, as a rule, drink them to excess whenever he could obtain them. What is really objected to, then, under the name of "vices of civilization," is simply the presence of ardent spirits in a colony; and, stated in these definite words, what is the practical force of the objection? A teetotal colony, rigidly excluding spirits altogether, may or may not be the only means of saving aborigines from the effects of their infatuation for drink; but the idea is, and will be, utopian, until the habits of the English race change. The social habits, dress, food, and favourite beverages of emigrants will be the same in the new country as in the old; and, though the liquors used by the settler prove to be a source of evil to the native, it is only here and there, perhaps, that an individual could be found who would abandon their use—one who would order his whole life with reference to the influence of his acts upon the aborigines. The hard-working emigrants generally could not be expected to give up the grateful cordials which they and their forefathers had been accustomed to, because their lot had been cast among a savage people with ungoverned appetites. It is found practically that the habits of the mass of the colonists require that ardent spirits should be offered for sale in all English colonies. These habits are too general and fixed to be altered or much influenced by any legislation. Another fact is established, namely, that, notwithstanding the severest penalties, backed by strong public opinion of the colonists themselves, against furnishing Indians with liquor, they obtain as much as they desire, on the simple condition of paying for it. Men are found who will run the risk of conveying spirits to the canoes or houses of the natives. Thus, the question is raised as to the utility of prohibitory laws against the giving, bartering, or selling intoxicating liquors to Indians. Such laws lead to their drinking vile, unwholesome mixtures, without in the least restricting the quantity which they consume.

Having stated my views as to the natural work of decay (if I am right) affecting the Indians as races, and as to the destructive agencies consequent upon intercourse with civilized men, I will now further remark on the effect thereby produced on the Indians themselves. It is a lamentable spectacle, and I do not wonder that kindly men, who witness the result of such intercourse, are more in the mood for declamation than for observation and argument. The effect is this:—The Indian loses the motives for exertion that he had, and gets no new ones in their place. The harpoon, bow, canoe-chisel, and whatever other simple instruments he may possess, are laid aside, and he no longer seeks praise among his own people for their skilful use. Without inclination or inducement to work, or to seek personal distinction,—having given up, and being now averse to his old life,—bewildered and dulled by the new life around him for which he is unfitted,—the unfortunate savage becomes more than ever a creature of instinct, and approaches the condition of an animal. He frequently lays aside his blanket and wears coat and trousers, acquires perhaps a word or two of English, assumes a quickness of speech and gesture which, in him, is unbecoming, and imitates generally the habits and acts of the colonists. The attempt to improve the Indian is most beset with difficulty at this stage of his change from barbarism; for it is a change not to civilization, but to that abased civilization which is, in reality, worse than barbarism itself. He is a vain, idle, offensive creature, from whom one turns away with a preference for the thorough savage in his isolated condition.

It is during this time of change, immediately after the arrival of intruding settlers, that the aborigines in our colonies are exposed, for the first time, to the temptation of strong drinks. The effect upon Indians of an excessive use of the description of ardent spirits which they generally get, is such as no one who has not seen can conceive. The appearance of an Englishman in a state of intoxication gives no idea of the effect of drink upon a savage. It is to him a consuming indulgence, producing madness, rage, and frantic excitement, followed quickly by disease, languor, despair, and death. This lamentable result is hastened by several circumstances. Owing to the operation of prohibitory laws against selling liquors to Indians, the only liquors which they are able to procure are, as above said, of a bad quality; these pernicious mixtures are consumed in excess by men whose minds are crushed and spiritless. Again, the physical constitutions of the drinkers are unused to stimulants of any description, and are probably affected and weakened, at this time of change, by an alteration of diet. Further, it has been observed that some unknown circumstances of their habitual contact with a superior people render the bodily system of savages specially subject to disease; particularly, as it appears, to sexual diseases, when resulting from the cohabitation of civilized men with native women.

CHAPTER XXVIII.

CONCLUDING CHAPTER.

Can Nothing be Done to Save the Native People ?—My View of the Case —The Home Government Primarily Responsible—Practical Suggestion as to the Means of Improving Isolated Tribes—Results of Missionary Work hitherto.

And patience, experience ; and experience, hope.—ROMANS, Chap. v.

THE question will now be asked, can nothing be done to prevent or counterbalance the injury to the aboriginal races consequent upon the occupation of their country by English emigrants ? I am afraid that little indeed can be done by governments, societies, or individuals, to preserve savages from their seemingly appointed decay, or to improve those tribes which have been most in contact with settlers. It may, however, be possible to benefit isolated bodies of savages by civilized teaching and example, though the improvement may not extend to the prolongation of their national existence. Alas ! that travellers and missionaries have contributed so little solid information towards the solving of this problem. Whether the endeavour is part of the duty of the Crown, or of the Colonial Government, or should be left to the spontaneous efforts of benevolent associations, may form a question to some minds. I regard the subject in this way. The Home Government sanctions and encourages the colonization of a new territory. With this sanction, and under the protection of the English flag, a society is formed which, in its first stages, harbours, it must be admitted, an unusual number of eager money-makers, discontented politicians, fugitives from justice, and adventurers of all sorts, needy, unscrupulous, and immoral. This portion of colonial society has an evil influence upon all around it, and, of course, upon the character of any neighbouring Indians. To argue that the Home Government is not in some degree concerned with this, and is not morally bound, either to compel a colonial settlement to some adequate measure of counteraction, or itself to take the matter in hand, is to say that the parent is neither bound to correct the child, nor can be called upon to repair the mischief arising from his own neglect. I am speaking, of course, of the early stage of a settlement, when it would be possible for the Home Government to interfere effectually on behalf of the aborigines, before the colonists received from the mother country a constitution and independent power of self-government. In granting constitutions to colonies, the Crown should have insisted on provisions as regards the treatment of the natives; it should have reserved to itself a greater authority than it is now able to exercise, through its colonial governors, in directing the policy of colonial legislatures towards the aborigines. The rule of policy which requires that colonies must work their own way by their own energies, without expecting assistance from the parent country—a rule open, I think, from a national point of view, to various objections—is one that cannot, with justice, be strained to comprehend the treatment of the aborigines. The question is not whether colonists shall be assisted to build up their own fortunes, but whether certain conditions of their social state shall, without any mitigation, be allowed to exercise a deadly influence upon their fellow-subjects; whether they shall not be urged or impelled towards some system of counteraction which shall cancel or compensate for injuries so inflicted upon the native population. As already hinted, our best efforts might be futile; but there would be glory in the trial, and there would be some use in it, too, if it only showed clearly to the public, how far beyond any human capacity are the solemn duties and overwhelming responsibilities of an English statesman. May God raise up men among us for such work, and give them sound minds and the spirit of prayer!

It must further be admitted, as regards Vancouver Island and British Columbia, that, notwithstanding laws for its prevention, a lucrative trade is carried on in many parts by the sale of spirits to the Indians. The destructive effect of this liquor traffic has been described in the last chapter. It is also the case that, wherever any considerable number of white men are congregated, there seduction, debauchery, and disease become the fate of the native females. Other injuries and discouragements, already alluded to—which, to a certain extent, are unavoidable—come upon the aborigines, through the occupation of their country by the settlers. Their hunting and fishing places are intruded upon, their social customs disregarded, and their freedom curtailed, by the unwelcome presence, and often unmannerly bearing, of those who are stronger than themselves. Admitting the lawfulness of the surplus of over-peopled civilized countries seeking homes, and building homesteads in new and thinly inhabited territory—admitting also their right to acquire property in such territory, in spite of the opposition of savages, who do not adequately occupy the land—it is a reasonable claim—a claim, indeed, of simple justice—that the injury done to the native population, as a whole, should be counterbalanced, not according to the Indians' poor ideas of gifts of food or blankets, but by a wise and paternal action of the Crown, in some practical way, on their behalf. It is unlikely, as already stated, that it would be possible entirely to prevent the evils mentioned. But it is surely incumbent upon those with whom the responsibility primarily rests to strive in every way to mitigate these evils; in such case, perhaps, though, in spite of these efforts, many Indian communities would be destroyed, others might be benefited, and perhaps regenerated.

Much disappointment might be expected as the result of any Governmental action. Still, it is probable that isolated bodies of savages, removed from intercourse with civilization, would to a considerable extent, by their improved condition, repay the care and efforts of the Government. Not being familiar with the existing official machinery of the Colonial Office, and not knowing the actual power of interference on behalf of its uncivilized subjects still remaining to the Crown, I cannot suggest the mode of organising a central authority to direct these efforts; but for practically carrying out the object, I can say that it would be advisable to choose a position which would secure the gradual spread of any good effects which might ensue—say a large native village, at a distance from civilized settlements, and connected by language with a good many neighbouring tribes. Each establishment might consist of about five men, carefully chosen in England, on verified testimonials of their peculiar fitness. They must be men of courage, energy, temper, and proved morality, and at least two should be acquainted with some trade or occupation, in which they might instruct the Indians—a gardener, for instance, would be a most useful man. The party should be under the command of one as a leader, and they all should undertake to forego the use of alcoholic drink; for moderation in such a thing is not appreciated nor believed in by the Indian, who would make his instructors' restricted use of liquors an excuse for his own extreme intemperance. Great care should be taken to select men voluntarily inclined towards such work, and they should be sought out by qualified judges interested in the matter, rather than obtained by advertisement. It would be an advantage for the leader—if he were a man of education, temper, and sound judgment—to be authorised to act magisterially against any white men coming among the Indians for unlawful purposes; but his commission should not extend to the Indians, as they would not, except out of personal respect to him, be willing to acknowledge his delegated authority. A magistrate in such a position should never employ Indian constables to apprehend white men; the latter will not surrender to Indian policemen, though provided with a proper official warrant. These instructors should not attempt to dictate to the Indians, nor seek by trade, nor in any way, to make gain out of them; their influence, which would only come gradually, and after a considerable period of experience in, and use of the language, would depend on their own prudence, intelligence, and uniform endeavour to understand the character of the natives, and really to benefit them. The general duties of these instructors, I would propose to be as follows: —to teach the Indians any useful employments and arts that they were capable of learning; to improve their moral ideas, and to instruct them in Christian truth, as far as possible: in this latter respect, acting as missionaries, or at least, preparing the Indians for the efforts of the missionary. The annual cost of such undertaking would not be more than that entailed by liberal salaries to those engaged, and the occasional transmission of supplies. The outside, or west shore of Vancouver Island would probably be, in that part of the world, a good place for this attempt, as all the tribes there speak one language, and there are few white men on the coast. The language and customs of the savages might first be studied in the neighbourhood of Barclay, otherwise called Nitinaht Sound, and a gradual acquaintance be made from that centre with the several tribes of the West Coast, until it was seen where actual settlements could be formed with the best hope of ultimate success.

In conclusion, I will name the results, to the present time, of missionary efforts among the savages of the north-west coast of America, and these efforts, to my knowledge, have been zealous, earnest, and unremitting. The reports of the missionaries themselves will no doubt afford full information; but as the result of my own observation, I must state that the attempts made by the missionaries, and of which such favourable accounts have been forwarded to England, have, as far as I have been able to judge, had no real, sound success, as regards any large body of the people—though I know of several apparent conversions of individuals. How far the moral condition of the native people generally might so far be improved by regular and systematic employment—if they would accept it—in various departments of agricultural and other labour, as to afford a more promising soil in which to sow the seed of Christian doctrine and truth, I am not prepared to say.

VOCABULARY OF THE AHT LANGUAGE,

with a List of the Numerals.

An Alphabetical List of Words† obtained at Nitinaht (or Barclay) Sound, but fairly representing the Language of all the Aht Tribes on the West Coast of Vancouver Island, including Words invented since their contact with White Men, which latter are marked *.

Ah-ah, yes.
Aâpso, arm above the elbow.
Aâpsoonilh, arm-pit.
Ah-ah-che, eyebrows.
Ah-ahp-quimulh, to wrestle.
**Ah-ah-he*, a hen.
Ah-ah-toh, to ask.
**Ah-asky*, a turkey (*i. e*, *ah-ah-he-asky*, bald hen).
Ah-ah-puk, industrious.
Ah-ahtl-tsoowit, equal.
Ah-cheitsah, which (of goods).
Ah-chuk, who (of people).
Ah-kook, this.
Ah-mah, a large grey diver.
Ah-toosh, a deer. ×
Ah-hummus, cheeks.
Ah-hupeemilh, shoulder.
Ah-peelsoo, in the centre ; central.
Ahousaht, name of a tribe.
**Ah-ohphah-kook*, sugar.
**Ah-wutsetsos*, a long dining-table.
A-thlah, to spue.
Ahk-shitl, a little below high water.
Ahtl-at'amaluxhool, to pull out the hair of the chin.
At-hohmilh, curly hair of man or beast.
Aichk, good-looking.
Aichomyts, thumb.
Ahm-ooye, yesterday.
Ahmaytlik, to-morrow.
Amewauts, a special name of the white-headed eagle before the head becomes white.
Akk-aht-a? of what tribe ?
Amenoquilh, a comer.
Ammitty, name.

† The syllabic division of words in this vocabulary, and perhaps also the use of the letter (or breathing) "*h*" to denote the broad sound, may be objected to by some as unscholarlike and superfluous ; but I hope that, as a whole, the orthography and the arrangement of the words will be intelligible to the reader.

Ammus-hulh, the bosom.
Annays, short (*i. e.*, not long).
Annah-ah, to gamble.
Anni, look!
Anni-mah, I see (in answer to *anni*).
Annoos, a crane.
Apuxim, hair upon the face.
Appoonit-nas, mid-day (also *hoop-cheilh*).
Appoon-uttyh, midnight.
Asky, bald (also *askumilh*).
Assits, a wasp.
Ash-sup, to break a string or rope.
Atlah, two.
Atla-newk-tsuuk, the fork of a river.
Attalh, black (also *uttalh*, with which compare *uttyh*, night).
Attoh, a beaver (probably connected with *attalh*, black).
Atsaykuts, the throat (also *win-nayk*).
Aychim, an old man.
Aychukasin, an ancestor.
Ay-is, a plant from which some sort of string is made.
Ay-entuk, always.
Ay-ook, a lake.
Ay-ha-ik, to cry.
Ay-yak-kamilh, fifth lunar month from November, inclusive.
Ayk-huk, to speak or cry (also to weep).
Aylh-mukt, nettles.
Aytl-chauna, by-and-by.

B.—This letter occurs seldom, except with the Nitinahts, who pronounce almost every M as B.

Chay-her, the place of spirits.
Cha-puts, a canoe.
Châ-tay-up, to cut off with a knife.
Chah-hatshitl, to be astonished, baulked, startled.
Chak-hots, Indian bucket.
Chahk-chahka, to press, to press down.
Chapook, a manned canoe.
Chastimit, a mink.
* *Choo-chuk*, a spoon.
Choochk, all (also *ish-ook*).
Choop, the tongue.
Chookwah, come.
Che-che-che, the teeth.
Che-is, salutation to a woman.
Chees-cheesa, a dance and song by women.
Cheh-neh, not to know.
Cheh-neh-mah, I do not know.
Chee-chitl, to pull or haul.
* *Chechamutlpyik*, a boat (connected with *chee-chitl*, to pull).
* *Chechik*, trigger of a gun.
Chekoop, husband.
Cheetuk, impudent.
Cheetashitl, cold (applied only to personal sensation).
* *Cheetayik*, a saw.
Cheetsyih, large iron fish-hook.
Cheeskuksootl, to shave.
Chay-tann-os, name of a hill.
Cheetamah or *cheetuk*, side-boards of an Indian house.
Chee-yahkamilh, the thirteenth lunar month, counting from November as the first.
Chimmus, a bear.
Chimmin, large wooden hook for halibut.
Chimilh, bed, including bedstead.
Chimmitsas, the right hand, or right side of a person or thing.
Chin-e-palh, to wrestle by holding the hair.
Chu-uk, water.
Chuk-she, push it along.

**Chukswih*, a waistcoat.
**Chupoox*, brass.
Chulcha, nails or claws.

E.

Eh-eh-she, be quick!
Eh-shetl-che, go!
Eiyemmah, a great many.
Eiyalh, wing feathers (*py-yalh* being small feathers).
Ei-yeh, many, a great many.
Ei-yeh-chinnik, a great many together.
Eesh-toop, things, small articles of property.
Eetâchles, uphill.
Eetâtus, downhill.
Eetowayes, to go to a distance and stay a long time.
Eechmah or *Eechuk*, the light fixed on the canoe for night-fishing.
Eehinakoom, ear pendant.
Eethloohoolh, the lips.
**Eishkook*, a bottle.
Eilchupamik, the common squirrel.
Ennitl, a dog.
Eher, great, large.
Ehersooquitl or *Ehersookl*, brave.
Enakoüsimilh, twelfth lunar month from November.
Ew-uttyh, a gentle wind.
Ew-ahtokuk, a strong wind.
Ewksah, wind from the sea.
Ewkstis, wind blowing up an inlet.
Ey-yahkshitl, to forget.
Ey-yohquilh, green blankets.
Ey-yohquk, green.

H.

Ha-ha-ook, a lizard.
Hâ-oom, food.
Hâ-ook, to eat.
Hâ-quatl, unmarried woman.
Hâ-quatl-is, young girl or daughter.
Hâ-witl, ebbing tide.
Hah-cet-leck, lightning.
Hah-han-noo-yik, boastful.
Hah-yew-itl, strong ebbing tide.
Hah-ho-pah, to admonish.
Hah-ohksâcheel, a generation.
Hahts-eh-tuck, all (also *ish-ook* and *choochk*).
Hân-nâh, naked.
Hat-tees, to wash all over; to bathe.
Heah-hay-hah, to breathe.
Hee-seesah, to beat with a stick.
Hemakah, look out!
**Himmix*, lard.
Himmik-kahoo, gooseberries.
Hinnasetsos, above, resting upon (relating to position).
Hinnays, the head of an inlet.
Hismilh, to bleed at the nose.
Hissin, a bright red berry.
Hissit, red.
**Hissits*, an axe.
Hissamis, blood.
Hissoolh, bloody, covered with blood.
Histokshitl, to come; (*wustokshitl sooa*, i.e., *wusseh-histokshitl-sooa*, whence come you?)
His-wah-soolh, to bleed out of the mouth.
Hit-tas, there, yonder.
Hit-to-myn, sandhill crane.
Hittahktlee, the base, the under side.
Hlem-eh-hlem-eh-hah, wings.
Hlook-tupt, veins or arteries.
Hloh-pilh, a bridge.
Ho-utsachitl, to return.
How-komah, a wooden mark.
How-wilh, a chief.
How-weutl, to cease, to stop
How-waykl, hungry, (*hâ-oom* food; *wayk*, not).
**Hoh-ha-um*, a percussion cap.
Hoop-ahlh, thimble berries.
Hoop-peh, to help.

Hoop-palh, the moon.

Hoop-cheilh, midday ; (also *ap-poonit-nas*).

Hokqueechis, to cover with a vessel, hat, or any stiff covering.

Hohpta, concealed (*hohpta ooyak kamis*, news to be kept secret).

Howtsshitl, to sprinkle.

Howksap, to upset, turn over.

Hohm, the blue grouse.

Hoik, the willow grouse.

**Hokidskook*, biscuit (*klyklydskook*, bread).

Hoxem, a goose.

Hooweulh, to dance (also *ooyalh*).

Houtsachepasym, to lend.

Howchuklisaht, name of a tribe.

Hucheemt, berries.

Huch-leetlh, west wind.

Huchimsuksah, a girl's brother (*kathlahtik* is a man's brother only).

Hummootisque, a bone.

**Huppah-yukkaik*, a brush.

Hys-shitl, the wild black currant.

Hy-yeskikamilh, third lunar month, counting from November as the first.

Hyn-nas, high, above, upper.

Hynnas-itl, to climb (up a tree or mast, not a hill).

Hynnoolh, the face.

Hynmuxhel, the mouth.

Hytoktl, worthless, untrue.

Hytokstootl, to tell a lie.

Hy-yakshitl, not to understand.

Hy-yu, ten.

Hy-yus-atyup (or *kutsquykup*), to lessen, to diminish.

Hy-ye, serpent, snake.

Ik-moot, old (of things).

Im-hah, shame.

Im-pig-walkinkl, the person walking second in a long line (the *g* soft).

Im-tah, unable.

Immich-sahta, the forehead.

Innimah, the nipple, milk.

Innik, fire.

Innik-quilh, to make a fire.

**Innik-ayik*, a stove.

Innikseh, firewood ; thence any sort of felled wood.

In-nits, around, surrounding.

Ish, and, with.

Ish-ook, all (also *hahts-eh-tuck*).

Ishim-yoap, to increase, or to set in order (I am not sure which).

Ishinnik, with, together with.

Ishinnikquaht, next door.

About a fifth of the whole vocabulary is formed of words beginning with *K*; and of these more than half commence with *Kl*.

Kââ, equivalent to "hand it me," "let me look at it."

Kââshitl, to die.

Kââsup, to wound.

Kah-hakkit, or *Kah-huk*, dead.

Kah-ohts, a nephew.

Kah-yupta, the arm or leg.

**Kah-pooh*, a coat.

Kah-oots, a large Indian basket.

**Kahchuk*, a fork.

Kahcheik, needle (also *neecheik*).

Kahsitimilh, fourth lunar month, counting November as the first.

Kapshitl, to take openly or by force, to ravish.

Kalh-kow-wih, bramble-berry.

Kathlahtik, a man's brother.

Kats-hek, a long Indian dress.

Kawkushup, a disease in the eyes.

**Kayhaik*, a telescope.

**Kay-holh*, sight of a gun.

Kaytsah, small rain.
**Kaytshitl*, to write.
Kayhashitl, to look through or along a thing; to take a sight.
Kayeep, to clean away, to take from one place to another.
Kayutl, a long time ago.
Keek-quth, submerged.
**Keitseh-kaytsah*, writing.
**Keitselh*, paper, letter, book.
**Keitsetsos*, a writing-table.
Kannatlah, a wolf (also *sahook*).
Kinnitsmis, a bruise.
Kistokkuk, blue.
Kittleyn, a crack, a shrink.
Kikleenkshitl, to be wrecked, to sink (of a ship).
Klah-choochin, a stranger.
Klah-chit-tuhl, to doctor the sick.
Klah-hix, a box.
Klah-huk-sih, the present generation.
Klah-klah-tanym, notch for the fingers at the end of the spear shaft.
Klah-klah-tym, a foot (also *kleesh-klin*).
Klah-klah-nakoom, hand.
Klah-oh, another, some more.
Klah-ooye, now.
Klah-haytsoh, a box with lid fitting over the sides.
**Klah-klah-pukkah*, to hammer a nail.
Klah-koh, thank you (also *oosh-yuksomayts*).
Klah-oh-appi, something instead of that (a word used in bartering).
**Klah-pukmah*, a nail.
Klah-quay, to beseech.
Klah-oh-quaht, the name of a tribe.
Klah-ich-nus, to-day.
Klah-ich-tins, young (of few days).
Klah-oh-quil, day after to-morrow.
Klah-oh-quil-ooye, day before yesterday.
Klakkamupt, a species of pine tree.
Klakkas, a tree.
Klak-shitl, spring.
Klukkupt, grass.
Klahts-lah-kupt-sem, leaf.
Klak-she, a parting salutation.
Klathlahenkatoo, the cramp.
Klattomupt, yew tree.
Klayhah-pannich, to go out for a paddle and to see, or to paddle and look about (compare *yet-spannich*).
Klay-hook, purple.
Klayhuk, to paddle, to go by paddling, to go as a steamer.
Klayhutshitl, thin.
Klayhulk, Indian matting.
Klayhupper, a small sea fish.
Klayohtshunkl, to commit fornication (of a woman).
Klayt-klayt-wha, to stride, to measure by stepping.
Klay-uktl, look out! take care!
Klay-chitl, to shoot with a bow.
Klayhmah, large red-headed woodpecker.
Klaytsawhk, a rat.
Kleehua, to laugh.
Kleeklaymis, to hunt, to pursue game.
Kleekklayhy-yeh, a marten.
Kleeshitl, just before sunrise (*kleesook*, white).
Kleeshklin, a foot.
Kleesook, white.
Kleetcha, man in the stern of a canoe.
Kleetshitl, to steer.
Kleetchaik, a rudder.
Kleetsuppem, a sail.
Kleetsmah, stuff to sit on in a canoe.
Kleehooamis, clouds.

**Kleekqushin*, boots.
**Kleeshklukkaik*, trousers.
Kleeselh, white blankets.
Kleetstoop, blankets (*generic*).
Kleeteenek, small cloak or cape.
Kleetsimilh, muffled up.
Kleetyik, small fish-hook.
Kleetseechis, to cover with a handkerchief, paper, or other yielding substance.
Kleklemahktlee, a grasshopper.
Klennut, a wooden wedge for splitting trees.
Kletshitl, to split with a wedge.
Klet-kleh-kan, tortoise.
Kliklenasm, a bracelet.
Kliklenastim, an anklet.
Klik-klik, a hoop.
Klilh-mah, firm, firmly knit.
Klimmukkah, to be sleepless.
Klimmukshitl, or *klohksahp*, to wake up another.
Klinnika, crooked, having one bend or crook.
Klinnik-klinnika, very crooked, having many bends.
Kloh-nym, an elk.
Kloat-lutl, to forget (also *ey-yahkshitl*).
Klohseah-how-witl, highest water.
Kloochim, mussels.
Kloochtsque, mussel shells.
Klo-quiltsah, name of a mountain.
Klookloothlalh, clean (of persons).
Kloothlalh, clean (of things).
Klohk-pah, warm, hot.
Klohpshitl, to wash the face.
Kloksem, a mast (compare *klakkas*, a tree, and for the termination, *kleetsuppern*, a sail).
Klooch-hunk, to commit fornication (of a man).
Klooch-inkl, just before sunset.
Klooch-moop, sister.
Kloopidg, autumn.
Klooshah, dry (also *klooshook*).
Klooshist, dry salmon.
Kloosmit, a herring.
Klootsinnim, board for a paddler to kneel on.
Klooshtsoque, thirsty.
Kloothlaht, a good workman.
Klooth-kloothlsik, to adorn.
Klooths-oquitl, kind.
Klootsmah, married woman.
Kloquisutlhl (or *moolquisutlhl*), a little above low water.
**Kly klydskook*, bread, flour.
Kochtsa, three.
Koh-hoo, a black duck.
Koh-pilh, to hang, to hang up.
Koh-quenapich, the small woodpecker.
Ko-ich-itl, to grow.
Ko-mah, the real bearded cod.
Kolh, a slave.
Kooh, ice.
Koquahowsah, a seal.
Koo-nah, gold.
Koot-kootah, to beckon with the hand.
Kopeik, the forefinger.
Kosh-kuts, a pipe.
Koquawds-athly, proud.
Kotowaut, half.
Kotsas, the left hand or left side.
Koulh, morning, sunrise.
Ko-us, a man.
Kouts-mah, the soul; also a shadow, a reflection.
Kowik, thievish.
Kowilh, to steal.
Kowih-tuppa, to open.
Kow-wih, the salmon-berry.
Kow-weept, salmon-berry bush.
**Kow-wits*, the potato.
Kulkah, the little finger.
**Kluk-kaik*, a key.

Kluk-sap, to unbind, to untie.
Klumma, a great wooden figure.
**Kluppay-uk*, scissors.
Klyemmi, equivalent to "give more" (often used in sale or barter).
Ko-ishin, a raven.
Kok-koop, a swan.
**Kokkumyahklassum*, a pin.
Koomits, a skull.
**Koquawtselh*, a portrait.
Kotsik-poom, Indian pin for blankets.
**Koquissunna-pyik*, corkscrew.
Kow-wishimilh, ninth lunar month, counting November as the first.
Kulkin-tupah, strawberries.
Kuskeep. a star-fish.
Kumatychea, to learn.
Kumotop, to understand.
Kummetkook, to run.
Kusseh, the eyes.
Kutcheim, the palate.
Kutsquyup (or *hy-yus-atyup*), to diminish, to make smaller.
Ky-yu-men, a panther.
Ky-yah-chitl, adrift.
Kyen, a crow.
Ky-yahtsa, drift, cordage.

Lebuxti (or *hklimuxti*), the heart.

Mah, equivalent to "take it," when you wish to hand a person anything.
Mahkatte, an eatable liliaceous root.
Mahtsquim, a housefly.
Mamakshitl, to fasten the dress or blanket by tying.
Mah-mahte, a bird.
Mah-pees, a bat.
Mahs or *mahte*, a house, a household, a collection of houses.
Maht-mahs, the entire population.
Macheelh, houseward, to the house.
Macheetl, to bite.
Mah-mayksoh, eldest brother.
Mahk, a whale, or porpoise, or large fish caught by the Indians in summer.
Mahlh, antlers, horns.
Mahptulh, an enemy; hostile.
Mahts-kulch, ugly.
Makquinnik, to buy.
Mammathleh, a white man; any person not an Indian.
Mathlook, cold (of the temperature).
Maylhi, like, similar.
Mayetlkuts, a small boy.
Meetsin, shade.
Mees-sook, to smell (also *myshitl*).
Meet-lah, rain.
Memetuk-mahk, a spider.
Milsyeh, a spear shaft.
**Mitwha*, screw of steamer.
**Mookshitl*, the hammer of a gun.
Moolquisutlhl (or *kloquisutlhl*), a little above low water.
**Mooshussemayik*, a hinge.
Mooshussem, a door, a lid.
**Mootsasook*, gunpowder.
Mooh, four.
**Mooh-wah*, steam, also, or "*youwha.*"
Moolshitl, flood-tide.
Mooshetuppa, to shoot.
Moostatte, a bow.
Mootsmahuk, a bear skin (probably the old word for a bear).
Mooxyeh, a stone, a rock.
Mowah, to carry.
Mowah-ishinnik-sup, to add, to carry to.
Much-koolh, covered with dirt, dirty.

Much-kulh, dirt.
Muchpelsokunhl, bitter.
Muk-koolh, blind.
Muktoop, string.
Mutamis-inkl, to fly upward.
Mutshitl, to fly.
Mutlah-sah, to tie or bind together.
Muschim, the common people, as distinguished from men of rank.
Mutlshitl, to bind round.
**Mutlsahp*, to lock (of a door).
**Mutlema-yaoom*, the iron hoop of a cask or tub.
Muttlyn, string bound round anything.
Myshitl, to smell (also *mees-sook*).
My-yalhi, the principle or personification of sickness.

Na-nash, to beg, to ask for.
Nahay (also *nahaıs*) give, or to give.
Nah-ah, to hear.
Nah-ayx-oh, uncle.
Nah-uktl, to feel.
Nah-tuch, the stock duck.
Nah-pee, light (or moonlight only).
Nanetsah, to see.
Nas, sun, or day.
Nashook, strong.
Nashay, or *nashetl*, or *natsoh*, or *nanetsah*, to see.
Nach-komuklinkl, to look back.
Nay-ye-ee, echo.
Nay-aytlik, to illumine.
Neetlach, to quarrel, to squabble.
Neecheik, a needle (also *kah-cheik*).
Neeputto, thread.
Neeuktl, deep laden (of a ship or boat).
Neetsah, the nose.
Netlah-kahte, a rib.
**Nenehktook*, peas.
Nismah, a country, territory, land.
Nithin, roe of fish.
Nish-shitl, to sneeze.
No-hah-shitl, to bury.
Noochee, a mountain.
Noonook, to sing.
Noop, one (also *tsow-wauk*).
Noop-pooh, six.
Noochuk, an egg.
Noomas, twins.
Nootimilh, round.
Nooquits, pitch stick, resinous wood.
Nooshah, or *nooshitl*, to make great gifts; to entertain for the purpose of making gifts.
Noo-wayk-soh, father.
Ny-yuk-patto, cradle.
Ny-yuk-uk, a baby.
Nukshitl, to drink.
Nuk-amayhamma, I want some water. (The Indian cannot break up this sentence into its component words or roots, he considers it one word.)

Oh-kookem, cross piece of the paddle.
Oh-puk, calm, describing absence of wind.
Oh-kokapem, a cork.
Oh-kumha, fine weather (sometimes used for "the sky").
Oh-oh-kamilh, seventh lunar month, counting November as the first.
**Oh-puxoonlh*, a button.
Oh-quinnik, a box with double sides.
Ohpka, to whistle.
Okshitl, to make water.
Oochkamis, clouds (also *kleehooamis*).
Ooquishstik, equivalent to "let me see," give me time to consider.
Ooshoolh, proud, scornful.
Ocyalh, to dance (also *hooweulh*).

Outlohkamilh, sixth lunar month, counting November as the first.
Okkuh, what ?
Oochkuk, cloud, fog, mist.
Ook-you, friend (also *oowah-tyn*).
Oomahkut, a colour.
Oomayksoh, mother.
Oon-nah, how much ?
Oo-oo-eh, to hunt, to pursue game.
Oo-ooshtuk, to work.
Oop-sup, hair.
Ooshimitso, to whisper.
Ooshyaksomits, an expression of civility, somewhat equivalent to "Thank you."
Oosteilh, low down, deep down, below.
Oostepittup, to bring down, to place in a lower position.
Ootachitl, to go (also *ootsashitl*).
Ootsmupt, a large tree.
Oouktlay, to finish.
Oowah-tyn, friend.
Oowahtsoh, third finger.
Oowayup, to begin.
Oowayuttah, to precede.
Oowhun, at the end.
Ooyahkkahs, to relate.
Ooyakkamis, news.
Ooye, soon, presently, lately.
O-uk-ooye, a long time ago.
Ootsamo, *Ootsequin*, *Ootsooquetta*, *Ootsuksemhuk*. Words in frequent use, but the exact meaning of which I cannot get with certainty.

Pah-quin, the skate fish.
Pah-pay, an ear ; also, the nipple of a gun.
Payh-eyk, to praise, to speak well of.
Pacheetl, give.
**Pah-pahts-uktl*, a loaf.
Pat-kook, things, small household property.
**Pay-ha-yek*, a looking-glass.
**Pay-pay-huyxm*, glass, a window.
Pe-pe-sa-ti, to work.
Pet-ek-say, the body.
Pish-shuk, bad (also *wikoo*).
Pishaht, bad workman.
Pilluk-pilluksht, a stone hammer.
Pooeh, halibut.
Poulteechitl, sleepy.
Poh-kleetum, small downy feathers.
Pooh-pootsah, a dream.
Potsmis, froth, foam (of the sea, or of a person's mouth).
Pow-wel-shetl, to lose, or to be lost.
Py-yalh, feathers (*eiyalh*, wing feathers).

Quaht-sook, to walk backwards (*yetsook*, to walk).
**Quas-setsos*, a chair.
Quawtlik, come (also *Chookwah !* sometimes both used together).
Quawtluk, sea otter.
Quisaht, the Indian settlements beyond *You-clul-laht*.
Quaw-te-ik, tired.
Quawtlquuch, the elbow.
Quawtoquk, devious, winding (of a path or trail).
Quayktluh, acid.
Queeahta, pointed.
Queëch-che-is, salutation to a woman.
Queel-queel-ha, to pray.
Queen-up-shilh, to attract.
Quees, snow.
Queeskidg, winter.
Quequenixo, the arm.
Quish-shah, smoke (applied thence to tobacco).
Quispah, on the other side.
Quit-te-yu, to fit together, to splice.

Quoy-up, to break a stick (*ash-sup*, to break a rope).

Satsope, a description of salmon.

Satsope-us, eleventh lunar month, counting November as the first.

Sah-ook, a wolf (also *hannatlah*).

Saeemits, a sort of grass or reed.

Sâsin, a humming-bird.

Sattoo, fir cone.

Sak-sah-api, to turn over.

Seeta, tail of an animal.

Seekah, sailing, to sail.

Sewah, we, us.

Sewahs, ours.

Seyah, I.

Seyas, mine (also *seyessah*).

Shâ-â-tyn, head of the salmon-spear.

Shaytlook, to change quarters (used of a general move from one fishing or hunting-ground to another).

Sheetla, brake-fern root, an article of food.

Shoh-shitl, rusted.

**Sikkah-ik*, a frying-pan.

Siskummis, flesh, meat.

**Sis-sidshook*, rice.

Sit-si-tehl, an animal, supposed to be the marmot.

Si-yah, far away.

Si-yah-yelh-syah, a superlative expression of the same.

Soo-a, thou.

Soowah, you, ye.

Sooas, thine.

Soowahs, yours.

Sooquitl, to bring.

Soosah, to swim.

Sootcha, five.

Soo-widg, the early part of summer; from *tsoowit*, salmon.

Sush-toop, beast or brute, including all fourfooted animals.

Sinna-mooxyets, a berry growing on rocks; probably thus derived — *sy*(*ah*), *na*(*tsoh*), *moox*(*yeh*), *yets* (*ook*).

Sloo-ook, roof-boards of a house.

**Soo-oolh*, a kettle.

Suchkahs, a cowl.

Summets, a squirrel.

**Sunday koilh*, the church at Alberni—from "Sunday," and *tuk-koilh*, "to sit").

Tah-chah, lowest water.

**Tah-haytlim*, ramrod.

Tah-klahdkamilh, eighth lunar month—from November as first month.

Tah-hap-e-chauna, by-and-by (also *aytl-chauna*).

Tah-kay-uk, straight.

Tah-kohstootl, to tell the truth.

Tah-kohtl, correct, true, undoubted.

Tah-pym, cross stick of the canoe.

Tah-tupwin, a spider (also *memetuk-mahk*).

Tah-mook, a kingfisher.

Tahkowin, stone hammer shaped like a dumb-bell (also *pilluk-pilluhshl*).

Tahkshitl, to spit.

Tahktsque, spittle.

Tam-mook-you, a single knot.

Tunnah, male infant.

Ta-ta-put-hi, to consider, think over, as in a meeting of the tribe.

Tahtsche, stomach.

Tay-quilh-yih, a chair.

Tatti-itskookquum, the second finger.

Tattoos, the stars.

Tautneetsin, descendants, posterity.

Tayahtaquâta, to make a mistake.

Tayilh, sick.

Tay-chitl, to throw (also *taytl-tay-yah*).
Tay-ish-tish, small hatchet.
Taytosah, to let fall unintentionally.
Tchoo, an exclamation inciting to immediate action.
Tchoo-upitlay, stop, stop working.
* *Teech*, well, convalescent.
Teechilh, alive.
Teelhah, bait (for fishing).
* *Teemelh-oomah*, a towel.
* *Teena*, a file.
Teetl-tee-yah, to rub.
Telhoop, the cuttle-fish.
Telh-toop, fish (the general term).
Tennak-mis, mosquitoes.
Tennanakshitl, to bear a child.
Tepittup, to throw down or bring down (*oostepitup*, to bring down).
Tim-mel-soo, a bell.
Tookamis, bark of a tree.
Toop-kulh, black blankets.
Toh-muktl, dark.
Toh-pelh, the ocean.
Toh-poolch, salt.
Tohuk, afraid.
Tokseilh, very high wind from the sea.
Toksohquin, an owl.
Toqukamilh, seal-skin.
Tow-quos, gills of a fish.
Toochee, the east wind.
* *Too-mees*, coal.
Toopkoop, black.
Toop-shitl, evening.
Tooshko, the dark-brown cod.
Tootah, thunder.
Tsaemupt, oak-wood.
Tsaimpts, water-grass.
Tsakoomuts, ground soil, earth.
Tsa-chu-uk, island (*tsakoomuts* and *chu-uk*, water).
Tsapin, a brown-headed diver.
Tsa-lsa-lach-tem, the toes.
Tsaoolhah, a wave or billow.
Tsasnoolh, bank of a stream or river.
Tsaykoomts, the neck.
Tsaychitl, to throw water.
Tsetsellukenakoom, the fingers.
Tsaykents, a small white-marked duck.
Tsay-uk-palh, to wrangle.
Tseeatlsoo, to obey.
Tseka-tseka, to talk, to talk much.
Tseuma, full.
Tsayhatte, an arrow.
T-sayk-im-en, iron.
* *Tsaykipkaylhool*, the smithy.
Tsay-yuk-koom, Indian wooden cup.
Tseetsahuktl, crab-apple.
Tseetsiktahsim, finger-ring.
Tseilh, Indian things for making fire—lucifer matches.
Tset-tset-tikatsim, seeds.
Tsimha, toothed pole for catching small fish.
Tsoh-pohitl, highest water.
Tsupquaw, to boil, (of water, intrans.)
Tsikhotyn, white-headed eagle.
Tsistoop, a rope.
Tstitsannha, angry (only used of a wordy anger. The anger of the heart and countenance is expressed by *we-uk*).
Tsokstelh, to fight with fists.
Tsok-kits, twenty.
Tsootsinnik, to wash the hands.
Tsoo-wit, a description of salmon.
Tso-quitl, to wash, to wash things.
Tsootshktuh, to wash the feet.
Tsots-howa, to fight with a knife
Tsow-wauk, one (also *noop*).

Tsow-wauts-hamma, a person having only one wife or one husband.

Tsow-wista, a canoe manned by one, or one man in a canoe.

Tso-youk, to wash the hair.

Tsu-uk, a river (*chu-uk*, water).

Tsow-wauchinnik, one walking alone, unaccompanied.

The words compounded with *Tsow* are used also with other numerals, as, *atlahtshamma*, a person with two wives or husbands; *moohista*, a canoe with four men; *atlahchinnik*, in company with one another; *kochtsachinnik*, with two others. (*See* numerals.)

Tup-win, to gird, to girdle.

Turquasseh, to sit down, as on a chair or stool.

Turqulleh, to sit or squat upon the ground (also *tukkoilh*).

Tush-she, a road or trail; also, a doorway.

Tuttayin, to bemoan, to lament aloud.

Uch-inna-his, small (also *unnahis*).

Uchispah, this side, this side of of (*quispah*, the other side).

Ukkaik, a knife.

Unnah-his-si-yah, near.

Unnahsatys, a few.

Upan-wilh, in the middle.

Upakowr, a point or promontory.

Up-pi, the back.

Upitsaska, the head.

Uttlmah, he, she; only used when the person is in sight.

Utsimixem, eye-lashes.

Utsin, backbone.

Uttyh, night.

Wah-haatlsoo, an expression of farewell.

Wah-haslkook, do not stumble; a farewell to a messenger.

Washitl, to do away, to destroy.

Waw-it, a frog.

Waw-kash, a word of salutation.

Wawkneh, a land otter.

Waw, to utter a shout.

Waw-waw, to speak.

Waw-waw-tsukka, to cough.

Waw-waw-tlookwah, the bark of a dog.

Wawkoahs, an Indian entertainment.

* *Waw-waw-shr-kook*, turnips.

Waw-win, to hunt by driving the animals together with shouts from unseen hunters.

Wayech, to sleep.

Weeuk, weak, not strong.

Weelhussem, a small berry.

Welshetl, to go home; to go to one's house.

Wĕ-uk, angry, stern (also used for "a warrior").

Wēht, the brain.

Welsohktl, cunning.

We-ukseh, a medicine making invulnerable.

Why-ak, that.

Wish-wish-ulh, blue blankets.

* *Wismah*, blacking.

Win-nayk, the throat (also *atsaykuts*).

Whoahtik, able.

Wik, not I.

Wiklyt, not, no.

Wiklitmah, not he; there is not.

Wikoo, bad (*pish-shuk* is the more common word).

Wikseh, wind.

Wiksim, to scold, to abuse, to drive away by scolding.

Wikmaektlah, to fast.

Wimmutomah, I do not understand.

Winna-pee, to stay, to stop, to remain.
Wishiksuktl, cruel, unkind.
Witshitl, to nod the head.
Wusseh, where, whence?
Wussemtuk, whence you, *i.e.*, where do you come from?
Wussokshitl, to cough slightly.
Wu-wu-puk, lazy.

Yah-ah, affection.
Yah-ah kloots-mah, to love a woman.
Yah-mah, sal-al berry.
Yah-uxem, a face pimple.
Yahk, long.
Yahkawimmit, long-staying, abiding.
Yahkpekukselh, a beard.
* *Yahk-pus*, a proper name, meaning bearded man.
Yahtoop, a whale (also *e-eche-toop*).
Yatchah, the dog-fish.
Yâulh, a word signifying distance.
Yay-yay-chim, the largest kind of whale.
Yatsetsos, a ladder.
Yatsquiup, to stamp on anything with the foot.
Ya-uk, pain.
Yelh, there, out there, out of sight.
Yetleh, he, she; only used when the person is out of sight.
Yetseh-yetsah, to kick frequently.
* *Yetseh-yetsokleh*, screw steamer.
Yetshitl, to kick.
Yetspannich, to walk out and look about.
Yetsook, to walk.
Yewch-kahta, pointed.
You-whis, light, not heavy.
Youquayksoh, eldest sister.
* *You-wha*, steam, also or, *mook-wha*.
Yuk-yeh-wha, to shake, (trans.)
Yuk-kaik, a broom.
* *Zah-wha*, a wheel.
* *Zoktâûs*, a cart.
* *Zocktikke*, paddle-wheel steamer.

NUMERALS.

1. *Tsow-wauk* or *Noop*.
2. *Atlah*.
3. *Kochtsa*.
4. *Mooh*.
5. *Sootcha*.
6. *Noop-pooh*.
7. *Atl-pooh*.
8. *Atlah-quill*.
9. *Tsow-wauk-quill*.
10. *Hy-yu*.
11. *Hy-yu-ish Tsow-wauk*, and so on to nineteen.
20. *Tsok-kits*.
21. *Tsok-kits-ish Tsow-wauk*, and so on to twenty-nine.
30. *Tsok-kits-ish hy-yu*.
40. *Atleyk* (*i.e.* two twenties).
50. *Atleyk-ish hy-yu*.
60. *Kochtseyk*.
70. *Kochtseyk-ish hy-yu*, and so on.
100. *Sootcheyk*. The same way of counting is continued up to
200. *Hy-yu-eyk*.

LIST of AHT TRIBES on the Outside Coast of Vancouver Island in 1860, with their Localities and Male Adult Population, the Names being stated in the Order in which the Villages occur going Northward along the Coast.

		Number.	Locality.
1.	Pacheenaht	20	Seaboard, south of Nitinaht Sound, and on the Nitinaht River.
2.	Nitinaht	400	
3.	Ohyaht	175	Barclay, otherwise Nitinaht, Sound.
4.	Howchuklisaht	28	
5.	Opechisaht	15	
6.	Seshaht	70	
7.	You-clul-aht	100	
8.	Toquaht	11	
9.	Klah-oh-quaht	190	Klah-oh-quaht Sound.
10.	Killsmaht	40	
11.	Ahousaht	115	
12.	Manohsaht	5	
13.	Hishquayaht	30	Nootkah Sound.
14.	Muchlaht	36	
15.	Moouchaht (the so-called Nootkahs)	150	
16.	Ayhuttisaht	36	
17.	Noochahlaht	26	
18.	Ky-yoh-quaht	230	North of Nootkah Sound.
19.	Chaykisaht	32	
20.	Klahosaht	14	
		1.723 men	

NAMES and supposed AGES of Men of one Tribe—the Opechisaht—in 1864.

	Names.	Ages.	
1.	Kal-lowe-ish	45	Hereditary chief.
2.	Quicheenam	55	Most influential chief.
3.	Tee-teech-it	45	Important men.
4.	Quassoon	45	
5.	Ta-hatchim	45	

Names.	Ages.	
6. Tsin-sick	20	Son of hereditary chief.
7. Wee-woom-tuck	25	Inferior men.
8. Klatsomick	25	
9. E-ees-siniap	25	
10. Georgees	25	
11. Klay-klay-has	25	
12. Too-tooch	30	
13. Klash-klookah	45	
14. Aytannos	15	
15. Klap-hytap	60	

In this tribe there were nineteen women, ten children (four boys and six girls), and three slaves (two male, one female).

AHT NAMES of MEN and WOMEN, 1860.

Men's Names.	Women's Names.
Ass-cha-ah-mick.	Kleeshin-nell.
Ar-wee-ell.	Wee-woom-tuck-shesh.
Ar-mish-e-nell.	Klah-miss-a-mah.
Klan-nin-ittle.	Kostan.
Kush-e-nishim.	Anah-hammes.
Kal-lowe-ish.	Nat-la-nah-his.
Ewona.	Hy-you-po-itla.
Mannaken.	Paona-ne-icksa.
Koo-lal-kut.	Jibo.
Kanas-keh.	Equata.
Anneets.	Kah-kah-hammes.
Ishka.	Kloo-yah.
Makouiña.	Witsa-how-a-klim.
Ewiz-zet.	Soa-wy-you-Koitla.
Sea-ossum.	
Seta-kanim.	
Wick-an-inish.	
Maquilla.	
Kleeshin.	
Quart-soppy.	
Quisto.	
Pat-low.	
Nish-watts.	
Estah-skoth-mick.	

Aht Names of Places.

Ock-tees.
Echachet.
Opetset.
Koabadore.
Chay-tann-os.
Chomata.
Malset.
Omoah.
Mackalay.
Tenahmah.
Sacket-sah.
Osmettikus.
Sarktees.
Newmah-kommes.
Nahmint.
Mook-a-tees.
Kloo-tus.
Keekah.
Keekin.
Tor-soppel.
E-kole.
Chee-anno.

Aht Names of Berries.

Berries.	Generic Name (Hucheemt).
1. Strawberry	Kulkintupah.
2. Salmon berry	Kow-wih.
3. Blackberry (bramble)	Kalh-kow-wih.
4. Thimble berry (Rubus Nootkanus).	Hoopahlh.
5. Gooseberry	Himmik-kahoo.
6. Black currant	Hys-shitl.
7. A berry	Weelhussem.
8. A berry	Hissin (connected with *Hissit*, "red.")
9. Sal-al berry	Yah-mah.
10. Crab-apple	Tseetsahahktl.
11. A blackberry growing on rocks...	Sinna-mooxyets (*Moox* or *Mooxyeh*, a "rock;" *yets* or *yetsook*, "to walk."

APPENDIX.

Note 1.

The aborigines of Vancouver Island may be divided generally into three nations—one including the tribes which speak the Quoquoulth, or Fort Rupert language; another including the tribes which speak the Kowitchan, or Thongeith; and the third those which speak the Aht language. The Komux tribe, who live on the east coast of the island, between the Kowitchan and the Quoquoulth tribes, are a distinct people, who are known to have come from British Columbia. The Quoquoulth language prevails on the north and north-east of the island; the Kowitchan on the east and south; the Aht language on the west coast of the island, between Pacheen and Nespod (Woody Point). The Kowitchan and Aht languages, or dialects of them, are also spoken on the southern, or American side of the Strait of Juan de Fuca; and I believe that the Aht language can be traced through all the tribes on the ocean coast as far south as the mouth of the Columbia River. These three supposed aboriginal nations in Vancouver Island—each including many independent neighbouring tribes—are almost as distinct as the nations in Europe. They do not readily understand one another's language, and their national customs and institutions are in many respects different.

I have selected for description in this book one set of tribes which inhabit the greater part of the outside coast of Vancouver Island, between Pacheen and Nespod (Woody Point), and to which I give the name of the Aht tribes, from the circumstance of all the tribal names ending in that affix. These tribes have been designated in the island, hitherto, as the "west coast" tribes. They have not been separately described by any former writer; nor does it appear to have been known that the different tribes of which the Aht nation is composed are nationally connected. No mission nor trading post, with the exception of the short-lived settlement at Nootkah, in the last century, has ever been established in this part of Vancouver Island.

A general name for this set of tribes was not easily found. *Maht-mahs* first suggested itself, as a word used by the Ahts in speaking of the whole population—a word which might be translated "the peoples," or "the settlements;" but it seemed rather to be a common noun than a proper name. Another word was *Klah-oh-quaht*, the name of a powerful Aht tribe dwelling in *Klah-oh-quaht* Sound, by which general appellation some of the natives on the inner side of the island designate those on the west coast. I could not, however, think of any more appropriate general name than the Ahts or the Quawteahts, which latter word is mythologically connected with the origin of all the tribes in this nation.

I may here remark that I have used in this narrative somewhat different names of places and tribes from those adopted by other travellers and by the makers of charts—not in any spirit of opposition, but in the belief that it is of some importance, if only for the sake of record, to determine, while possible, and make use of, the true original native appellations. My corrections are chiefly orthographical—to make the names correspond with the language of the people—and they are not intended to interfere with the established rule among travellers, by which, I believe, the first published name is considered indisputable, without reference to its absolute correctness.

NOTE 2.

THE Indians regard the English as a large tribe, whose principal village is distant. Their name of King-George men was given to the English because the first of the English who visited the Aht coast frequently talked of a great chief of that name. For the same reason, another white tribe—the Americans—are called by the Indians Boston-men, owing to their frequent mention of that great seaport in their own country. The Ahts distinguish an Englishman from an American as easily as they can point out a Klah-oh-quaht or a Nitinaht among themselves; and this not by the dress, but, as they described it, by the face, and the way the hair is worn. Owing, I believe, principally to the bad quality of the blankets and other goods offered in trade by American traders, the Americans are to this day regarded by the Ahts as inferior to the British.

Note 3.

The natives did not, during five years, invent new names for any of their domesticated animals. They called all of them, except the dog, by one name—the Jargon-Chinook word *moosmoos*, which specially means the ox, and is probably connected with the Walla-walla (in Oregon) word for the buffalo *moosmoos-chin*. The knowledge of this word, with a general application of it at first to any large animal, may have come down the Columbia River from Walla-walla to the Chinook district at its mouth, and spread gradually, with the use of the jargon, along the coast to the north, until it reached the west coast of Vancouver Island. I found that the dog was known to the Ahts before my arrival, and that they had a name for it; but they have no knowledge or tradition as to the "woolly Nootkah" dog, which travellers have reported as existing on this coast. They call the dog *ennitl* or *annitl*, a name which it may not be fanciful to suggest was composed from the Aht word *anni*, "look," and *shitl*, an Aht verb terminal, implying "movement" (see the chapter in this book on the "Aht Language"), and was bestowed on the dog on account of its quick sight and rapid movements. The *real* Chinook language, distinctly from the Jargon-Chinook, has separate words of its own for animals domesticated by civilized man, *e.g. keutan*, horse; *kamux*, dog; *piss-piss*, cat; *polotax*, hog. These words cannot be older than the time of the first travellers or settlers on this portion of the Pacific coast, who brought such animals with them; but the imitative word *moosmoos*, in various forms, coming, as it must have come, from the interior of the country, through aboriginal channels to the western shore, may be as old as the first bellowing of the buffalo heard on the North American continent by man.

Having mentioned the Jargon-Chinook, I may notice a statement made respecting it by Lord Milton and Dr. Cheadle. In a note, page 344, of their pleasant book, *The North-West Passage by Land*, they inform the reader that the Chinook-Jargon was *invented* by the Hudson Bay Company for use in trading with the Indians. This statement, which I daresay these travellers heard at Victoria, and without examination adopted, is erroneous, as their own good sense might have told them. It would imply that at some solemn "convention" of Hudson Bay Company traders and savage chiefs, chosen words were agreed upon which, from a stated time, were to be the signs for certain objects and actions, and that these words came into general use on the coast, thus exhibiting the philological phenomenon of a language definitely known to have been invented by man. The truth is, as stated in Chapter XV. of this book, that the Chinook-Jargon is simply a depravation of the Chinook language—an old language, which probably is the mother of all the dialects spoken on the coast between the Columbia River and the north of Vancouver Island. This original Chinook language, of which I possess a vocabulary, and which does not, as Dr. Wilson says (*Prehistoric Man*, vol. ii., p. 429), "baffle all attempts at its mastery," was spoken by the Chinooks and other tribes at the mouth of the Columbia River, and is now almost extinct, owing to the disappearance of the people. It was probably the first native coast language in this quarter that was learned by the traders of J. J. Astor, and the North-West Company; and these, with the traders of their successors, the Hudson Bay Company, in trafficking at different points on the coast, would naturally use the native language best known to them—the Chinook—which, it so happened, from the affinity of all the dialects along the coast northwards, would be understood without great difficulty by the different coast tribes. In the course of time, on the decline of the original Chinook-speaking tribes, the standard of reference for the language would be withdrawn, and dispersion and deterioration would ensue, until finally the old language would cease to be spoken, and would be changed and corrupted into the present contemptible *lingua Franca*.

The Newatees, mentioned in many books, are not known on the west coast. Probably the Klah-oh-quahts are meant. Newatee may be a locality in Klah-oh-quaht Sound. The blunders and confusion in the statements of the latest writers on the Indians of the north-west coast really alarm any one accustomed to believe the stories of travellers who are supposed to have got their information "on the spot." Error upon error is copied from one book into another. How, indeed, could any one, ignorant of the various languages spoken by the people, merely by sailing, or by knowing somebody who sailed along, say the coast of Galway, in Ireland, be considered to have qualified himself for giving a correct account of all the different inhabitants of the north-west of Europe?

Note 4.

Cook's book of *Voyages* has proved to be the most truthful and sensible book of the sort ever published. The short account he gives of the Aht natives is better than the hearsay statements made about them by subsequent writers, few of whom have ever visited the district.

Cook does not seem to have known that the west-coast Indians formed a nation, and he probably misnamed the people the "Nootkahs." *No Aht Indian of the present day ever heard of such a name as Nootkah*, though most of them recognize the other words in Cook's account of their language. The tribes called by Cook the Nootkahs probably were the Muchlahts, Moouchahts, Ayhuttisahts, and Noochahlahts, as these tribes have lived for a very long time, according to Indian memory and tradition, at the places Cook visited. The name Nootkah may have originated thus :—The first white visitor, on reaching the Sound, probably pointed to the mountainous shore, and, in addressing the Indians, threw his arm about to indicate that he wished to know the name of the whole district; and the natives, imagining that he referred to the mountains which appeared on every side, would answer according to their habit of frequent repetition, "Noochee! Noochee!" which is the Aht word for mountain. I may remark that this word *Nootkah*—no word at all—together with an imaginary word, *Columbian*, denoting a supposed original North American race—is absurdly used to denote all the tribes which inhabit the Rocky Mountains and the western coast of North America, from California inclusively to the regions inhabited by the Esquimaux. In this great tract there are more tribes, differing totally in language and customs, than in any other portion of the American continent; and surely a better general name for them could be found than this meaningless and misapplied term *Nootkah Columbian*.

NOTE 5.

THE Aht substitute for soap formerly was that with which English sailors, on long voyages, clean their duck trousers.

> Nay, in troth, I talk but coarsely,
> But I hold it comfortable for the understanding.
>
> *Beaumont and Fletcher.*

NOTE 6.

THE personal modesty of the Aht women—particularly when they are young—is greater than that of the men, who, it must be said, are often careless in the disposition of their only covering—the blanket. The women wear a shift, or some such thing, under their blanket, and seem anxious, generally, to cover their nakedness.

Note 7.

I have no special knowledge of aboriginal lingual districts outside of Vancouver Island; but the numerals of the following five languages, of the north-west of America, which, it will be seen, include the Kowitchan, show that the languages are closely related :—

Kowitchan or Thongeith : South-east and part of east of Vancouver Island.

Squawmish : Neighbourhood of the mouth of the Fraser River in British Columbia.

Douglas, Lytton : Names of English towns in British Columbia. I do not know the Indian names of the districts, but the language spoken there resembles the Squawmish, and exhibits instances of change to be discovered in the language, as we advance up the Fraser and its tributary, the Harrison.

Shewshwap : Is spoken in a large tract of inland country lying between the Fraser and the Columbia.

There may be observed a slight but significant similarity between some of the Aht numerals and those of these five districts.

Two branches of the British Columbian Indian languages—the Carrier and the Tshimpsean—seem quite distinct from each other and from the rest.

Note 8.

From a careful observation of the arts among the Aht natives, I am tolerably certain that no other materials than bone and shell were required by them for making their tools and weapons, up to the time when iron was brought amongst them, say, within the last 150 years. They used bone tools and bone fishing and hunting instruments long after they had a knowledge of iron—as lately, indeed, as a few years ago ; and at the present time, the mussel-shell adze, used in canoe-making, is preferred to one of any other material, and to the best English and American chisels. In felling large cedar-trees, and in other work, until the natives got the admirable American woodman's axe, they found their bone chisels more useful than any small-handled instrument of stone or iron, as the bone tool had the requisite toughness, bluntness, and penetrating power for working cedar-wood for their purposes. At the same time, it should be stated, the Ahts had a few stone and copper (the latter not smelted or moulded) instruments, when first visited by Cook—and probably earlier ; and ground stone chisels can be found amongst them at the present day.

But I think that these stone instruments could never have been in general use on the Aht coast, as the Indians never describe their utility, but produce old bone instruments for every purpose on being asked what they used before they had iron. I have little doubt that most of these tools, like the carved stone pipes found among several of the tribes, were obtained in trade, or as curiosities by the Ahts from the Indians inhabiting the coast of the mainland farther north, who, though perhaps originally, or anciently, a bone-using people, have been forced, by the comparative scarcity of cedar in their district, to make many stone instruments for cutting harder trees. The northern Indians, who are an entirely different people from the Ahts, possess, in their district, a soft blue slate, and are now skilful workers in stone: they have stone weapons and instruments remarkably well shaped and polished; but, at the same time, these northern Indians are fiercer and more uncivilized than even the Vancouver Ahts. What, then, is the value of the quality of stone implements as a test of civilization? The numerous tribes of the great Tshimpsean nation are as thoroughly uncivilized as men can be: they are removed, apparently, but little from mere animal existence, though their boldness, their stature and bearing prevent them from being *gens de pitié*. Nevertheless, their skill in working stone is greater than that shown in the existing specimens of the supposed highest stone age: it is, indeed, remarkable, as any one who has seen shop-windows in Victoria filled with their carvings can testify. They make figures in stone dressed like Englishmen; plates and other utensils of civilization, ornamented pipe stems and heads, models of houses, stone flutes, adorned with well-carved figures of animals. Their imitative skill is as noticeable as their dexterity in carving. (See Papers by G. M. Sproat, in the Transactions of the Ethnological Society of London for 1866 and 1867.)

LONDON:
PRINTED BY SMITH, ELDER AND CO.,
OLD BAILEY, E.C.